Inside Jewish Day Schools

The Mandel-Brandeis Series
in Jewish Education

Sharon Feiman-Nemser, Jonathan Krasner,
and Jon A. Levisohn, Editors

The Mandel-Brandeis Series in Jewish Education, established by
the Jack, Joseph and Morton Mandel Center for Studies in Jewish
Education, publishes scholarly monographs and edited volumes of
compelling research on Jewish educational settings and processes.
The series is made possible through the Mandel Foundation.

For a complete list of books that are available in the series,
visit brandeisuniversitypress.com

Alex Pomson and Jack Wertheimer
Inside Jewish Day Schools: Leadership, Learning, and Community

Inside JEWISH DAY SCHOOLS

ALEX POMSON AND JACK WERTHEIMER

Leadership,
Learning, and
Community

BRANDEIS UNIVERSITY PRESS

WALTHAM, MASSACHUSETTS

Brandeis University Press
© 2022 by Alex Pomson and Jack Wertheimer
All rights reserved
Manufactured in the United States of America
Designed by Eric M. Brooks
Typeset in Calluna by Passumpsic Publishing

For permission to reproduce any of the material in this book,
contact Brandeis University Press, 415 South Street, Waltham MA
02453, or visit brandeisuniversitypress.com

Library of Congress Cataloging-in-Publication Data
NAMES: Pomson, Alex, author. | Wertheimer, Jack, author.
TITLE: Inside Jewish day schools: leadership, learning, and community/
    Alex Pomson and Jack Wertheimer.
DESCRIPTION: First Edition. | Waltham, Massachusetts: Brandeis
    University Press, [2022] | Series: The Mandel-Brandeis Series in
    Jewish Education/Sharon Feiman-Nemser, Jonathan Krasner, and
    Jon A. Levisohn, editors | Includes bibliographical references and
    index. | Summary: "This book takes readers inside Jewish day
    schools to observe what they actually do. Many different types of
    Jewish day schools exist, and the variations are not well understood.
    Nor is much information available about how day schools function.
    This volume is conceived as a guide to those wishing to understand
    the contemporary Jewish day school"—Provided by publisher.
IDENTIFIERS: LCCN 2021033869 (print) | LCCN 2021033870 (ebook) |
    ISBN 9781684580699 (Cloth) | ISBN 9781684580705 (Paperback) |
    ISBN 9781684580712 (eBook)
SUBJECTS: LCSH: Jewish day schools.
CLASSIFICATION: LCC LC715 .P66 2022 (print) | LCC LC715 (ebook) |
    DDC 371.076—dc23
LC record available at https://lccn.loc.gov/2021033869
LC ebook record available at https://lccn.loc.gov/2021033870

5 4 3 2 1

Contents

Acknowledgments | vii

INTRODUCTION Inside the Black Box | 1

PART I Lower and Middle Schools | 15

   1 Progressively Maintaining the Middle: Hillel Torah Day School, Skokie, Illinois | 17

   2 A Forward-Looking Community School: Hillel Day School, Detroit, Michigan | 43

   3 The School as a Gateway: Brandeis Marin, San Rafael, California | 69

   4 Nurturing Students' Reflectiveness and Wellness: The Pressman Academy, Los Angeles, California | 97

   5 Doing More with Less: Akiva School, Nashville, Tennessee | 122

PART II High Schools | 145

   6 Recentering the Centrist Orthodox Day School: Rav Teitz Mesivta Academy, Elizabeth, New Jersey | 147

   7 It's All in a Name: The Anne & Max Tanenbaum Community Hebrew Academy of Toronto, Toronto, Canada | 174

PART III K–12 Schools | 203

   8 How a Day School Transforms Itself: Hebrew Academy (RASG), Miami Beach, Florida | 205

   9 The Yeshiva as Teiva (Ark): Yeshiva Darchei Torah, Far Rockaway, New York | 230

CONCLUSION Vital Jewish Day Schools | 254

Appendix: Day School Sectors by the Numbers | 283

Glossary | 287

Notes | 291

Index | 299

Acknowledgments

We acknowledge with appreciation the advice and encouragement graciously offered by a number of individuals. Over the years, Mem Bernstein and Arthur Fried have displayed their confidence in the value of our research and writing in numerous ways. We, like so many others, have been recipients of their gracious support and thoughtful advice. At the inception of this project, Yossi Prager proved himself an advocate of our work and also a trusted critical reader. Before choosing our nine schools, we conferred with a number of well-placed connoisseurs of day school education, some working in schools and others at foundations with a strong interest in Jewish education. Their guidance steered us well and stimulated our thinking. We thank Rachel Abrahams, Jonathan Cannon, Sharon Freundel, Moshe Krakowski, Ilisa Cappell, and Tali Aldouby Schuck. Wendy Rosov and the team at Rosov Consulting supported this project from its inception. Wendy was an incisive thought partner and strong advocate for the work from beginning to end. Pearl Mattenson read, and helped improve, first drafts of most of the chapters. As readers of an early draft of this book, Jane Taubenfeld Cohen and Elliott Rabin offered clear-eyed and constructive feedback and suggestions, which helped us improve our manuscript. Neal Kozodoy helped us reshape the Introduction. Special thanks to Sharon Feiman-Nemser for her trenchant response to the book manuscript and also to Jon Levisohn and Jonathan Krasner, her coeditors of the Brandeis University Press series on Jewish Education.

Our greatest debt is to the heads of school, board members, administrators, teachers, students, and community supporters of the nine schools in our sample. Their warm hospitality, openness to our many inquiries, and special efforts to accommodate our schedules transformed the process of our gathering information about their schools into a joyful and often eye-opening experience. Their generosity in opening their schools' doors has provided us, and our readers, with an unusually deep view into the universe of Jewish day school education at the end of the second decade of the twenty-first century.

Inside Jewish Day Schools

Introduction

Inside the Black Box

Jewish day schools have sparked a good deal of controversy virtually since their inception. Though they differ from one another in important ways, they share the commonality of being all-day educational settings, which, with a few exceptions, enroll only Jewish students—and that exclusiveness has spurred a good deal of debate. To some observers, including one of the most prominent Jewish educators during the first half of the twentieth century, such schools insulate their students from their gentile peers: "What we want in this country is not Jews who can successfully keep up their Jewishness in a few large ghettos," wrote Samson Benderly in 1908, "but men and women who have grown up in freedom and can assert themselves wherever they are. A parochial system of education among the Jews would be fatal to such hopes."[1] As late as 1954, when *Commentary* magazine published a positive appraisal of the then-expanding day school movement, a "shocked" reader wrote that such an education "makes for arrogance and creates a lack of genuine understanding of the differences among people," fostering instead "a spirit of exclusiveness" and "snobbishness."[2] More recently, the journalist Peter Beinart wondered whether "earlier generations were correct—that full equality in an overwhelmingly Christian country is, in fact, reliant on Jewish willingness to participate in a common system of education?"[3]

Yet for others, Jewish day schools serve as unparalleled settings for immersive and intensive Jewish education. "Jewish day schools," wrote one champion of such schools, "offer students access to Judaism's unique tools for human thriving—and Jewish tradition has some powerful tools."[4] Nor does that immersion in Jewish study come at the expense of other commitments to the general well-being of society, proponents of day schools contend. They once "called us segregationists, un-American, East European," wrote the head of an Orthodox movement that is the largest single promoter of day schools. "But now the day school has proved itself. The community has seen that its graduates do not necessarily become rabbis or fiddlers on the roof, but are

1

doctors, lawyers, and space scientists who also happen to be conscious and proud of their identity as Jews." A national consultative body studying Jewish education concluded its work in the early 1990s by depicting Jewish day schools as "arguably the most impactful [*sic*] single weapon in our arsenal for educating Jewish children and youth."[5]

Though such debates have persisted since the establishment of the first day schools in America, they have become more restrained in recent years, perhaps because day schools have proven their mettle. But many parents and also Jewish communal leaders have raised other concerns. Some parents worry privately that their children would be disadvantaged if they attended a Jewish day school. They fear that these schools can't possibly provide the most rigorous academic opportunities available at many independent schools and some of the best public schools. They simply lack the resources, including the funds to hire the best teachers—or so some believe. Nor, it is claimed by others, can Jewish day schools offer the vast range of extracurricular options— clubs, sports teams, art, music and dance programs—available in other types of schools. *Will our children be shortchanged?* they wonder. Not surprisingly, given the intense preoccupation with getting their children into the most prestigious universities and colleges, parents also worry whether Jewish day schools, especially high schools, serve as effective launch pads to gain admission to the best-regarded institutions of higher learning.

An additional concern focuses on the dual curriculum offered by Jewish day schools: Will attention to two very different types of study lead to a dilution of both? Every kind of day school offers some Judaica instruction; many also devote school time to prayer. In some schools, half the day or more is devoted to Judaics; in many others, between 10 and 40 percent of class time is set aside for engagement with Jewish texts and culture. How, parents wonder, can such an arrangement possibly compete with a school offering only general studies?

Not least, parents are concerned about the value proposition: the average cost of tuition in Jewish day schools is nearly $23,000 annually per child.[6] Some of the most expensive schools, mainly in New York City and Los Angeles, charge twice that sum or more. Not for nothing do some parents committed to a day school education refer, only half in jest, to day school tuition as a highly effective form of birth control. Even upper-middle-class families with school-aged children may have to defer family trips and the purchase of luxury goods if they are to meet the steep costs. Naturally, they ask themselves whether the outlay is worth it. What are they getting for the steep tuition fees?

These questions have implications not only for individual families making decisions about where to enroll their children; they also have large implications for Jewish communal life. This is because day schools offer an unparalleled Jewish education to young people: no other educational vehicles can match day schools as providers of skills and content learning in Jewish studies. Day schools therefore serve a critical role in preparing the next generation of Jewish leaders and active participants. When it comes to debates about the best means by which Jewish individuals and Jewish communities might flourish, some of the fiercest disagreements are centered on the potential contribution of day schools.

To understand Jewish day schools and address the issues thus far posed requires a perspective grounded in real schools, not abstractions. Simply put, without understanding how these schools function—what the school day is like and how students spend their time—it's difficult to evaluate their value and impact. Accordingly, this book takes readers inside Jewish day schools to observe what they actually *do*. It will become apparent immediately that many different types of Jewish day schools exist. Those variations are not well understood. Nor is much information available about *how* day schools function. As one of us put it in a different context, "The Jewish day school remains a black box, what happens inside hidden from view."[7] Even alumni who graduated fifteen or more years ago have little knowledge of what actually happens in day schools currently (unless they enroll their own children).

The operative term here is *currently*. Most Jewish day schools go about their business today in radically different ways than they did even a generation ago. They think about learners very differently, they relate to students differently, and they bring different types of resources to bear as they work to educate students and their parents.

This book therefore is conceived as a guide to those wishing to understand the contemporary Jewish day school. It informs readers about how styles of pedagogy have shifted dramatically in both general and Jewish studies. It examines where new technologies, including digital learning platforms, are present in these schools—and where they are not. It attends to the resources brought to bear when schools seek to guide the social and emotional development of students. It explains how Jewish studies function: what is taught, how the curriculum has shifted, and how schools find ways to integrate material from Jewish and general studies. And it makes evident how these schools provide a range of extracurricular options to help students demonstrate their talents in sports, the arts, Jewish self-expression, and caring for others.

Capturing twenty-first-century Jewish day schools in action, then, is one goal of this book. A second goal is to identify important challenges facing these schools—and how they respond to those challenges. In doing so, our purpose is neither to portray Jewish schools as overwhelmed by difficult realities nor to idealize how superlatively schools have mastered all the challenges they face. No school is perfect, and none we examine in this book has figured out how to address all of its challenges flawlessly. Rather, this book portrays how a sample of imperfect yet well-managed schools address issues that tend to beset many other Jewish day schools. In this sense, the book speaks to educators interested in learning about other day schools and to members of school boards and other stakeholders seeking to place their own school into a wider context.

Even as our primary focus is on what happens inside Jewish day schools, every school we studied has a profound impact on the lives of people it touches. Jewish day schools shape students, their families, and their communities. To be sure, we have only limited information on the long-term influence of such schools on the adult lives of their alumni,[8] but we have learned about their immediate impact as reflected in the behavior of students toward one another, family conversations, and the place of the school in the Jewish lives of parents. Every school also plays a social role, both as a setting where parents meet and befriend peers and as an institution making an impact on its local Jewish community. Every school is embedded in a wider communal context and helps shape its local environment.

The Jewish Day School Sectors

Why were these schools established in the first place? A brief historical overview is in order. Though a handful of Jewish day schools existed in the nineteenth century, the movement to establish such schools, especially on the high school level, is a phenomenon of the decades since World War II. During the war years, the organization Torah U'mesorah was founded with the explicit aim of planting Orthodox Jewish day schools in every American city with a critical enough mass of Jews. Initially the goal of these schools was to serve as a "fortress" or "bulwark" against the ravages of assimilation. Some came to regard them as institutions for training a Jewish elite who would serve as the future leaders of the community. But in time, Orthodox schools saw their mission as ensuring the continuity of Jewish life and culture.

Several distinctive school sectors emerged in the Orthodox world, with a key demarcation based on how general studies and, more broadly, contemporary American culture was perceived. In the Haredi sectors, sometimes called the "ultra" or "right-wing" Orthodox, the mores and cultural outlook of modern societies were regarded as a threat to Jewish life. Hasidic schools, founded by various sects tracing their origin to late eighteenth-century Eastern Europe, conduct most of their classes in Yiddish or a variation of what some have called Yinglish—Yiddish with sprinklings of English words. Most of the school day is devoted in Hasidic schools to the study of Jewish texts. Boys and girls are educated in separate buildings, usually at some geographic distance from each other, and the two genders are exposed to different Judaica curricula. Yeshiva schools (whose participants are referred to as Yeshivish) are organized similarly, though they tend to be somewhat more open to incorporating general studies into the school day; their language of instruction is English heavily laced with Hebrew, Aramaic, and Yiddish terms, and they are more open to their students going on to higher education, provided it takes place at carefully selected colleges or night schools. By contrast, Modern Orthodox schools tend to be coed, even if many separate boys and girls during Jewish studies classes. They intentionally prepare students to function in the broader society, with the result that virtually all go on to attend schools of higher education, including graduate schools. An intermediate grouping of Centrist schools provide strong general studies classes but educate boys and girls separately and urge graduates to choose colleges with large populations of other Orthodox Jews and preferably continue to live at home.

The postwar era saw the creation of non-Orthodox day schools. Arriving on the scene later than their Orthodox counterparts, schools under Conservative auspices (usually called Solomon Schechter day schools to honor the leader who placed his impress on the Jewish Theological Seminary and the Conservative movement), and then in considerably fewer numbers schools under Reform auspices, opened their doors during the second half of the twentieth century. Both types of schools are coed, seek to deliver a rigorous Jewish and general studies academic course of study, aim to compete with the best of American public and private schools, and are guided by the ideology of their religious movements. They were joined by community day schools unaffiliated with one of the streams of Judaism and generally aspiring to offer a pluralistic education respectful of all varieties, including secular Jewish identification. In recent years, community day schools have overtaken the combined Conservative and Reform sectors numerically. Once perceived as settings solely for the minority of Jews who identified as Orthodox, Jewish day schools came to be understood during the last quarter of the twentieth century as a viable option for Jews of all types.

If, as appears likely, roughly two hundred day schools had been established throughout North America as of 1960, by the second decade of the twenty-first century, close to one thousand all-day Jewish schools dotted the combined U.S. and Canadian landscapes.[9] According to the most recent national census of Jewish day schools in the United States, 906 operated in the 2018–19 school year, and collectively they enrolled some 292,172 students from early childhood through high school programs.[10] Canada's roughly 57 Jewish day schools and yeshivas enrolled slightly fewer than 18,000 students in the 2018–19 school year. Collectively, in the recent past, Canadian day schools enrolled 43 percent of Jewish school-aged children for at least nine years, twice the proportion as in the United States.[11] In both countries, then, in any given year, roughly half of school-age Jewish children *receiving a formal Jewish education* are enrolled in a day school. (Since students in various part-time settings tend to be enrolled for fewer years than their day school peers, overall the majority of young non-Orthodox children still are enrolled in a supplementary program, receive private tutoring, or are exposed to no Jewish education.)[12]

Some explanation of this dramatic expansion is in order. In Orthodox circles, enrolling children in Jewish day schools became de rigueur by the fourth quarter of the past century. Modern Orthodox Jews embraced day school education as a necessity during the postwar decades. They were concerned about ensuring their children would attain high levels of Jewish literacy, wary of powerful assimilatory forces in society at large and convinced that day schools would prepare their offspring for full participation in civic, economic, and cultural life of their North American communities while also providing the tools for them to engage actively in Jewish life. For those living in more insular Orthodox enclaves, day schools were an integral part of the landscape into which they aspired to socialize their children. And indeed, the largest growth in schools and student populations has been in the Hasidic and yeshiva sectors—those most focused on Jewish textual studies and skeptical of the value and impact of general studies.

For parents outside the Orthodox camp, day schools have held the allure of offering their children a grounding in Judaica, along with general studies. Added to this, schools under Conservative, Reform, and communal auspices became more attractive options during busing experiments in public schools, when parents concluded that public education in some localities was inferior, when independent school options were deemed viable, and when affluence encouraged some parents to give day schools a second look. Some Jewish subpopulations also have been drawn by particular qualities of non-Orthodox day schools; for example, Israelis in the United States appreciate the Hebrew language and Israel studies offerings of day schools; some secular Jews want their children to learn about their Jewish cultural heritage; parents of different denominational outlooks value the exposure of their children to the range of Jews and Jewish expression on display in pluralistic day schools; and not least, some parents are attracted by the warm atmosphere, attention devoted to each student, and wholesome environment that day schools provide.

Setting Priorities

As they shape their educational environment, day schools are faced with a host of difficult choices, as will be made amply clear in every chapter of this book. Like most other schools, they must grapple with limitations of time, resources, and personnel. How, for example, might the finite number of precious hours with students best be spent: in classrooms, assemblies, informal school settings, or outside the school building? Given constrained financial resources, how should a day school balance its investments in new technologies, curricula, staff positions, plant facilities, and scholarships for students? And as many schools struggle with high personnel costs, should they prioritize the hiring of mission-appropriate teachers or import *shlichim* (emissaries) who bring a touch of Israel and the Hebrew language to the school, both of which may prove costly?

Jewish day schools, moreover, encounter additional dilemmas. Many schools conceive of their mission as addressing not only the needs of their own students but also those of the wider Jewish community. Ideally, they endeavor to aid every family wishing to enroll children, regardless of financial circumstances. That, of course, places great burdens on schools to raise scholarship funds. It also requires balancing the school's communal mission to enroll students regardless of their academic abilities and their aspiration to serve as elite academic institutions. To accomplish the latter aim, they will have to admit students selectively and limit enrollment to only the most talented students. Similar difficult questions arise concerning the inclusion of students with learning or emotional disabilities. Especially in the current environment when parents expect schools to pay close attention to their children's academic achievement, emotional well-being, and social skills, schools, as we shall see, now must address concerns that barely registered a few decades ago.

Fulfilling their religious mission also poses dilemmas for day schools. Some schools are pressed to exclude families whose levels of Jewish religious practice do not conform to the stated ideology of the school community. In Orthodox schools, some parents lobby to have their children placed in classes with schoolmates whose religious observances at home are identical to their own. They seek as much religious homogeneity as possible. But that excludes students who may be brought closer to observance through their exposure to the school's teachings, certainly another religious mission some schools set for themselves. In community day schools, by contrast, some parents chafe under school policies regarding Jewish observances, such as limiting lunch food brought to school by children to items with kosher certification and insisting that birthday parties may not be held on Shabbat, the Jewish Sabbath. A school's infringement on family practices may be deeply resented. How to navigate religious differences is a source of perennial tension in many day schools.

This raises an additional concern: Will classes teach about Jewish religious practices prescriptively or descriptively? Valuing their autonomy and fearful of day schools turning their children into religious "fanatics," some parents fret that a day school education will border on indoctrination. Parents may worry that their children will become "too Jewish" or make demands on parents to incorporate more Jewish rituals into home practices. Some fear that their children will judge their own levels of Jewishness as inadequate. As they work to allay those concerns, schools struggle not to adopt a completely neutral stance toward Jewish living, for if they do, what message does that deliver to students about the mission of the school?

In a further challenge, day schools also contend with tough questions about the content and delivery of their general and Jewish education. More than in the past, parents expect day schools to offer high-level academics in general studies. They do not want their children shortchanged. Schools, as we will see, are investing heavily in cutting-edge curricula for STEAM classes (in science, technology, engineering, art, and math) and language arts, and the hiring of high-quality teachers in those fields. They are opening robotics labs and makerspaces (a place in schools where students develop creative projects, often collaboratively, using tools and materials physically and virtually available to them) for children to learn how to translate their learning into handcrafted material objects. Schools are mindful of diverse learning styles, and they invest in ways for different kinds of learners to absorb material and give expression to what they have learned. Introducing new educational methods incurs heavy costs to purchase new online curricula and pay for continuing education for the teaching staff. Choosing which disciplines to upgrade first often becomes a juggling act because budgets are limited.

Jewish studies subject matter poses its own set of challenges. Traditional religious instruction was not learner centered. Teachers served as the "sage on the stage," systematically uncovering layers of meaning in sacred texts. In more advanced settings, students studied together in pairs (*Hevruta*), thus taking some ownership of their learning. With day schools having embraced more progressive pedagogies over the past few decades, schools must decide whether to convey material in one fashion during general studies classes and a completely different style in Jewish studies classes. In the former, problem-based learning and design thinking are gaining ground, as is blended (or technologically assisted) learning. Students are encouraged to discover answers at their own pace. In Jewish studies classes, even the most fervent supporters of new methods among parents may be uneasy about abandoning centuries-old study methods. And even when the decision is made to teach Judaic materials differently, online resources are not nearly as advanced or available as for general studies courses. Moreover, Jewish studies teachers who themselves were educated using the older methods may resist embracing new approaches. When and how to revamp Jewish studies pose dilemmas for schools.

Finally, the teaching of Hebrew language perennially raises challenges. Because the language has evolved over the long course of Jewish history, modern Israeli Hebrew is a vastly different language from the tongue spoken during the biblical era or the Middle Ages. The study of Jewish sacred texts requires familiarity with earlier registers of Hebrew, while reading and speaking modern Israeli Hebrew is an entirely different enterprise. Deciding on which register to emphasize is still another challenge day schools face, one made even more complex because those who seem best suited to teach sacred texts may have little competence to teach modern Hebrew. Should a school hire a separate teaching staff for modern Hebrew as opposed to the Hebrew of sacred texts? Many schools do precisely that, a decision that incurs heavy financial costs.

All of the schools included in this book are faced with the range of challenges outlined here. How they resolve these questions varies considerably and makes for the distinctive culture of each school.

The School Sample

Several considerations went into the process of assembling the nine-school sample highlighted in this book. We endeavored to include schools that have not been the subject of much study by others and eschewed the usual suspects in favor of lesser-known but also strong schools. Geography too was an important consideration. Our nine schools are scattered in different parts of North America: two are in the Greater New York area, though outside the city, where the largest concentration of Jewish day schools is found. Another two are in the Midwest; two are in the South; two are on the West Coast; and one is in Canada. They also differ considerably in the size of their enrollments, with one school enrolling fewer than one hundred students, while the largest educates almost twenty-five hundred students. A deliberate decision was made to include a day school that alone serves the Jewish population in its city, even as others are located in areas where they face stiff competition from neighboring Jewish day schools. As readers will note, some schools offer only elementary and middle school grades, if that; others are K–12; and a few others are stand-alone high schools.

Our nine schools were selected too with an eye to providing a broad representation of the ideological spectrum. Only one of our nine schools can be classified as Haredi, although more than half of all students enrolled in all-day Jewish schools are in Hasidic or yeshiva schools. Access to Hasidic and Yeshivish schools is a major impediment facing observers of Jewish education: such schools tend to be wary of outsiders and not to value the work of academic researchers. At a different end of the spectrum, we chose not to include a school under Reform auspices because there are only eleven and they are similar to many community day schools. The different permutations of modern and Centrist Orthodoxy are represented by three schools. One of our schools is a Solomon Schechter lower and middle school, and four are pluralistic community schools.

We are acutely aware that day schools, like schools in general, are not static. During the writing of this book, two heads of schools we studied departed, as have an even greater number of administrators and teachers. Since then, schools have continued to evolve in their programming. As this book neared completion, the coronavirus epidemic of 2020 hit, forcing schools to shift classes online and limit in-person learning. The portraits we present are snapshots in time that date to the period between spring 2018 and fall 2019. Yet even as the nine schools we studied evolve in response to new circumstances, the trends we trace have not changed dramatically, and most of the challenges we observed still shape the schools. (At the end of the concluding chapter, we briefly take stock of how the nine schools in our sample fared during the first seven months of the COVID-19 crisis and how directly their responses reflected changes in their approaches during the years prior to the crisis and their distinctive cultures.)

As to our method of research, both of us visited all nine schools, typically at different times of the year and separately. The lead author of a chapter spent more time in the school, usually for five days, while the secondary author was present for two or three days. During those visits, we made sure to spend a day shadowing the head of school and a day shadowing a group of students from one of the oldest grades; these provided rich opportunities to gain a sense of the school's leadership, learning cultures, and rhythm. Where possible, we joined students for *Tefila*, prayer services. We spent a good deal of time in classrooms observing teaching styles and interactions between students and studying how teachers approached pedagogy. Occasionally we had opportunities to observe students in the course of special events, such as ceremonies and performances. We interviewed the full range of individuals who inhabit the schools and shape their policy: students, teachers, administrators, board members, and parents. In some cases, our trips coincided with board meetings or student recruitment programs, which our hosts generously permitted us to observe. We spoke with alumni too. In every case, we interviewed community leaders, such as professionals at federations of Jewish philanthropy (which offer some financial support to day schools), and local rabbis whose congregants enroll their children in the day school we were studying at the time.

Inspired by the pioneering work of Sarah Lawrence Lightfoot, whose book *The Good High School* serves as a model of insightful school research, we too have opted to name schools (in every case with permission); we have endeavored to present portraits of schools and also to draw conclusions about the critical building blocks they have assembled to offer a good day school education. Like Lightfoot, we chose our schools seeking out "goodness," not perfection. Also, like her, "our selection was not scientific. No random sample was taken, no large-scale opinion surveys were sent out in order to identify good schools. They were chosen because of their reputation among school people, the high opinion of them shared by their inhabitants and surrounding communities, and because they offered easy and generous entry."[13]

Though it is impossible to find schools with an orientation representative of all Jewish day schools of their sector, the portraits presented in this book touch on many of the most pressing challenges day schools face. Our examination of how these schools go about their work, the voices included in our chapters, and the stories we tell about the people we met—students, teachers, administrators, board members, and communal observers—are designed to present Jewish day schools in the round, as living, evolving organisms. Collectively, our portraits of these schools also provide answers, even if only indirectly, to the questions posed at the outset of this Introduction that are on the minds of parents, educators, and other stakeholders.

How This Book Is Organized and May Be Read

Our approach to gathering data and then writing each of the chapters in this book has been akin to the various ways one might approach a jigsaw puzzle. Sometimes it is easier to start with a corner piece, sometimes with a line of pieces from along a puzzle's border, and sometimes with a set of particularly striking pieces somewhere in the middle of the puzzle.

It was hard to predict in advance the most useful way to pick up the trail of a school's story. When we started our work, we presented a consistent wish list to all of the schools, including the types of personnel we sought to interview and the kinds of settings we wanted to observe. Although we were drawn to these schools because they were well known for some feature or another, typically we did not know ahead of time what would prove to be of a special interest at a school. In each case, the narrative hook was quite distinct. For example, at Brandeis Marin, a lower and middle school in the Bay Area, it was the head of school's educational vision for how day school education can prove compelling for a very wide range of Jewish and non-Jewish families. At Hillel Torah, a K–8 school in Skokie, Illinois, it was how the school's leaders had enabled the fusion of cutting-edge educational practices with the core curriculum tasks of a Modern Orthodox day school. At the Rav Teitz Mesivta, it was the work involved in turning around a long-established high school and enthusing a skeptical faculty to embrace a child-centered vision for the yeshiva day school, while constrained by acute financial challenges.

Reflecting these different foci, each chapter starts and finishes in different and distinct places. None follows a single tick-the-box template. Each chapter has its own unique trajectory. To help orient readers and draw out some initial comparative analyses, each chapter concludes with pointed observations about connections and exceptions: the commonalities shared by some of the schools and where schools find themselves in unusual circumstances and chart their own unique approaches.

In the final chapter, we draw together what we believe this collection of studies reveals about day schools as a whole. The Conclusion reflects on the roles the schools play in the lives of students, families, and communities and on what we perceive to be the common keys to performing these roles well.

Readers need not necessarily read the following chapters in their order of appearance. Some might find it enlightening to read the chapters along a denominational/ideological continuum, starting, say, with Yeshiva Darchei Torah, a New York area, male-only institution, the most traditionalist school in the sample, and ending with Brandeis Marin, a progressive community day school on the West Coast with a small minority of non-Jewish students. If school size is of special interest, then it would pay to start with Nashville's Akiva Academy, the only day school in its community, and with fewer than eighty students in kindergarten through sixth grade. At the opposite extreme is TanenbaumCHAT, a high school located in a competitive day school marketplace and boasting over one thousand students.

We have chosen to organize the chapters according to the grade level schools serve. The first section of the book gathers the accounts of five K–8 or K–6 institutions. The next section presents examples of Jewish day high schools. Finally, there are two chapters about schools that run from kindergarten through twelfth grade. This organization reflects a well-grounded expectation that the cultures of schools and the social-emotional challenges their students face are strongly determined by the ages of those they serve. Through this study, we learn that this is true but only partly so. There is much in the earlier elementary/middle school chapters about the ways in which schools serve families and about the role of parents in schools. The chapters in the second half of the book, even those that describe K–12 institutions, are concerned much more with how schools respond to the societal pressures that bear down on them: intense academic pressures, addiction to technology, and mental health issues. There is very little mention of parents in these chapters.

As we discuss in the concluding chapter, for all of their differences—and there are many more than we note here—it is instructive nevertheless to reflect on commonalities in these nine schools: What, for example, are their shared roles in respect to students and communities, and what are the common challenges they face in terms of finances, leadership, and staffing? We encourage readers to reflect on the patterns they perceive through the juxtaposition of these nine accounts before they turn to our perspective in the final chapter.

I

Lower and Middle Schools

1

Progressively Maintaining the Middle

Hillel Torah Day School, Skokie, Illinois

> Hillel Torah Day School combines the traditional verities of Modern
> Orthodox day school education (intensive exposure to Hebrew, an
> Israel-centered calendar, prayer every day, and extensive text study)
> with a progressive, child-centered educational orientation. This chapter
> reveals what happens when school leadership acts with great clarity of
> purpose—how, in this instance, that purposefulness sees expression
> in an intense commitment to child-centered education and a serious
> investment in Hebrew in all of its forms. It also results in creative and
> at times unconventional moves to ensure that students are served by
> educators who can bring the school's mission to life and model its central
> principles. In a day school subsector that is pulled by market forces to
> the religious right and religious left, this is a school that demonstrates
> the special benefits of a strong educational direction, or what its
> leadership would call *hashkafa*, a religious worldview.

Three episodes observed during the course of the same morning at Hillel
Torah North Suburban Day School convey a sense of the student experience
at this kindergarten to eighth grade Modern Orthodox school.

Every day, approximately twenty-five boys in the school's oldest two grades
come together for both *shacharit* and *mincha* (the morning and afternoon service) in a classroom that does double duty as a prayer room. On days when Torah
is read, the girls also join; otherwise, they have their own separate service. The
proceedings are always led by the students, usually with a fair degree of competence. To all intents and purposes, it is no different from the weekday services
in the synagogues their fathers attend.[1] Usually the group is supervised by a senior member of staff and another member of the faculty. On this occasion, the
supervising teachers arrive late. Nevertheless, more or less on time, the boys get
started with the *minyan* (prayer service) by themselves, with impressive, if not

flawless, decorum. When the teacher arrives, the service is already well and truly under way. There is no need even to pause.

A couple of hours later, in a different corner of the school, beyond a classroom door plastered with hand-drawn self-portraits of the students, "kindness awards" and "Smores learning artifacts," second-grade students are absorbed in a writing workshop. They start out gathered on the carpet where they're all independently doing an exercise laid out on the interactive whiteboard in front of them. Once it is complete and without any obvious teacher intervention, they disperse to tables where groups continue their work. They share writing resources from pots at the center of these tables. One group is working with a teaching assistant on spelling tasks. Another group is gathered at a semicircular table around the lead teacher in a guided reading activity. A third group, completely independently it seems, is proceeding with a word-study workbook exercise. Everyone seems to know what they're supposed to be doing. They appear remarkably content.

Back in the middle school, soon after, a seventh-grade group of thirteen girls and boys start a Gemara (Talmud, the foundational compilation of rabbinic Judaism) class. They began learning Gemara at the start of the year, about six months earlier, so they're very much beginners. Taking laptops from a common trolley, each student sits at a separate table and begins the class by taking a ten-minute online quiz of common Gemara vocabulary. Once they have finished, the students are asked to spend the next five minutes reading out loud to a partner from the passage they've been studying this past week—"not just scanning with your eyes," says the teacher. A couple of students take turns to read to the teacher at his desk. With Pesach (Passover) less than a month away, the teacher next distributes a workbook of new material from Masechet Pesachim (the tractate concerned with Passover matters). He explains that the students' first job is to mark up the unpunctuated text to decipher the structure of the Gemara; they're not expected yet to understand every word. He encourages them to use the skills they've developed over the past few months. And so, working in small groups and checking back to material they've previously studied, the students pick their way through this puzzle. When a student gets stuck, he goes over to another group and calls, "Heh, I have another question for you." It's striking that the student doesn't simply turn to the teacher for help. In fact, while the groups are puzzling over the material, the teacher is continuing to listen to students read, another way of checking if they understand the flow of the text. In a class made up of beginners, it's remarkable how independently the students are working during almost the entire lesson. The teacher, for his part, has needed to address the class as a group only very occasionally.

Despite the different school settings involved, the consistent display in these episodes of the same attributes and aptitudes is striking. In each instance, students indicate both an ability and a readiness to act independently. Their ability to do so is surely the result of learned roles and accumulated skills, cultivated, most likely, within the framework of classroom routines since these are habits that typically need to be developed with concerted cultivation. At the same time, the students' readiness to act with so much independence from a young age indicates their comfort within an environment that evidently gives them frequent opportunities (and even requires them) to act with autonomy and self-sufficiency—not to rely always on teachers but to draw instead on their own resources and those of their peers. To find the consistent expression of this paradoxical mix of structure and autonomy in this setting—a Modern Orthodox, religious Zionist day school in Chicago —is surprising. It invites further exploration. What are the educational principles and organizational processes that have made this fusion of attributes possible? What are the purposes and aspirations that have nourished these attributes? To what extent might they be reproduced in other settings?

Widening the Frame

From the outside, Hillel Torah looks like a great many other Modern Orthodox day schools in America. More than sixty years old, this institution has catered to multiple generations from the same families in the same suburban Chicago location. The facilities have not fundamentally changed over the years. There are tens of Modern Orthodox day schools in America with a similar profile, serving communities that, following World War II, were among the most active adopters of a model of Jewish education that promised Jewish, often Hebraic, literacy alongside preparation for a decent college education. Built around a dual curriculum of Judaic and general studies, these schools embodied what their ideologues called *Torah Im Derech Eretz* or *Torah U'Mada*—access to Jewish culture and world culture in equal measure.

Today, these schools continue to be the bedrock of the day school market. It's no surprise, for example, that programmatic components of the Jewish studies and Hebrew curriculum used at Hillel Torah are also employed by a great many other schools: Tal Am—the elementary-grade Hebrew curriculum most widely employed in the day school field; Bishvil Ha-Ivrit—a widely used middle and high school Hebrew curriculum; and Bonayich—a more recently developed curriculum and framework for the study of Talmudic texts for middle school and high school students. These programs were developed for a market sector that has seen tremendous stability over many decades. Modern Orthodox schools have been the equivalent of anchor tenants in the day school curriculum marketplace. While non-Orthodox day school options rapidly expanded toward the end of the last century, they have contracted in recent years for a variety of sociological and financial reasons. By contrast, over the past two decades, the number of students enrolled in Modern Orthodox day schools has been characterized by the most recent day school census as exhibiting "modest growth."[2] Total enrollment in these schools has increased by 1 percent in twenty years, hovering at around twenty-seven thousand students. In recent years, this sector has been decisively outgrown by various ultra-Orthodox school sectors. It has also been subjected to repeated warnings of implosion under the burden of continually rising tuition and due to what commentators call "a slide to the right," that is, the pull of ever more stringent Orthodoxy. And yet despite the dire prognoses, Modern Orthodox day schools continue to survive, if not thrive, in many communities across America. They are safe bets for parents, many of whom attended similar, if not the very same, schools themselves.

This stability is both an asset and a liability. Absent the prospect of losing families to tuition-free public schools, still a marginal phenomenon in the Modern Orthodox community but a real and present danger for non-Orthodox institutions, these schools have not experienced special pressure to innovate. Outside the unusually congested marketplace in the New York tristate area where any number of subtly differentiated alternatives compete with one another, Modern Orthodox schools are not under special pressure to keep up with the competition. Some wrestle, for example, with swings in their feeder markets due to rising house prices or some other local circumstance, but most cater to what is essentially a captive market. There might be some ferment at the edges created by parents seeking, on the one hand, more intense *limmudei kodesh* (sacred Jewish studies) or, on the other hand, more up-to-date STEM education, but essentially the great majority of their customers aren't about to leave, unless, that is, to Israel, an ideologically and financially appealing option for a small stream of families every year.

This is the educational microclimate inhabited by Hillel Torah, a long-established school with a current enrollment of 425 students, most of whose families have been members of the same three or four congregations for decades. Certainly the school faces challenges—financial, ideological, and educational—but this is a school that has achieved an unusual degree of equilibrium. It is blessed with a highly respected head of school who at the time of this study was completing his tenth year in the position. The school's enrollment is steady, and its finances are relatively stable, although about a third of families are not able to pay full tuition. In terms of Jewish education, it maintains an unusually intense commitment to its ivrit b'ivrit program (teaching Judaic studies in Hebrew) at least until the end of the elementary grades. In the middle school, a strong Judaic studies faculty is admired for offering relevant and appealing role models for the students.

What makes Hillel Torah so interesting is its combining of the traditional verities of Modern Orthodox day school education (intensive exposure to Hebrew, an Israel-centered calendar, prayer every day, and extensive text study) with a strongly child-centered educational orientation. Even in a Modern Orthodox day school context where parents typically seek the best of all words, these attributes don't always sit well together, if indeed they both are present. In a community context where the only real enrollment competition is from a non-coed day school ideologically to the right, it's worth pondering what drives the school's determinedly child-centered educational orientation; it does not seem to be marketplace pressure. Spend a few days at Hillel Torah, and it's remarkable how often you encounter verbal and visual expressions of a commitment to deliver ever more effectively on this distinctive educational vision. What accounts, then, for this unusual blend of educational and ideological commitments?

Putting the Pieces Together

As we talked to the head of school, Rabbi Menachem Linzer, it becomes evident that his own biography has been an important element in shaping this fusion. The child of educators, Linzer had what he calls a mixed day school experience as a child. In fact, once he decided to give up on a career in the sciences ("the world didn't need another engineer!") and chose to devote himself to Jewish education, part of what drove him forward was his desire to create a different kind of school experience from the one he'd had as a young adult. Linzer himself is a paradox: an intellectual with a passion for experiential education. One of the most formative educational experiences of his life was his relationship with Rav Aharon Lichtenstein, one of the most serious *halachists* (decisors of Jewish law) and Jewish thinkers of recent generations, with whom he studied in Israel and whom he welcomed to the school on one memorable occasion. At the same time, he'll readily tell you that one of the most enjoyable parts of his job today is playing guitar and singing each week with the youngest grades in the school. To put this unusual mix in insider terms, he's a guitar-playing Gushnik (the Gush being one of the names of the yeshiva co-led by Rav Aharon for more than thirty years).

No doubt, Rabbi Linzer's own passions offer a kind of rough template for what one finds at Hillel Torah. More profoundly, though, the educational approach he has helped shape at the school is a blend of what he observed and absorbed at two markedly different New York day schools where he worked as an educator before coming to Hillel Torah. (This blending is a powerful testament to the ways in which educational traditions evolve and advance.) After completing *smicha* (rabbinic ordination) at Yeshiva University, Linzer took his first full-time job at the Ramaz Upper School, where he taught Gemara for eight years. Supported by a skilled department chair, he thrived in a serious academic environment that enabled and encouraged him to work with students at a very high level—what he calls a Bes Hamedresh level, one found in serious study halls. His job wasn't just about academics. He took on pastoral responsibilities as a grade adviser, doing Israel guidance, supporting student clubs, and playing guitar at *kumsitzes* (informal musical gatherings), but the academic dimensions of the experience demonstrated how schools can successfully and productively embrace a rigorous curriculum with high standards in both general studies and Judaics.

An opportunity arose to take up a first administrative position at another flagship in the New York area: a Modern Orthodox institution, the SAR (Salanter Akiva Riverdale) Middle School, a diametrically different educational institution from where he had been. It was a challenging stint at a time when the school was going through some major transitions, but his experiences there overturned his own thinking about education. Sitting in meetings where the education team would spend forty minutes talking about one student, he learned what it meant to truly give attention to children. Coming into a classroom where students had taken all the books off the shelves in order to build car ramps, he saw what real student engagement looks like. For someone who had by then spent a quarter of a century in one day school or another, it was nothing less than a revelation.

After four years at SAR, Linzer was given a chance to take up the position as head of school at Hillel Torah. He describes it as an opportunity to weave together the best of what he had experienced over the previous decade: a commitment to high standards and rigor in ways that are appropriate in a K–8 institution, while at the same time giving children a chance to express their creativity, giving them the attention that helps them grow. This is the yin and yang that has made Hillel Torah tick these past few years.

Linzer himself is the first to say that what Hillel Torah is today is far from being all about him or his personal story. He's had the good fortune to work with and learn from some outstanding educators and, no less important, he has been able to partner with some unusually generous and wise lay leaders. This may indeed be the case, but it is also evident from observing his collaborative leadership style and from hearing how others talk about his style that no matter how fortunate he might have been, he has been remarkably open to learning from partners and colleagues, whatever their level of seniority. Ego has not been an obstacle, even while he has been driven by a general sense of what he was trying to achieve.

Growing into Growth

The prevailing educational philosophy at Hillel Torah has certainly changed over the course of Linzer's tenure these past ten years. Those who have been associated with the school for a long time will say that Hillel Torah was for many years "very old school." The instruction was teacher centered and the students generally passive. Characterizing the classrooms as traditional would have been an understatement. As we have already seen, that is not the case today. How this has happened is a textbook story in school change.

Rabbi Linzer came with a general sense of the direction in which he was hoping the school would grow, but he was a new head in a conservative institution, and those who hired him were not especially interested in educational change. Board members, most of whom were parents, certainly wanted what was best for their children, yet, like parents in many other schools, their image of what was best resembled the best parts of their own education; they were not looking for something radically different. In any case, while Linzer may have had aspirations to take the school in a new direction, he did not claim to be an expert in teaching and learning in elementary education. It was not as if he arrived with a plan in his hands.

The key in this instance, was to gradually co-opt and recruit fellow travelers on a journey when at first the destination was only dimly perceived. Linzer was fortunate that when he took up his position, Tamar Friedman was already in place as head of Judaic studies. Friedman, an experienced educator with a deep commitment to ivrit b'ivrit (teaching Jewish studies classes in Hebrew), was unusually receptive to trying out new ideas despite her already well-formed views about language learning. She has continued to be a strong partner over many years. The school's senior team has also included over the past ten years general studies educators who have been particularly interested in the promise of new thinking and child-centered educational ideas. One head of general studies who occupied the position for three years before emigrating to Israel was especially pivotal in introducing what have become some of the school's signature programs. The growth mind-set of the leadership team was, and continues to be, a special strength of the school. The current head of general studies was recruited from a community day school in a search that specifically sought a creative educator for this role. Coming to the end of her first year, she has already been able to help the school continue to evolve.

An additional important contributor to the school's evolution has been the unusual willingness of Hillel Torah's senior team to place bets on new faculty who come straight out of college, something that many schools are reluctant to do. In the first years of Linzer's tenure, as an older generation of teachers started to move on, the school took a chance on hiring younger educators who may have lacked classroom experience but displayed latent talent and whose preparation programs had exposed them to cutting-edge educational thinking. These younger faculty have been especially adept, for example, at integrating technology into the classrooms and in coaching their colleagues to do so. A number of them have now been working at the school for more than five years, and as they have matured as educators, they have played critical roles in continuing to advance new educational thinking.

At first it was hard to bring about change, particularly while an older generation of faculty lingered. Over time they either opted to move on, were encouraged to do so, or bravely submitted themselves to the often painful work of learning new ways of doing things. With the passage of time, however, there has been a flywheel effect—first, as the turnover of staff has brought about an acceleration in the pace of change and, second, as the focus of change has sharpened. If at first it was generally unclear to Rabbi Linzer himself, let alone to those he was trying to inspire, how traditional commitments could be fused with new educational practices, today one need only step inside many of the classrooms to see what this vision looks like.

Across the curriculum and across the grades, teachers are using the responsive classroom approach, a student-centered, social and emotional learning framework for teaching and discipline. (This is the framework that shaped the second-grade classroom described at the start of this chapter.) Hillel Torah is the only day school participating in an experimental program of Chicago's Museum of Science and Industry to integrate different kinds of STEM activity within project-based learning across the curriculum, with aspects of Chanukah having served as the focus point for much of this work in its first iteration. Finally, in a number of settings, students are exploring restorative circles, a practice designed to enable conflict resolution and emotional expression. This approach started out in the art room and is now found in a number of classrooms and even in staff meetings.

The point about these examples is not that they reflect what used to be called curriculum integration (the blending of Jewish and general studies subject matter), but that they indicate how contemporary educational practices and norms have become consistently infused across the curriculum and across the grades They reflect, first, a strong appreciation of the extent to which the social and emotional climate in schools is important to the quality of the learning in every discipline. Second, they model how students typically learn most when they are active producers of knowledge themselves, a fundamental tenet of contemporary education.

It's worth noting that the school's current mission statement—one that constitutes a succinct bringing together of the different academic and child-centered educational traditions we previously described—was not produced until six years into Linzer's tenure, until, that is, many changes had taken root or until it became that much clearer where the school was headed. The mission was not a compass helping the school's leadership navigate those early changes; in fact, it is quite possible that the board would not have bought in to this particular mission at an earlier stage. Instead, the mission has served more as a snapshot of the destination to which members of the school community can now see they are headed. As articulated today, the mission is as much a description of what Hillel Torah has become as it is an expression of what it might still be. This is what it says:

> We are a dynamic, Modern Orthodox day school preparing the Jewish leaders of tomorrow. Our progressive, child-centered approach promotes academic excellence in Judaic and *general studies*. Rooted in Torah learning and values, we encourage children to develop a life-long commitment to Medinat Yisrael [the Jewish state], the Jewish people and the global community.

Where the Board Makes a Difference

The school's volunteer leadership has also played an important role in nurturing Hillel Torah's current educational identity, although this might not be so obvious at first glance. At the time Linzer was appointed, the board functioned in a highly traditional fashion, or at least in a manner that was typical of a great many other Jewish day schools. Almost all of its members were current parents, and they were locked into a somewhat adversarial relationship with the school's administration, much as parents were with the teachers. This situation was epitomized by the role of the Vaad Hachinuch, the board's education committee. This well-meaning group met almost once a month and micromanaged a whole range of decisions, from which curriculum was purchased to whether there should be snack machines on the premises. Under such circumstances, it was no wonder that Linzer's predecessor was accused of trying to shut out the board. That was his way of trying to keep them at arm's length.

Today, thanks to the contribution of some farsighted board leaders working in concert with the senior administration, the educational decisions, and certainly the day-to-day operational decisions, are now left to the professionals. The board is focused much more on fulfilling its fiduciary and governance responsibilities. It is concerned with the long term and not with what is happening next week or next month. This does not mean that board members don't help guide the school's educational direction. It's just that they do so through the systems that are appropriate to their areas of responsibility and their expertise. The Vaad HaChinuch is gone. Today, a head support and evaluation committee provides appropriately channeled assistance to the head in a timely fashion, and a governance committee works hard to ensure that the board stays on task and that new board members learn efficiently what those tasks are.

In a scarcity economy, where there are never enough resources to do everything the educational personnel or parents would wish for, every educational policy decision comes with an opportunity cost. Now, with a much clearer sense of the school's identity and of its own role, the board has become highly disciplined about ensuring that financial resources are deployed in mission-appropriate ways while a subgroup of its members explore how those resources might be further deepened. For example, they continue to support a policy of enabling two *shaliach* couples (teachers from Israel working on time-limited contracts) to be in the school at any one time as a critical means by which to sustain the school's commitment to ivrit b'ivrit, although the full costs of employing a shaliach are about 30 percent greater than they would be for a local teacher. In a series of fiscal moves that have been critical to enabling the implementation of a child-centered educational philosophy, the board has committed to ensuring that a teaching assistant is in every class in the elementary grades. It has expanded the proportion of the budget devoted to learning resources (supporting children with special learning needs) and has invested heavily in educational technology.

Although the board is still composed almost entirely of current and former parents, its role in relation to the parent body has changed. Instead of being a funnel for complaints *from* the parents to the school administration (parents now know that they should take any concerns directly to the relevant professionals), board members have become advocates and communicators *to* the parents. With Rabbi Linzer spending a few hours of his week in conversations and meetings with board members, ensuring that they're up to date about the issues with which the school is engaging, they have become important spokespeople on behalf of the school and its educational vision.

For Linzer, a major part of his role is cultivating a sense of shared investment among different members of the school community. That does not always come naturally no matter how many stakeholders he tries to engage. For example, one of the things he finds most difficult about day school education is that teachers are not paid more. Currently, the starting salary for a teaching assistant is about $20,000 and for a teacher $40,000. He would like to pay teachers more. That's not just a tactical issue that would make it easier to hire or to retain teachers. He sees it as a moral principle. As teachers' work becomes ever more sophisticated and as they have become ever more professional, he is of the view that teachers surely deserve better compensation. And yet if teachers were paid more—something the administration has explored by examining different ways to structure pay levels—the parents would end up bearing the brunt, something that's just not possible given that they're already paying more than $18,000 a year in tuition. It's impossible to square this circle. In the end, the best that the school's professional and lay leadership can do is work to ensure that teachers don't feel they're being taken advantage of, whatever they're being paid. This is one of the reasons the school invests heavily in programs and packages to help see that teachers do indeed feel appreciated, a goal pursued particularly by working in tandem with the PTA to support events and programs that make that clear. With a sense of shared mission among educators, parents, school administration, and board members, all parties can move toward a common goal.

Hebrew First and Foremost

Although the shift toward a more child-centered educational vision hasn't exactly played out under the radar, the school's reorientation educationally is not widely known. It is not something that has necessarily earned Hillel a national reputation, and it has not shifted the enrollment calculus for parents. Reputations are hard to shift, and while one doesn't need to spend long in the school to sense the kind of child-centered philosophy that animates a great many of the classrooms, to a large extent Hillel Torah is still known as an educationally conservative institution: a middle-of-the road Modern Orthodox day school in the middle of the country. If you ask people beyond Chicago, and certainly if you ask community leaders in Chicago itself, what distinguishes Hillel Torah from other day schools, they're much more likely to say something along the lines of, "You walk into that school and Israel is everywhere" or "Now that's a school that takes Hebrew seriously."

These responses are not misplaced. Over decades, Hillel Torah has been a field leader in how it has sustained a Hebrew-rich and Israel-centric Jewish educational program and culture. It still is, thanks to a number of factors that are worth reviewing. At the same time, what is less well known is that while Hebrew continues to be absolutely central to Hillel's identity, in recent years the school has found ways to calibrate this emphasis, especially in the higher grades. This is a development that is no less instructive for why it has happened and how it has been accomplished.

At Hillel, from kindergarten through fourth grade, during the half of the day that students devote to Judaic studies and Tefila, you hardly hear English spoken in the classroom. In fifth and sixth grades, this continues to be the case most of the time. Only in seventh and eighth grades does the balance shift toward spoken English. The Hebrew one hears is authentically Israeli. A minority of the teachers might have learned Hebrew as a second language, but their inflection and style are very much Israeli. Those who teach in Hebrew are native Hebrew speakers. In fact, six of the fourteen lead Judaic studies teachers are Israeli. Four are shlichim, temporary teachers from Israel on two- to four-year contracts, and two are shlichim who have stayed and have played key roles in the department over many years. In addition, at any given time, there are between two and four *bnot sherut* in the school, young women from Israel who spend a year abroad as part of their national service.

There are many schools where shlichim are seen as a stop-gap solution to the challenge of finding appropriately qualified Hebrew teachers locally; critics complain that they're never going to properly understand the culturally unfamiliar lives of their students, but at least they do a job that few locals can. Other schools view shlichim as an expensive luxury; with the recruitment and relocation costs involved, there's limited payoff given that by the time these people get settled and understand their work, they're already winding down. It has become a cliché that in the first year of their tenure, they're learning the ropes, and in the last year they're planning their departure. That leaves one or two years of productivity if schools can persuade them to stay for more than two years.

Hillel Torah has made hiring shlichim a centerpiece of its approach to Jewish education. Thanks in large part to the leadership of Tamar Friedman, the long-standing head of Judaic studies, the school takes a great many careful steps to maximize the payoff from this investment. First, Friedman is incredibly careful about those they hire. She explains that it's not enough to rely on the recommendations of third-party agents who act on behalf of schools to find appropriate candidates: "You have to plant yourself in their schools . . . visit their homes . . . meet their children." These are the ways to get a sense of people—how disciplined they are in managing their lives and how they relate to young people. She also always looks to recruit couples, both of whom are expected to teach. It would not be efficient to hire one member of the family, although of course that raises the bar higher still in that she needs to find pairs of educators who both have genuine potential.

Once a couple is appointed, the Hillel team follows a well-established protocol to enable them to hit the ground running. Few other schools scaffold these appointments to such a degree. Over the six months before the shlichim leave Israel, they participate in a training program that introduces them to the school, its programs, and its ways of doing things. It's not unusual within this framework for these new recruits to observe Hillel classrooms by video from Israel. The shlichim are also paired with a mentor from whom they continue to receive intense guidance and feedback during their first year in the school. Once they arrive in the United States, their mentor guides them in observing other teachers' classes. They see how their colleagues manage classroom discipline and what motivates students in someone else's classroom. With continuous guidance and support, there is a sense that time and again, the shlichim who come to the school truly grow as educators, returning to Israel much better equipped than when they came.

Away from the classroom, the school has developed all kinds of systems to minimize the stress and distractions shlichim might experience when starting a new job in a new country with unfamiliar norms and practices. One of the senior members of the department helps the newcomers decipher emails and school announcements and often summarizes them in Hebrew. Outside school, from the time they arrive, a team of parent volunteers makes sure their new home is ready and they experience the smoothest of transitions. Someone helps them set up a bank account, find a car, and take care of any number of personal financial matters. They have a schedule of invitations for Shabbat meals and more. If they come with children, they'll be introduced to future classmates while they're still in Israel and then playdates will be organized once they arrive. They experience a kind of swaddling that minimizes the culture shock and the relocation stress. These are all ways of enabling the shlichim to fulfill their primary functions, achieve success, and, if everything works out, commit to a full four-year term if desired. (If they stayed any longer, they would lose tax benefits in Israel, so four years tends to be the upper limit for their hire in the United States.)

A Special Vintage

All of these ingredients come together in the seventh grade Chidon class. Chidon is an international Bible competition that climaxes each year with a grand final in Jerusalem over Yom Haatzmaut (Israel Independence Day). For years, Hillel Torah students have entered the preliminary rounds of the competition in Chicago and then moved on to a national round of competition. Occasionally, to great excitement, a student makes it to the international final in Israel. Every day, Rabbi A, a third-year shaliach, meets his seventh-grade class for Chidon—essentially, an opportunity to study Chumash and Tanakh (Bible) with a competitive edge.

Rabbi A readily admits that when he and his wife first came from Israel, he was the less comfortable of the two in the classroom. She was a natural—he not so much. Today this is not apparent. Given the goal—mastery, even memorization, of large quantities of Bible in Hebrew—the energy and excitement in his classroom are astonishing. Until about halfway through his seventh-grade class, the instruction is conventional. He begins with a quick check that students are familiar with a selection of names and places in the Book of Judges. He then transitions to a workbook exercise in which, led by a series of models on the interactive whiteboard, students mark up different pieces of the text in a teacher-prepared workbook. He encourages volunteers to jump in and complete quotes. The pedagogy is sound enough. It's striking that both he and the students speak almost entirely in Israeli-accented Hebrew.

After about twenty minutes, it's as if a surge of electricity courses though the class. Each student picks up a laptop from a cart and logs on to a quiz about material they've recently covered. Quickly, the students' names pop up on the interactive whiteboard screen, and once they're under way, they're tracking how they're doing compared to one another. Rabbi A warns them that less than 80 percent will mean taking the quiz again. As the clock ticks down, it looks as if they're all going to be safe.

This, it seems, was the warm-up for the main event. Now, switching to a different online program, students are randomly assigned to three-person teams for a different quiz. In this case, they're required to confer before they answer a question; they can't depend on one team member doing all the work. Witty, student-generated team names appear on the interactive whiteboard, and we're under way with the noise level progressively increasing. Here, it seems, the mission is not to avoid the retest but simply to show classmates who has what it takes. This is about the thrill of competition. There are amusing waves of oohs and ahs as the scores get updated on the screen and Rabbi A reacts to what he sees. He circulates to check in with those who didn't get an answer right, but this is a case where he doesn't need to make sure that everyone's on task. This group is well and truly in the zone.

When the quiz ends with less than ten minutes of the lesson remaining, the students urge Rabbi A (in Hebrew) to let them do another round. He theatrically agrees. The software generates a new set of groups. It turns out, to the students' disappointment, that there isn't enough time to finish. Rabbi A has to literally push the students out the door. This is a Tanakh (Bible) class they don't want to leave.

For an observer, this is an intoxicating experience. The task of memorizing biblical materials has perennially scarred day school students. Generations have plowed their way through questions such as, "About whom was it said? Who was king when? Which place was?" Here, communicating with their teacher in Hebrew, these young adults were completely enraptured. They were having fun, and evidently most knew their stuff. Yet there was more going on here than the adept use of technology. There was smart pacing, the clever use of theatrics to elevate an educational experience to something truly formative, and subtly fine-tuned teacher attention to individual students—and, without wanting to belabor the point, all of this was happening in Hebrew. The technology gave space to the teacher to work with individual students. He then made the best possible use of that space. Rabbi A may not have been a natural when he arrived, but it's evident he has been a quick study.

Standing on Guard

Of course, an episode like this can be deceptive. When the pieces all fall into place so snugly, the outcomes seem almost inevitable: bring over some cannily identified shlichim from Israel, cultivate their potential, throw in a seasoning of technology, and you have a tick-all-the-boxes lesson. The old-timers in the school would say that such outcomes are rarely won so smoothly.

In fact, in seeking to bring about such outcomes, Tamar Friedman sees herself engaged in a continuous effort to hold back the tide. She uses the Hebrew expression la'amod al hamishmar—standing on guard. She's engaged in a constant battle to maintain norms and standards. It's not that there is opposition to ascribing so much importance to Hebrew or that there are forces resisting the school's historic commitment to employing shlichim. That might be the case at other schools, but not at Hillel Torah, perhaps because the benefits have been so vivid, as witnessed in Rabbi A's class.

Friedman's vigil is much more about resisting the relentless erosion of what it takes to maintain high standards in Hebrew. Teachers—even first-language Hebrew speakers—can easily slip into speaking in English with students, especially outside the classroom. When students don't readily respond to them in Hebrew, they switch to English. That might mean that students will more easily understand a point, but repeated over time, patterns and expectations are established that are hard to disrupt. As Friedman repeatedly tells her team, "They don't need to hear your broken English!" By the same token, in the classroom, it can often happen that students will use English to answer a teacher's question. She's insistent that teachers resist. "If they don't, they're turning their students into passive language users."

She tells a story of how earlier that week, in the run-up to Yom Haaztmaut she popped in on the seventh-grade students while they were preparing for a Yom Haatzmaut fair, something that their grade has traditionally organized.

She saw they had prepared signs where the prices were in shekels but the products were listed in English. She insisted they replace everything in Hebrew. "We're not celebrating the Fourth of July!" she exclaims.

Over the course of a regular day, she spends an unusual amount of time in classrooms, observing and helping staff. She's a skilled classroom teacher herself, and she's focused on identifying opportunities for teachers to engage students more actively or deepen their learning. One suspects that her constant presence has an additional purpose: call it an enforcement effect. The staff know about her expectations and can never be sure when she'll next pop in. Circulating the corridors and classrooms, she is continually on watch for the encroaching tide.

This is what it takes to maintain a culture committed to Hebrew. It entails making symbolically important moves to communicate the school's values. That's part of what lies behind Friedman's assertiveness, for example, in relation to the Yom Haatzmaut fair. But her vigilance is also rooted in a theory of language learning, of the cues and habits that shape the brain. Without pushing students constantly to be active users and producers of the language, they simply won't develop proficiency in it.

More Than Language

Strange as it may sound, the deep investment in Hebrew at Hillel—hiring shlichim and doing all it takes to maintain the intensity of the Hebrew program—is not only, and perhaps not primarily, about developing proficiency in the language. It's about ensuring that Israel, and especially contemporary Israeli culture, is close to the school's heartbeat, a paramount value for Hillel Torah since its founding. Hebrew is a key to accessing much of this culture and to feeling at home within it through jokes, music, movies, and social media memes. Without modern spoken Hebrew, one can't completely understand the State of Israel today, and—on a much smaller scale—without modern spoken Hebrew, one can't understand much of what is happening at Hillel Torah, such as the displays around the school and the conversation between adults in the school corridors. The shlichim play an important role in contributing to this environment, as do the *bnot sherut*, especially when it comes to the physical environment.

The *bnot sherut* are at the forefront of decorating—literally, plastering— the school with images and expressions from Israel. The school's entrance hall is forever being redecorated with some new theme, whether it is to do with the Jewish calendar as viewed from an Israeli perspective or through the often humorous depiction of current events in Israel: another general election, Israel's Breishit spacecraft, or the Eurovision song contest. Teachers invariably don't have time to decorate the corridors themselves, and so this is a task that generations of *bnot sherut* have made their own. It makes a decisive contribution to the feel of Hillel Torah as an Israel-rich school. It's a large part of why when you walk into the school, Israel hits you in the face, in the best possible sense.

In essence, Israel is at the heart of space and time at Hillel. Developing "a lifelong commitment to Medinat Yisrael" might be identified as one of a number of concerns toward which the school's mission is dedicated, but spend a few days at Hillel and it feels as if this outcome is especially valued. Just as the State of Israel gives meaning and focus to corridors, classrooms, office spaces, and other public areas in the school, so contemporary Israel shapes important moments in the school calendar. It provides the content for some of the most beloved events of the school year. So-called minor festivals in the Jewish calendar—Chanukah, Tu b'Shvat, Lag Ba'omer—invariably include an Israel-connected angle, a hook-up with people in Israel, fun activities modeled on what is hip in Israel at the time, or simply images of how this festival is being celebrated there. In the final months of the school year, Israel is at the center of a series of peak moments in the calendar: Yom Hazikaron, Yom Haatzmaut, and Yom Yerushalayim.[3]

Yom Haatzmaut looms over all else, in part because it is experienced within a highly ritualized framework that enables students to know what to expect from one year to the next. The preschool students always take a virtual flight to Israel, tweaked each year so as to include some kind of surprise. In the middle school, besides festive prayer followed by dancing in the corridors, there is always a special show—a *tekkes*—performed by the eighth grade, typically including *daglanut*, a parade of Israeli flags—a venerable part of state celebrations in Israel. Each year, there is also an Israel fair, a series of round-robin activities, that is always the responsibility of the seventh grade and put on for the lower grades. Involving intense rehearsal and preparation during the prior weeks, these events carry powerful associations for their participants. They are often what students most remember about their time at the school.

In bald terms, these experiences do not differ much from what happens in a great many other schools, especially those that are shaped by a strong Zionist ethos. What seems to elevate them at Hillel are three things: first, a great many members of this community are connected to friends and close family in Israel, including many of the school's alumni; second, the sizable contingent of current staff who are Israelis; and, third, the extensive use of spoken Hebrew at these events and during their preparation. These features add a kind of authenticity and intensity to these experiences—an as-if-you-were-there quality—that might not be quite so palpable in many other schools.

A few days before Yom Haatzmaut, the eighth graders have been released from regular classes to focus on preparations for Yom Haatzmaut. Their tekkes is directed, as in past years, by a husband and wife team who came originally from Israel and have been pillars of the Judaic studies faculty ever since. All of the direction is in Hebrew. Some students respond in Hebrew, some in English. There's a long schedule pinned to the door of the lunchroom, where rehearsals are taking place, telling students when to come to practice their scenes.

Up on the stage, a series of scenes play out interspersed with a soundtrack of Israeli classics and hits from today. Some of the narration, provided by students, is in English and some in Hebrew. The scenes, often involving song, dance, and plenty of humor, depict moments from Israel's history and life today: the UN vote that brought the state into existence, waves of immigration, different communities in Israel today, army life.

With Yom Haatzmaut just a couple of school days away, anxiety levels are at a high pitch. There's plenty of nervous laughter. Periodically, students who are not yet due on the stage are cleared out of the room. They're getting a little too excited. A steady stream of faculty pops in to see how things are going. Evidently many people have a stake in this, and with so few school days to go, there's quite a lot of work to do.

Balancing Priorities

Despite the intense commitment to conducting Judaic studies in the lower grades in Hebrew, this intensity eases off in the middle school grades. As many other Modern Orthodox schools do, Hillel Torah introduces the study of Torah She B'el Peh (oral law), and specifically Gemara, in the middle school grades. For many years, the school tried to find teachers who could teach rabbinic texts effectively and do so in Hebrew. They would turn to shlichim or would hope to find the rare individuals in the United States who could do everything demanded of them. Often, because they couldn't find appropriate candidates, they ended up turning to Haredi or Yeshivish individuals who were capable Torah teachers but were hardly aligned ideologically with the school's modernity and its Zionism.

Over the years, there was increasing pressure to do things differently, fueled by the fact that Hillel Torah was starting to lose families to its closest competitor on the religious right, a school that did not run an ivrit b'ivrit program and offered a *limmudei kodesh* experience in which students learned from and formed a relationship with a *rebbe*, a rabbi/teacher who serves as a mentor. Rabbi Linzer's appointment created an opportunity to explore a different way of doing things. He was a strong proponent of the idea that in middle school, the priority was that those who teach limmudei kodesh be role models for their students. They should be American (ideally, day school graduates themselves) who could demonstrate through their own example what it means to be a modern, Torani, religious Zionist. (*Torani*, here, serves as shorthand for religiously serious.) Hebrew was important, but it wasn't more important than the other values that were at the core of Hillel's identity as a Modern Orthodox day school. The middle school is the time to prioritize a love of Torah learning and observance and to hire staff who could make that happen.

Although this proposed shift did provoke concerns among some that it would be the thin end of the wedge, resulting in a retreat from ivrit b'ivrit in the lower grades as well, the concept was well received by the board and parents and accepted by the faculty too. Tamar Friedman, one of the fiercest proponents of ivrit b'ivrit, was of the view that toning down the intensity of Hebrew in the middle school would not result in students losing what they had gained in earlier years. That's not how language learning works. If you can shape the brain during the elementary years, you lay down a foundation for life.

While the school community was ready for a recalibration in emphasis, it might have been difficult to pull off if it wasn't for one piece of good fortune. About a year before Rabbi Linzer's appointment, Yeshiva University opened a Community Kollel (a local hub for full-time Torah study) in Chicago. The Kollel served as a base from which a small group of newly ordained rabbis and their wives engaged in all manner of community education activities, in synagogues and schools, and through programs run under their own auspices. In other communities, this model had been a successful means by which to intensify Torah teaching aligned with a Yeshiva University Modern Orthodox *hashkafa* (ideology), which at the turn of the last century was engaged in a rearguard fight against forces from the right and left. Each cohort of Kollel rabbis typically stayed in a community for a couple of years and then moved on to full-time rabbinic or communal work elsewhere in the United States.

The Kollel's opening in 2008 started to bring to Chicago a small stream of young couples who were ideologically aligned with Hillel Torah's own ethos. They also invariably came with experience as informal Jewish educators; some had advanced degrees in education. Most had not intended to stay longer than a couple of years in Chicago and didn't do so. And yet, as Rabbi Linzer describes it, the school seized on the opportunity to draw from this talent pool and worked intensively to convince a handful of the Kollel members to come work in the school. (Going hard after these individuals was not as obvious a strategy as it seems today and is another indicator of Linzer's instinct to invest faith in educators of not yet fully realized potential.) Today, more than half of the faculty teaching Judaic studies in the middle school at Hillel Torah originally came to Chicago under the aegis of the Kollel. (The Gemara class at the start of this chapter was being taught by a Kollel alum, for example.) Their presence has transformed the atmosphere in the middle school. They bring a breath of fresh air to the teaching of Chumash, Navi, Halacha, Mishna, and Gemara.[4] And, no less important, they have formed lasting relationships with the students that continue long after they graduate. They have left a positive imprint on the lives of Hillel Torah students and in doing so have contributed to an important updating of the school's image.

Halacha with Humor

With just a couple of weeks to go to Pesach, Rabbi L's coed eighth-grade class is devoted to prepping the students for the Seder. Rabbi L was one of the first rabbis at the Yeshiva University Kollel. He and his family stayed in Chicago so he could take a part-time position as the rabbi of a small congregation that some Hillel Torah families attend. Looking for additional work, he came to Hillel Torah and has stayed, becoming a beloved mentor to generations of Hillel Torah students.

Parents expect their children, no matter what age, to bring fresh Torah insights from school to their family Seder tables. In the worst cases, this expectation can result in students' being force-fed *divrei torah* (Torah insights) they barely understand that they then regurgitate at home. Rabbi L's approach is different. He'll certainly make sure his students arrive at the Seder with a bag full of sharp insights and ideas; in fact, for the past few years, his former students have been coming to his home for a pre-Pesach class where they expect to continue picking up new nuggets. What's different is that rather than pumping his students with off-the-shelf Torah tidbits, he uses Hagaddah-inspired questions to explore with them what can only be called the philosophy of *halacha*, the principles that lie behind different aspects of the seder night. All of this is sprinkled with a wry sense of humor. In this, the most teacher-centered class observed over a number of days in the school, he has no trouble holding the attention of his adolescent students with witty repartee and whimsical observations.

"Why don't you make a *bracha* (blessing) at the start of the *magid* (narrative) section of the Haggada?" This is the lead-off question that drives the class. Each student has a copy of the Haggada in front of them, formatted with the Haggada text on one page faced by an empty page for taking notes. They write as the conversation goes back and forth between teacher and students.

To get to the answer this question, Rabbi L steers the class through a series of broader questions: "What else don't you make a bracha on?" "What's the difference between the commandment to tell the story (*sippur*) and remembering the story (*zechira*)?" Along the way there are additional quirky questions that help piece together the picture: "If there's a commandment not to kill, should that come with a bracha?" "Should you make a bracha if you eat bacon?" These questions all help clarify the principles behind the circumstances when making a blessing is appropriate.

The conversation moves forward, with most of the class weighing in at some point or another, even if it's with quirky questions of their own, such as, "What bracha do you make on quinoa?" (The rabbi's responds, "Why would you eat quinoa!") And as the class moves forward, Rabbi L writes notes on the interactive whiteboard in English, inserting key concepts in Hebrew. He doesn't write fully formed sentences; it's for the students to finesse those. Ultimately the divrei torah they produce are in their own words.

The atmosphere in class is relaxed. The rabbi engages in some good-natured banter with the students, and they respond in kind. Occasionally he reminds the students to raise their hands if they want to make a contribution, but in truth, the discussion is free flowing thanks in large part to the fact that students seem to be bringing a great deal of general textual knowledge accumulated over the years. This enables the discussion to move quickly from basic content to a higher conceptual plane. It also allows Rabbi L to explore the moral implications of what they're exploring—in this instance, the notion that "people need to be ready and able to get along with people with whom they don't agree. . . . If you tell me that your family *minhag* (custom) is to drive to McDonald's on Yom Kippur, I can't write you off." It's at these moments that textual study becomes a springboard to profound life lessons.

Mission over Market

Rabbi L's warm style and the life lessons he offers are important elements in the experience that Hillel Torah offers students today. Alongside a highly progressive educational experience in both general and Judaic studies, the school provides the primary components of a traditional Jewish education. Middle school students develop robust Judaic textual skills, become Jewishly knowledgeable, and have an opportunity to be both inspired and instructed by male and female Torani personalities.

One might have expected that being able to offer all of these things on top of an ever more cutting-edge general education, there would be a positive impact on the school's enrollment. The school is surely an ever more appealing proposition to prospective families. And yet over the past decade, there hasn't been a great change in the numbers attracted to the school. In the lower school there continue to be about forty-five students in each grade and in the middle school grades about thirty students. The attrition is usually due to families emigrating to Israel (Aliya), to all intents and purposes success stories within the universe of Hillel's values. For example, fifteen students were due to make Aliya with their families during the summer after the school year during which we gathered our data.

The challenge for Hillel Torah is demographic and ideological. Over the last couple of decades, Hillel has faced competition from the Arie Crown Hebrew Day School, an institution positioned ideologically to its right with leadership coming out of the ultra-Orthodox Lakewood yeshiva. Arie Crown is located in West Rogers Park, about a fifteen-minute drive from Hillel. Young Orthodox couples have been attracted to renting apartments in this neighborhood. If they start families while they still live in these first homes, Arie Crown is equally accessible in transport terms. Additionally, irrespective of proximity, a sizable number of parents on the right wing of the Modern Orthodox community are increasingly attracted to what Arie Crown offers: boys and girls are taught separately; families are expected to filter their Internet at home; girls do not perform in front of men or learn Gemara; and each year students are assigned a rebbe. Ironically, a sizable number of those who are attracted to this model are some of the most religiously committed Hillel graduates. These students, like those who have emigrated to Israel, can be considered—in terms of Hillel's mission—success stories, in this instance with respect to their religious seriousness.

These trends reflect a social situation that has challenged the Modern

Orthodox community across America for the past few decades, a steady drift from the middle of the road to more stringent expressions of religious orthodoxy. The response of Hillel's leadership to this situation is instructive. It has been measured and fully consistent with the school's mission. As we have seen, the school has worked to intensify the Torani features of its middle school. Hiring the Kollel couples has been a large part of that. When hiring shlichim and *b'not sherut*, it has in recent years sought out those who come with a more religious profile; female shlichim cover their hair, and the men are referred to as Rav. These are small markers of a more Torani orientation.

The school has also been much more proactive when it comes to recruitment. It has started to hold prospective parent events in West Rogers Park. The school has been running student *shabbatonim* in the neighborhood. Pictures included in the school's marketing material have started to reflect the religious dimensions of life at Hillel. These moves have helped increase the school's appeal to more right-wing Modern Orthodox families. There is evidence this is having an impact. Some young families have relocated to Skokie.

What Hillel's leadership did not do was fundamentally alter its curriculum and ethos: the equal expectations of boys and girls, the balance of Hebrew and Judaic studies, or Israel's special place in the school. In short, it has remained faithful to the Modern Orthodox and religious Zionist ethos on which the school has historically rested. As a consequence, the makeup of the families in the school has largely been unchanged: about a third come from the liberal end of the Modern Orthodox community, about a third from its right wing, and the remainder from somewhere in the middle. Unpleasant scuttlebutt in the wider community has claimed that students' birthday parties are not always kosher and that families are not always *shomer shabbat* (Sabbath observant) or that the school has become more liberal over the years. These claims don't seem to have any basis. They probably say more about shifts in the broader community context in which the school exists than about changes in the school's priorities. Hillel continues to hold firm to the signature values of Modern Orthodox day school education. And for Rabbi Linzer, there is every reason to do so: Hillel Torah provides a wholesome coeducational experience. It is a socially healthy environment in which to appreciate what it means to live out the principles of Torah u'Madda, a dual curriculum of sacred and general studies.

Viewing the stickiness of Hillel's student enrollment, it's hard to resist the conclusion that while America's Modern Orthodox day schools may have been one of the most stable sectors in the day school marketplace these past twenty or so years, these schools essentially constitute a niche sector. They are likely to appeal to a narrow slice of the community who share a particular *hashkafa* (religious ideology) but are probably not going to appeal to a wider market from the right or the left. That's not a reason for despondency or disappointment. On the contrary. It argues for a clarity of purpose and self-confidence in serving this particular community. This, one might say, has been the MO of Hillel Torah's philosophy: exceptional clarity of mission, purposeful pursuit of that mission, and a special commitment to finding the right staff to bring that mission to life. The tireless search to serve students as effectively as possible through an education that is both consistently child centered and grounded in the verities of Modern Orthodoxy and religious Zionism has value for its own sake. It is not about beating the market.

CONNECTIONS AND EXCEPTIONS

Although only thirteen years old when they graduate, the students at Hillel Torah corroborate how, with appropriate resources, Jewish day schools are capable of nurturing Jewish cultural virtuosos: students who can communicate competently in Hebrew, study traditional Jewish text with a good deal of independence, and lead religious services. Like the students in the higher streams at TanenbaumCHAT (chapter 7) and at the Rav Teitz Mesivta (chapter 6), the oldest students at Hillel Torah display a level of Jewish literacy far in advance of what most American Jewish adults ever achieve. It leaves one to ponder what it would take for greater numbers to achieve this kind of cultural competence. Is it so much contingent on the time invested?

The educational transformation that has played out at Hillel Torah over the past ten years suggests that cultural virtuosity isn't only a question of hours of repeated experience. With its introduction of child-centered pedagogies across the grades and across the curriculum, Hillel Torah looks in educational terms much like the other elementary schools in our sample: Brandeis Marin, Hillel Detroit, the Pressman Academy, and Akiva School. These day schools are all at the front end of the curve in their use, for example, of project-based learning, the responsive classroom approach, and blended learning. With such diverse Jewish cultures in these schools, it is evident that child-centered educational practice is not driven by just one model of schooling or school leadership.

Where Hillel Torah departs radically from these other schools is in the low-key role it plays in the lives of parents. We characterize Pressman and Brandeis as "repair shops," intentionally setting out to repair the damage caused to parents by their own disappointing experiences with Jewish education as children. This is not a feature of Hillel Torah; many of the parents are themselves graduates of the school. As adults, they lead rich Jewish lives of their own; they do need not any kind of supplement from the school, let alone an antidote. And because they inhabit already tightly knit Jewish social circles, they don't need the school to build community in a personal or social sense.

That said, there is one critical way in which the school does contribute to community. Like Yeshiva Darchei Torah in Far Rockaway (chapter 9), the school serves as a physical anchor for a particular segment of the wider Jewish community. If the school did not exist, most of its families would probably move elsewhere so important to them is it that the school be aligned with their Modern Orthodox religious hashakfa.

Unlike the Hebrew Academy in Miami (chapter 8), the other Modern Orthodox school in this sample, Hillel Torah need not function as a broad tent. As in all other Modern Orthodox schools, there are constituencies that would like to pull the school to the right or the left, but unlike the Hebrew Academy, Hillel does not seem to be drawn one way or the other. This, it seems, is a consequence of the demographic luxury of being located within a substantial population of ideologically aligned families in one of North America's largest Jewish communities. It is also because the school's leadership has the confidence to pursue a strong and singular ideological direction, whatever the consequences.

Leadership, as in so many other schools, is determinative at Hillel Torah. As is the case at TanenbaumCHAT and the Rav Teitz Mesivta, the head of school's own biography as a graduate of similarly aligned day schools makes him an exemplar of what it means to have had one's life shaped by the school's central values. There is perhaps no more powerful way of advocating for the school's distinctive mission.

2

A Forward-Looking Community School

Hillel Day School, Detroit, Michigan

The evolution of Detroit's Hillel Day School reflects a broader national pattern in which pluralistic models of Jewish day school education have sprouted from liberal denominational forerunners.[1] This chapter reveals both the benefits and challenges associated with this widespread trend. Hillel's Jewish pluralism has helped the school continue to thicken the connective tissue of local Jewish communal life (an outcome that also owes a great deal to the school's continued diligent cultivation) and has made it difficult, at the same time, to cultivate a Jewish culture that is both appealing and engaging to all those it recruits. This is a project that continues to be a work in progress. Benefiting from generous philanthropic support, the school offers a striking instance of what it takes first to reinvent the Jewish day school in the service of twenty-first-century learning and, then, what is involved in ensuring that parents understand and support an experience of schooling profoundly different from their own.

A paradox lies at the heart of Jewish day school education: even though Jewish day schools are distinctive primarily for their intensive Judaic content and immersive Jewish ambience, most parents enrolling their children in day schools not under Orthodox auspices are far more concerned about the quality of the general studies classes than offerings in Jewish studies. It's not that these parents have no interest in the Judaic side, but their focus is on the teaching of good Jewish values (by which they generally mean fair play, compassion, respect, and discipline—values not limited to Jewish culture), along with basic Hebrew-language skills, a modicum of knowledge about Judaism and Jewish culture, and the fostering of some connection to the Jewish people and Israel. Above all else, though, the school must field a serious general studies program. To be sure, as one proceeds toward the more insular end of the Orthodox spectrum, a commitment to Judaic literacy rises in importance. Yet even among the Modern Orthodox, it simply won't do if a school fails to offer strong preparation for serious high school learning and eventually a path to acceptance at sought-after colleges.

Hillel Day School in suburban Detroit, a K–8 educational center with 450 students plus a 144-student early childhood center during the 2017–18 school year, illustrates how this dynamic operates in practice. A proudly pluralistic community day school, Hillel attracts children from the entire spectrum of Jewish outlook. Its largest contingent from a single synagogue is drawn from a Reform temple, while the majority of its students come from Conservative homes. Rising numbers also are being drawn from Modern Orthodox families dissatisfied with the general studies offerings at the Orthodox schools in the area. And a fair number of secular families with little interest in Judaism also send their children.

What binds these disparate families together into a community is Hillel's strong commitment to offering cutting-edge approaches to education, mainly in general studies. In recent years, the school has remade itself into a laboratory for progressive educational experiments, introducing project-based learning and new curricula, trying out new uses of time and space, and accommodating different learner styles within its student body. To make this possible, the school has engaged in a massive physical reconstruction to create spaces for innovative learning experiences.

All of this effort, in the words of the school's president, has transformed Hillel into "the cool kid on the block," a serious competitor to the best private schools in the area and one that is increasingly attractive to families. As a parent put it, "Hillel conveys its warmth and aliveness when you walk in the door," in contrast to an elite private school nearby. It also offers "a much more individualized educational experience than the public schools." In this sense, it offers a "phenomenal general education—that's what will bring people to the door." Even parents who are not especially committed to a Jewish education are quickly won over.

And yet precisely because the school has introduced a model of learning that downplays grades and rote learning, continually explains to students why the subject matter they are studying is important and creates opportunities for students to express in their own distinctive ways what sense they have made of their new learning, some parents remain anxious: they fear the very progressive approaches that have elevated the school may not prepare their children for challenging high school–level work. By contrast, it appears that most parents have little that is critical to say about the Jewish studies side, even though it is widely acknowledged to be the weaker one.

It Starts with Leadership

Founded in 1958 as a Conservative day school, Hillel has undergone a series of major transformations over the past fifteen years, changing its curricula, expectations of students, means of student assessment, homework requirements, physical plant, and its affiliation as a Conservative day school. The strong consensus at the school and in the wider community is that the driving force behind these changes has been Hillel's school head, Steve Freedman.

Steve is a most unlikely day school head. He did not have an intensive Jewish education as a child, but after college he found his way to work in the congregational school sector, teaching Jewish history at a Hebrew high school, where he started to make his mark. Then he started a journey of more advanced study at Gratz College in Philadelphia and eventually the Jewish Theological Seminary in New York City, graduating with a master's in Jewish education. Though he held various educational positions, mainly in congregational part-time schooling, and at one point served as an assistant day school principal, he came to Hillel as a novice when it came to running a Jewish day school. He did, however, have one extracurricular experience that has stood him in good stead: during his early years, he developed a passion for directing theater, an experience he claims to be not unlike the role a school head must assume.

Hired at Hillel in 2003, he was the first head of Hillel who was not a rabbi, did not have a doctorate, and could not speak fluent Hebrew. But he did have extensive experience in Jewish education and, most important, came with a promising description of the role he intended to play at Hillel, then a floundering school where parents and board members did not know or accept the limits on their prerogatives to manage the school. The message he delivered to the search committee was unequivocal: *he* would run the school. This was especially appealing to the board chairman at the time, who told Steve, "I don't have a price. I hope you don't have one either," a tough stance at a time of financial challenge. Since his hiring, Steve has taken the reins firmly, though not without recurring flash points.

First, soon after he was appointed, came an uproar when he announced that in the coming school year, Hillel would have a dress code for students and also parents entering the school building. Some parents were up in arms, but the storm passed fairly quickly after a parent meeting with the school administration. Then came a second battle: he insisted on Hillel sponsoring an eighth-grade class trip to Israel. In both instances, parents demanded the board step in; some resented the dress code; others feared for the security of their children on a trip to Israel. Steve adamantly insisted that neither was within the purview of the board. "I maintained that Israel was a curricular issue—not a decision for the board to make and that all I wanted was their blessing. Sure, we had some protests from parents, but the board stayed out of it. Now, thirteen years later, no one remembers a time the eighth-grade class at Hillel didn't go to Israel."

Then came a succession of even more contentious decisions. In his second year, Steve began to educate the board about the distinctions among parochial, public, and independent schools. This occurred in the wake of a Michigan Appellate Court decision to exempt a Catholic parochial school from union elections required by Michigan's Employment Relations Commission. The question at Hillel was whether it would oust the teachers' union in light of the court's decision. This was a fraught issue that unnerved teachers and some parents. Teachers established a picket line, fraying nerves even more. But through careful managing, Steve was able to navigate the shoals and, most important, reassure the teachers that they would be treated well and fairly. Though some teachers have left for a variety of reasons, Hillel has on staff individuals who have been in the school for decades—one for nearly a half century. Its reputation has attracted public school teachers who are willing to take a pay cut, and it often has the luxury of choosing between multiple candidates for general studies positions. The key was to communicate to teachers that they were cared for and would be rewarded when they did well. In fact, teachers receive both cost-of-living and merit raises as a way to recognize excellence.

An even more contentious issue arose in 2008 when the school moved to disaffiliate from the Schechter Conservative day school system and join what was then known as Ravsak, or community day school network. Affiliation with the Schechter network identifies the day school as committed to the ideology and practices of the Conservative movement in Judaism. This requires schools to maintain religious practices such as daily prayer (*Tefila*), keeping kosher, being closed on Jewish holidays, and limiting enrollment to children deemed Jewish according to Jewish law, Halacha. Despite the shift in affiliation, Hillel has maintained its commitment to religious observances, and its bylaws state explicitly that Hillel is a "halachic" day school in all its dynamism."

What lay behind the debate about changing Hillel's affiliation were two concerns: first, Conservative synagogues in the Detroit area were suffering a membership decline that was bound to suppress enrollment, and concurrently, leaders in the community saw an opportunity to broaden the school's appeal to families identifying with other sectors by eliminating its denominational label.

At board and parent meetings, some attendees expressed their dismay that the school's Jewish orientation would be diluted. They saw value in the school's adherence to Halacha, a commitment of the Conservative movement. In opposing this perspective, the arguments in favor of joining Ravsak summarized neatly by one board member: "[This] is about the future of the school and the Detroit Jewish community. How do we best position the school and provide as many families as possible a serious Jewish education for their children if this is what they seek? How do we open doors as widely as possible for the future? How do we teach mutual respect in our Jewish world if children don't have opportunities to learn and be together? A school is the place to break down these barriers within the Jewish community. A Jewish day school is the best hope for a vibrant Jewish future."

After hearing presentations by the national heads of the Schechter and community day school (Ravsak) organizations, the board voted to approve the shift. But matters did not resolve with that decision. A previous board chairman tried to organize several other former leaders to campaign for the ouster of Steve Freedman; that went nowhere. Yet even today, some on the more traditional side of the spectrum worry aloud about the adverse impact of the school's openness to all kinds of families: given the lack of commitment to Jewish observances on the part of many parents, they ask whether all children admitted to the school are appropriate to Hillel's mission and whether their presence is diluting the clarity of its religious message. But the shift in affiliation went through in part through the resolute stance of the board chairman, who took much of the heat. And then matters calmed down. One of the strongest opponents of the shift now has his grandchildren enrolled in the school's early childhood center.

Still another important step prompting a good deal of hand-wringing and disagreement was the decision in 2009 to investigate the feasibility of Hillel opening an early childhood center (ECC). In this case, considerable opposition could be expected by local synagogues. The latter had long sponsored preschool programs, often relying on them to serve as portals of entry for young families to join synagogues. Why, some asked, would Hillel jeopardize its good relationships with local synagogues by becoming a competitor to their programs? Was this politically wise when Hillel sought and required Federation and foundation funding, both of which might dry up if it made the wrong enemies? Besides, why would a Jewish day school embark on an effort that would result in lower membership in synagogues and potentially fewer children enrolling in synagogue-sponsored Jewish education? Further concerns were raised about the insurance and other costs of opening an ECC.

The argument in favor of the move noted that synagogue-based early childhood programs were in numerical decline and costing synagogues dearly. Moreover, it was not necessarily the case that teachers in synagogue programs would be put out of work; Hillel could hire some of them. Of course, the benefits to Hillel were part of the calculation: the ECC might serve as a feeder, thereby increasing enrollments and exposing more Detroit-area children to an immersive Jewish education.

The latter set of arguments ultimately won the board over. By 2018, Hillel enrolled 144 children in its ECC; between 60 and 75 percent went on to matriculate in the school. The ECC arm was so successful, in fact, that Hillel embarked on a major physical expansion to accommodate the preschool division in anticipation of eventually enrolling 180 children.

The purpose in noting these various controversies is to highlight the role of the school head in leading change. In each instance, he laid the ground-work at meetings for board members and groups of parents. And in each instance, he was prepared to take the heat from dissatisfied parents. His approach to these matters bears attention. Although he prepared stakeholders for changes being contemplated, he did not wait until everyone was on board. Certainly, he did not spring a new decision without proper consultation and community-wide discussion. But he also was clear that he would lead change rather than settle for becoming the embodiment of a new course that had already won widespread approval. In short, he displayed a strategic sense with attention to important tactical moves designed to gradually win over his stakeholders.

His course of action entailed risks. The rewards, however, were great: not only has the school gone in important new directions; it has done so without too much off-putting agonizing, and it has held together as a community. Most important, the school is widely perceived as having taken the right steps and that perceptions also brought extraordinary financial support.

Educational Vision

Steve Freedman's greatest challenge, and the one undoubtedly most important to him, has been the remaking of Hillel's educational program. To further this aim, he has committed himself to playing two primary roles:

As an advocate of schoolwide learning who is eager to experiment and learn from what happens. His approach is pragmatic: "let's see if it works."

As the school's chief communicator who prepares the ground for change and controls the school's message.

To begin with the first of these, Hillel is committed to adopting current progressive educational approaches. In recent years, the school has incorporated problem-based learning in its general studies program and introduced new curricula, including some based on the Common Core. Classes are highly participatory and active, aiming to help students become reflective thinkers. The school is learner centered and constructivist, which means that students are encouraged to make their own meaning out of material presented to them. To further this aim, the school has created new opportunities to stimulate students to translate what they have learned into artistic or other physical form. Encapsulating its approach in pithy form, the school likes to take note of its seven C's: creativity, collaboration, critical thinking, communication, core Jewish values, community, and character.

The underlying assumption of this approach is that twenty-first-century learning must prepare students for a radically new world, and this requires Hillel to adopt new approaches if it is to succeed at that task. Hillel accepts that children are wired differently today. They're more comfortable working in groups, they need to be bombarded with stimuli, and they have the tools to work independently of their teachers.

Equally important, the new technological age brings information to our fingertips with a quick Google search. Students today, the reasoning goes, need to learn how to learn and understand why the subject matter is worth learning. It won't do any longer to focus classes on "covering" material. The challenge of education today is to stimulate students to learn in their own ways and help them incorporate their new learnings in their own ways.

Educating toward twenty-first-century skills necessitates a new approach to learning best captured by a poster in the school quoting Albert Einstein: "Imagination is more important than knowledge." So too are character, responsibility, and respect. What, then, is passé? Rote learning, memorization of facts, the regurgitation of "correct" answers, and the teacher as sage on the stage. To make the case, Steve Freedman likes to cite a study in which high school students returning after the summer vacation were administered the final exam from the previous spring. Very high percentages had forgotten what they had memorized. Memorized learning does not stick well, whereas acquired skills don't fade nearly as easily.

Hillel's new emphases, unsurprisingly, have met with some resistance. Some parents periodically express concern that their children will be short-changed by new ways of learning. A parent in the school captures the ambivalence well: "Buying into twenty-first learning is a huge change when the school is ahead of much of the world. We struggle with it as a board and as parents. We expected school to be a place of homework, tests, grades. I'm not freaked out. We want to believe. *Our kids don't live in the world we did.*" Parents understand that the new approach may be good for their children, that a new era requires new skill sets and strengths. But they also perceive so much in life as a race and worry that their children will be left behind. Some chafe at the school policies of not assigning homework in the lower grades, of eliminating grades for students in K through 4, of stressing imagination and varied learning styles over the kinds of education that they themselves received. Moving away from twentieth-century learning modes, they fear, will short-change their children, leaving them unprepared for high-level school work.

What this means is that the school has to coax parents out of their comfort zones. In contrast to the schools where change occurs only after a buildup of parent pressure, Hillel's dynamic goes in the opposite direction: its educators pull parents in a new direction that some regard with skepticism or fear. And the chief educator of parents and teachers is the school head, Steve Freedman.

Perhaps in light of this responsibility, it makes greater sense that Steve has a love of directing theater. At Hillel, he manages the various stakeholders and decides when the time is ripe to introduce changes. Interestingly, much of his educational approach is based on experience and self-teaching. He has not attended any of the major programs run to develop heads of Jewish day schools, but he reads voraciously and then translates what he has learned for others.

Steve defines his second role as "chief storyteller." He relies on members of his staff to relay what parents are feeling or worrying about. He tells stories and develops a narrative to explain what the school is aiming to accomplish and why change is necessary or desirable. And then he thinks carefully about how to stage change. Are teachers prepared for it? Do parents understand it? He employs blogs, letters, and different types of gatherings to communicate with parents and his teachers. He and the school principal host teachers in their homes to talk about their common journeys and plans. At these meetings, he shows videos about advanced thinking in educational circles. The challenge is to get enough parents to attend meetings, the best place for him to communicate about the school. He has had experience with theater and knows how to use the stage to his advantage. In short, he translates the latest educational literature he finds compelling into language that will be accessible to his main stakeholders.

He also meets with parents to help them understand why certain changes are *not* opportune. Parents periodically push for the school to expose students at younger grade levels to sophisticated course material. Steve then explains why in the school's view, students are not yet deemed ready for certain types of subject matter. For example, he brought along data to a meeting with parents who were pressing for their children to begin studying algebra. His data established the optimal time for students to begin this type of math.

One way he communicates is by issuing an annual state-of-the-school report. These presentations usually consist of reiterating the fundamental questions the educational leadership consistently asks, reporting about progress the school has made, and examining prospective initiatives in the works. A typical page in his reports illustrates how he frames the educational questions central to the work of the school community:

1. What do we want students to know?
2. How do we know they know it?
3. What do we do when they don't know it?
4. What do we do when they already know it?

To keep these questions uppermost, he has also introduced changes in how students are taught and assessed. Every class through grade 4 is taught by two teachers to maximize the attention students will receive. In those grades, homework has been eliminated, although parents are encouraged to read books to or with children every evening and are given an extensive list of home-based activities they may try with their children to stimulate their imaginations. And gradually, the school is moving away from student evaluations in the form of grades; instead, assessment reports answer "I can do" questions—statements about competencies, such as, "I can write a sentence introducing a paragraph." Part of the assessment of students in the middle school is based on their own sense of competence in various areas.

All of this also requires bringing teachers onboard with the school's thinking. That involves a careful navigation between pushing too quickly and risking losing teachers in the process, and alternatively delaying much longer than is healthy for the school. Perhaps nowhere is this tension more evident than in the higher grades because seventh- and eighth-grade teachers tend to view themselves primarily as conveyers of content. They want students to absorb material and are reluctant to devote time to asking why it is important that students absorb material other than because it will help them do well in high school. The school is working to move teachers away from a focus on teaching about cells and chemistry, for example, that takes no account of "why students should learn about them." The new approach stresses the role of the educator in explaining reasons why a subject is taught.

To help teachers adapt to the new approach, Hillel invests in sustained teacher learning. For example, a coach comes to the school three times a year to work with fifth-grade teachers. Teachers are also sent to training workshops and conferences. The school invests $80,000 of its own budget in addition to government funding and grants it has received in order to provide professional development for its teachers.

Freedman also spends time with teachers. He sees himself in a different category from the senior administrative team. Although he confers with that group regularly, he also meets with teachers for the purposes of hearing them out and helping them navigate change in the school's educational approaches. Over the years, teachers who could not or would not adapt have left the school. Those who remained are deeply committed and seem to have grown with the school. It's not something the school speaks about openly, but clearly teachers best matched to the growth sensibility the school cultivates flourish, while those who do not move with the program are let go.

The Leadership Team

Though it is hard to appreciate Hillel's recent trajectory without understanding the leadership skills of its school head, he would be the first to concede the importance of his leadership team and the significant role its members play. The team consists of the K–8 principal, the director of early learning, director of curriculum, dean of Judaic studies, dean of student learning, and rabbi. We highlight the roles of three members of this team.

One is Joan Freedman, director of curriculum, who was trained as a Jewish family life and general studies teacher. When she first arrived at Hillel, her role was defined as librarian and enrichment teacher. But when it became evident that the school lacked formal curricula in most areas of general studies, she assumed responsibility for curriculum development. Under her guidance, the school aligned its math and language arts curricula to the Common Core. Along with Hillel's science team, she attended national conferences, which served to stimulate them to develop a coherent science and robotics curriculum.

Strikingly, though, Joan Freedman has distanced herself and the school from conventional understandings of curriculum. She constantly pushes teachers to ask themselves why students ought to study a particular subject matter. What is the rationale, for example, for Hebrew-language instruction in that language (ivrit b'ivrit)? When they reply that Hebrew serves as the bridge to Jewish civilization or that it connects students to Israel or that as a foreign language it is good for brain development, she then presses teachers about how their "why" is reflected in the classroom.

In her approach to curriculum, Joan Freedman insists on depth rather than breadth as the most important goal. It used to be, she relates, that a textbook would contain as many as twenty units. Teachers would be expected to "cover" them all. Now Hillel has dispensed with textbooks, and the twenty units have been compressed to a more manageable four or five major themes. The goal, moreover, is not to "cover" the material but to help students understand key concepts. One teacher gave an example: it used to be that second-grade Hebrew was expected to cover a set amount of material and vocabulary. More often than not, teachers could not complete the assigned goal, but that did not prevent third-grade teachers from picking up where the students should have been at the end of the previous grade rather than where they actually did conclude the year. And remarkably, it did not occur to the teachers even to ask themselves how much students had learned at the end of the previous year. Now there is far more attunement to the actual learning experiences of students.

Not the least of the curricular changes under Joan has been both a streamlining of the major themes to be covered each year and a simultaneous effort to bring multiple disciplines to bear on subject matter. So, for example, when students study census taking in a Mishna text (the foundational text of the Talmud), they also look at places within the school where gathering data might improve the educational experience. The Mishnaic census, then, is not understood in a "Jewish" vacuum but is related to the current lives of students. (As a result of several such projects, Hillel has taken to heart student sentiment and has changed both the physical layout of the school and some programs.)

The integration of studies with real-world applications is a hallmark of the approach Joan favors, as a few examples illustrate. When a class was studying the nature of Jewish community, it heard from a student's grandfather who had visited the Jewish community in Uganda. Students then came up with ways to contribute modestly to that community by making toys and using the proceeds of their sale to send as Tzedakah (a charitable contribution) to the Ugandan Jews. In an example from general studies, students learning about cities were given an opportunity to hear from a city planner in Detroit. Similarly, an eighth-grade class learning about the Pythagorean theorem had a rich conversation with a visiting mathematician.

A separate coordinator, Saul Rube, serves as dean of Judaic studies. In recent years, the school has gradually introduced some progressive learning approaches in these domains, though it remains a work in progress. Under Rube's leadership, Hillel also was an early joiner of the Standards and Benchmarks project, which is designed to help schools think through their goals and method in Bible (Tanakh) study. It also joined with Ayeka, an initiative to infuse Judaic studies with a more spiritual sensibility.

The school principal, Melisa Michaelson, conceives of her main role as an instructional coach and leader whose job is to hold teachers accountable for meeting the needs of the children. She observes classes and then works with teachers. In some cases, she models lessons and offers advice on how teachers might fulfill their own goals. In others, she sets clear goals for teachers and meets with them over the course of the year to chart progress on attaining those goals. Though her purview is general studies, she is convinced parents are attracted to Hillel because of its values, which they link to its Jewish commitments.

An Ecosystem for Sustaining Community

In order to house Hillel's ambitious reimagining of student learning, the school has undergone a massive transformation and expansion of its physical plant. Wandering through the school, an observer remarked that Hillel looks like a cross between a children's museum, Google headquarters, and a boutique hotel with funky furniture. The spaces do not have conventional school names. At the center of the school building is a vast public area known as the Mercaz (center in Hebrew). This space is used for multiple purposes at the same time: for a teacher meeting in one area while a class is held in another, and off in another sector, kindergartners make themselves comfortable on oversized chairs. The space is available for teachers whenever they feel it beneficial to move their students out of formal classrooms. Multiple prayer serves are also held in the cavernous Mercaz space. Overall, the goal of the Mercaz is to offer a flexible space for all kinds of activities.

Off to one side of the Mercaz is the fishbowl, a glass-enclosed space most often used by the leadership team for its meetings, though classes also meet there at times. And then in the far reaches one can find a beanbag room and a brainstorming room. A *kikkar* (square in Hebrew) provides an open learning space.

Just beyond the Mercaz lie several large rooms known as the innovation hub. Chief among them are makerspaces, where students come with their classes or, if they wish, on their own before or after school hours to use various materials to translate what they have learned into physical form. Various makerspace rooms house computer-generated printing, 3D machinery, heavy tools, small gadgets, and electronic components. One room is stocked with materials for producing artwork employing different types of materials —paper, cardboard, and acrylic, for example. The innovative space is used for formal art classes, cooking, learning about coding, and robotics. And adjacent to the makerspace is a large greenhouse where students learn about plant growth and cultivation.

The innovation hub, including the makerspace, art, and music, is designed to help students make meaning by making things. The underlying logic for investing in such a space is that not all children benefit from a traditional classroom experience. Furthermore, not all students excel in showing off what they have learned by performing well on tests. Some students are more artistically inclined; others relate to technology or the material arts. The makerspace frees up students to engage in more creative learning experiences. A class learning about Israeli cities, for example, builds scale models of different cities, including information about the topography, surrounding areas, and water sources. Third and fourth graders prepare for Yom Ha'atzmaut (Israel's Independence Day) by engaging in research about Israeli technological or scientific innovation and then building replicas.

From the perspective of the administration, the makerspace has also freed up teachers to think in a more tactile and practical way about their teaching.

Educators who in the past had conformed to conventional, frontal teaching now think about ways to help students learn the same subject matter but in a far more hands-on fashion. For example, while studying the Tal Am Hebrew curriculum, a teacher realized that she could help students internalize the vocabulary for articles of clothing and body parts by having them construct wooden cut-out figures and then clothe them. Children build the school Sukkah while they learn about the religious requirements for such a booth and also about math. The makerspace has spurred curiosity among both students and teachers.

By helping students make objects to concretize what they have learned, the makerspace helps them become producers, not only consumers. A visitor to the makerspace may find the experience disorienting because of the noise level, but also cannot fail to note how students are enjoying themselves and certainly are comfortable with the educational experience. On one visit, an eighth-grade science class was observed building a roller-coaster using bicycle tires for the purpose of learning about laws of physics. The atmosphere was reminiscent of an amusement park, but the purpose was serious study.

The innovation hub is also heavily used by Judaic studies classes. For example, students grow parsley that they will use at their family Passover Seder. But in a more complex way, students translate their learning into physical objects. Thus, when learning about biblical concepts such of purity and impurity (*tahor* and *tameh*), or obligation and exemption (*hayav* and *patur*), students produce physical objects to embody these dualities. Similarly, when learning about Jewish holidays or concepts, students are invited to pour their creativity into making physical representations. For example, one group of boys made a knife that converts into a gavel to illustrate Haman's initial power and eventually how justice prevailed. Another put together a house of cards to illustrate the precariousness of Jewish existence, but the cards were well glued and therefore did not fold, a metaphor for Jewish perseverance in the face of persecution. Students also work in the makerspace on creating floats for the annual Salute to Israel parade and learn there about famous Israeli inventions.

Hillel has invested in a coordinator for this space who helps students design and then make objects. The school has built facilities with attention to aesthetics, the possibility of collaboration and teamwork, as well as play. Even students in the upper grades are active in the makerspace. Simply put, this approach succeeds because it helps make learning fun. But at the same time, it injects a degree of unpredictability, which is unsettling for some parents who are used to a more formal learning environment. Clearly, the maker-space embodies Hillel's commitment to individualized learning experiences and offering opportunities to all kinds of learners to express themselves. As of 2018, Hillel was one of only a few day schools to have created a makerspace and undoubtedly runs the largest such effort in a Jewish school.

For all its experimentation with new teaching modes, the one area Hillel is not much invested in is flipped learning. Neither parents nor students in the middle school were comfortable with heavy reliance on computer technology or using teachers mainly as guides. Some blended learning occurs in Hebrew classes. But the school found that especially in math and science, students need more teacher involvement.

The Jewish Studies Challenges

Jewish studies at Hillel combine elements of more traditional learning modes with the experimental. The subject matter in each year consists of Hebrew language, the study of Jewish rituals and holidays, biblical and later rabbinic texts, and eventually big questions about Jewish identity. On the more experimental side has been the school's decision to drop grading students in Jewish studies classes and instead provide narrative assessments. And of course, the opportunity to use the innovation hub as a teaching instrument is another instance of greater experimentation in Jewish studies.

A visitor to Hillel can't miss the omnipresence of Hebrew, images of Israel, and Jewish sayings adorning walls throughout the building. Signage is in Hebrew; hallways are plastered with murals and posters reflecting Jewish concepts. And in classrooms, the walls are festooned with Judaic references and photographs of Israel and its heroic leaders. The school works to create a Jewish ambience in which students are steeped.

Both Hebrew-language study and Jewish content matter are handled differently by grade level. To begin with the former, up to grade 5, a fair amount of Jewish studies teaching is conducted in Hebrew. This is the case in kindergarten, and it continues through the lower school. (Attention to Hebrew begins in the early childhood program.) Beyond that, Hebrew is spoken only in Hebrew-language classes. (In some grades, an advanced class in Bible is taught in Hebrew.) By grades 7 and 8, students claim they have "forgotten" all their Hebrew. This is not true, of course, but around puberty, students in many day schools tend to become more self-conscious about making mistakes and therefore try to avoid speaking up in Hebrew. Their teachers tend to be more confident of the Hebraic knowledge of students; they see the problem as an unwillingness to use the language rather than a matter of ignorance. On the eighth-grade class trips to Israel, students generally don't function in Hebrew.

As is true in almost all schools not under Orthodox auspices, the school day at Hillel is not divided equally between Jewish and general studies. In grades 1 through 4, between one and a half and two hours are devoted to Judaic Studies daily. From grades 5 through 8, of the thirty hours of weekly class time, between eleven and twelve are devoted to Jewish studies. (In all grades, daily prayer is not included in these figures.) Above and beyond those times, students are exposed to Jewish studies during makerspace visits, schoolwide programs, class trips, Shabbatonim (Sabbath retreats), and assemblies.

The primary subject matter of Jewish studies classes are the holidays, the study of biblical texts, and, from fifth grade, Mishna study. Through Hillel's involvement in the Standards and Benchmarks program, far more coherence in the teaching of these subjects has emerged, and idiosyncratic teaching styles have been smoothed.

In the higher grades, students are exposed to more challenging approaches. Sixth-grade classes in Jewish studies incorporate project-based learning. As an example, the class learns about the census reported in Bamidbar (the Book of Numbers), which leads into a discussion about evaluating needs and how using data plays a role in making changes. Starting in seventh grade, there is a diminution in emphasis on the acquisition of skills. The focus instead is on discussing big questions raised by the study of Halacha and history.

The capstone comes in grade 8 when the primary focus beyond Hebrew language is a specially designed course, Siyyum (culmination). Drawing on different media and a wide range of Jewish source materials, this course explores each of the seven core values of Hillel. Among the topics discussed are: Who is a Jew? What is a Jew? What are the differences in being a Jew in a hostile versus welcoming environment? Twice a week, students also learn about the Holocaust. And during that final year at Hillel, students embark on a class trip of several weeks to Israel, a trip often described as "transformative."

A word here about Tefila. The value Hillel places on situating students in independent groups is reflected not only in learning but also in *Tefila*. By giving students in the lower school the opportunity to divide into smaller groups, the school nurtures a strong worship community. Students seem completely absorbed. Particularly striking was the enthusiasm of grade 4 students. Dispersed throughout the Mercaz in small groups, these nine-year-olds exude an innocence and invest energy in their prayer, loudly chanting words in a very public place. Situated in nooks, on comfortable chairs, or on swivel chairs, they eagerly belted out the prayers with gusto as they sit in small, self-sufficient groups. With barely any teacher direction, they recited the second paragraph of the Sh'ma with special enthusiasm.

The same cannot be said for Tefila in the higher grades. Tefila is mandatory daily for grades 5 to 8. On Monday and Thursday mornings, there is Torah reading, as is the traditional practice. On Tuesdays and Fridays, more experimental approaches are used, and the quality fluctuates considerably. On Wednesday, these grades have Tefila for *mincha*, the afternoon service, not in the morning. Experiments involving drama, music, and yoga have been tried in an effort to involve students actively in Tefila. By the admission of the school's leadership, "Tefila for the older grades is painful," and that was especially the case in 2017–18, the year the school was observed for this study.

It needs to be said that Tefila is a difficult challenge in many Jewish day schools, roughly beginning for students around age 12. As one Hillel student put it, it's the same every day—and that routinized activity tends to bore students. One teacher at Hillel described Tefila as "the Vietnam of Jewish day schools." Another claimed students find it to be a "misery." But he also noted that teachers at the school do not model behavior during Tefila: their own lack of engagement is obvious to students. And then there is the school's lax enforcement of uniform disciplinary policies, he claims. A few students can subvert the entire effort through their acting out and efforts to draw peers into the same kinds of undermining activities. Steve Freedman has deemed the current situation "unacceptable" and has hired two rabbis with the hope they will bring "joy and spiritual inspiration" to Tefila for grades 5 to 8. He also acknowledges that "parents want their children to have a positive prayer experience." But matters may prove more complicated: some parents through their own lack of interest in synagogue attendance set a model for their children that is diametrically opposed to what the school is trying to fix.

Here, then, is one of the unresolved challenges facing the school. By virtue of its pluralism, it attracts students from families that do not share the same religious commitments. It's well and good to tout the virtues of a Jewish education steeped in a pluralistic ethos that is the sine qua non of Jewish community day schools in general. But that pluralism comes at a price. Some students have received messages from home that prayer is unimportant or silly. Some students come to Hillel talking up the joys of eating shellfish and other foods forbidden by the Kashrut standards set by the school. Others ridicule the use of phylacteries (*tefillin*). Some have been persuaded by their parents that Jewish studies is at best a frill. What really counts, they say, are general studies. A teacher at Hillel acknowledges that challenge: "The diversity of the population makes the creation of Jewish culture challenging. You need people who love minyan to lead it. . . . We're trying to figure out how to give families what they want while moving them forward." The makeup of the parent and student bodies, in short, complicates Hillel's efforts to instill core Jewish commitments in its students.

Furthermore, Hillel sends an unintended, subtle message to students about its own priorities. For a variety of reasons, the general studies side not only occupies more of the students' time but is also delivered in a manner far more consistent with progressive education and far more sophisticated than the Jewish studies side. Although teachers of Jewish studies have been trained in problem-based learning, only a few have embraced it enthusiastically. Jewish studies teachers have been more reluctant to give up their tried-and-true approaches in favor of new types of pedagogy, such as PBL, though as new teachers are recruited, that is changing.

Still, there is a fair amount of diffidence even among the top leadership of the school about how best to educate its students when it comes to the Jewish side. Teaching text does not work for many students, and the teaching of Judaism must be handled with great sensitivity to denominational differences. The uncertainty is reflected in comments by teachers of Jewish studies too. As one noted, "Today there is so much more attention to kids' inner worlds, but figuring out what that means in Jewish terms is not easy." As for pedagogy, one teacher speaks of Jewish studies being "twenty years behind general studies" in the sophistication of its pedagogy. Even the fact that Jewish studies classes are not graded, whereas general studies classes after fourth grade are graded, sends a message about the seriousness of one as compared to the other.

And so the school relies heavily on what it can do best, and perhaps is the safest bet. Hillel offers a warm, loving environment where students feel part of a community. Teachers feel a strong responsibility to nurture a warm atmosphere in the classroom; their relationships with one another are seen as models of the kinds of caring, kindness, and goodness they seek to nurture in students. Hillel excels in communicating how to have a Jewish heart. When a student is absent, the class calls to express its good wishes and to convey that they miss the absent student. Rewards are giving weekly to recognize students who have behaved in a particularly *menschlich* (decently humane) fashion. Hillel prides itself on its Jewish *neshama*, its soul. And there's no mistaking its commitments to Israel, the Jewish people, and the Jewish community of greater Detroit. A teacher explained what students take away from Hillel: "It's not so much literacy or mastery of texts and language, but a very strong sense of connection, of feeling part of something larger than themselves. They know what it means to be part of a Jewish environment and to feel loved." None of this is to be taken lightly. Indeed, it is one of the selling points of Hillel because parents value the human dimension of the school and regard it as Hillel's special Jewish quality.

It Takes a Community

Hillel has benefited immeasurably from the unusual communal setting in which it is situated. Moving from the center to the periphery, we begin with the parent body. Parents are hardly a monolithic group. Some are skeptical about what the school adds, especially because in most suburban areas, the public schools are "good enough." This is a sector of the parent body that Hillel personnel work to reassure about the school's value proposition, stressing its warm ambience, its nurturing of each child, its communal cohesiveness. Then there are other parents who are Hillel alumni (and, in the near future, also children of alumni) who cannot conceive of sending their children elsewhere.

Hillel's staff perceive many parents as far more comfortable in the Jewish environment of the school than in a synagogue. In essence, the school serves as a far more compelling Jewish community and also is less intimidating or off-putting to Gen-X and millennial parents. The school creates an environment for parents to ensure that *they* benefit from enrolling their children at Hillel. The school runs a family camp, family get-togethers around Sukkot, "movies and munchies" social events, mystery Shabbat dinners (with the mystery being where you will end up), adult-oriented programs on how to make a Seder table, recipes for holiday meals, and so on. While these efforts are designed to build community within the parent body and strengthen ties between parents and Hillel, they also create a learning environment for parents. Hillel thus teaches parents as well as students.

During interviews, a number of parents spoke about taking on trust that the school was moving in the right direction. If their child is coming home happy, something must be working. Even so, some did express a nagging doubt about how well their children will perform in a high school run along more conventional lines with tests and grades. They fretted over how much of a shock their children will experience during the transition after Hillel.

To get at some of these issues, we cite two interviews with parents somewhat characteristic of parent sentiment. One parent interviewed captured a good deal of the ambivalence mixed with overall satisfaction with the school's ambience. With a strong background in educational evaluation, she identified two primary strengths that appealed to her: she likes the dual language approach because she believes it helps students learn how to process, and she is impressed by the twenty-first-century learning experience. Her children are exposed to a more deliberate approach to learning, not rote learning. "It's important for them to learn how to learn." Hillel students, she believes, "have the freedom to explore." But the fact that students are not assigned homework makes it harder for parents to judge. She also is concerned about the elimination of traditional grading. This is a running tension many parents feel between a willingness to try new approaches to pedagogy and yet worry that by abandoning older models, Hillel is shortchanging its students. Still, her overall assessment of the general studies teachers is high: "They're amazing." On the Jewish side, she notes, the children "develop a love for Torah stories." The Jewish dimension is not pushed at students, but the school does have some expectations of them. Teachers care about the children and work very hard. "There's a lot of love and kids feel nurtured and protected," she adds. As to her main concerns, she worries whether children at Hillel will learn perseverance, by which she means learning that at times, it's important to do work even if it's boring. And she worries that her children "will not be where they should be in high school."

Though hardly typical due to her advanced knowledge of education, this parent hit many of the notes typically heard from parents about what they value in the school and what leaves them a bit unsettled. Symptomatically, she expresses no discomfort with the Jewish side of the school. But when it comes to the more experimental efforts in general studies, she expresses the concerns of older parents who tend to favor homework, grading, teaching students to do the work even if they find it dull; in brief, she still favors a school experience similar to her own. Younger parents at the school seem more receptive to the new orientation of learning.

A second mother candidly addressed her initial skepticism about sending her three children to Hillel. She decided to do so because she was impressed by how well Hillel students participated in the services during their bar or bat mitzvah and also how well behaved they were in synagogue. The innovation hub has made a great difference, she believes, in how her children have responded to the school. Her daughter felt she was in a more serious and creative school. "These spaces," she claims, "have changed the culture both for students and teachers." They make coming to school "more exciting. This is an inspiring place. . . . Sitting in circles with other students can be inspiring. Writing on walls together with other students collaboratively is so different." Her son was bored and unhappy with math classes, but "the makerspace enabled his mind to explode in new directions." In high school, he has taken off. Hillel graduates, in her experience, do very well at the local Jewish day high school.

She also stressed Hillel's warmth and its palpable *Ruach* (spiritedness). Hillel students who have moved on to high school like to return to Hillel to hang out with their former teachers. As for their parents, she notes how "important it is to be a Hillel family. This group pulls together and celebrates together." It also offers support at times of family crisis, caring for families at times of illness and death. The school works to create strong peer groups within the parent body as well.

Moving outward from the parent body is a second concentric communal circle consisting of the primary Jewish institutions of which Hillel is a major component. A parent who also is an alumnus describes how Hillel is part of a fabric that also includes some synagogues and the community camp, Tamarack, as well as certain neighborhoods. Families involved with Hillel tend to find their way into these other settings too. In the matrix created by the web of major institutions, Jews find friends and associates. Some adults remain close friends with elementary school classmates from Hillel and then go on to volunteer together for the same causes and watch their children befriend one another. (A further contributing factor is the tendency of ethnic groups in the Detroit area to stay among their own.)

To a significant extent, this phenomenon of bonding across a small number of institutions reflects midwestern Jewish communal life, rooted in stable suburban neighborhoods, multigenerational families, a strong volunteer culture, and philanthropic ethos. To be sure, the shifting economy of the area, and especially Detroit, has proved challenging to that communal life. But for the younger families who have remained in the greater metropolitan area, that culture continues to embrace them. Some have speculated on the eventual impact of newcomers to the reviving downtown of Detroit and how well they will integrate. But for now, a tightly woven community with Hillel as a key element is functioning well.

Symptomatically, the local Federation of Jewish philanthropy regards Hillel as an asset and provides financial support beyond what most other communities offer. Not only does the Federation provide a per capita sum for each enrolled child, it also disburses $4 million from a restricted fund covering day school scholarships for families needing extra help. (That sum is not given solely to Hillel families; all day school families in the area benefit from it.) The Federation has helped raise endowment funds for Hillel. Unlike the place of day schools in most other communities, Hillel is an agency of the Detroit Federation.

The rationale for this heavy involvement by the Federation is based on a number of considerations. As a pluralistic school, Hillel is in sync with the preference of the Federation to bring all Jews under a common umbrella rather than fragment them based on denomination, ideology, or other potentially divisive banners. Moreover, it is widely understood that a high proportion of the community's leaders were educated in the day schools. One funder called Hillel "The beginning of the supply chain for the community." Hillel is perceived as an asset. Moreover, Hillel parents and grandparents are major volunteers in the Federation. Hillel is good for the Federation, and the Federation's acknowledgment of its importance benefits the school.

Above and beyond Federation support, Hillel has an ace in the hole—or to be more accurate, it has several aces: major funders willing and eager to provide large multimillion-dollar gifts. The multistage reconstruction of the school's physical facility, with its Mercaz, innovation space, and soon an ECC wing, all have been made possible by large capital gifts. Other school initiatives also have benefited from philanthropic generosity few other Jewish day schools can boast. To put this into perspective, barely half of Hillel's operating budget is covered by tuition, a prescription for disaster at most day schools but workable because of long-term funding commitments the school has received. Roughly a third of its annual expenditures are covered by private donations. This has meant that no family is turned away on financial grounds, a policy that was merely a dream a decade earlier when nearly one-third of applicants had to be turned away due to severe limits on scholarship funds.

Luck has played a role in all of this, but the school has also helped make its good fortune. Hillel is smart in its approach to finances. The school rents out its facility as a communal space for activities such as the Melton Adult Education program and millennial engagement activities. It also serves as a kosher catering venue. And it has applied successfully for state aid for shared time services.

Most striking, when a major funder approached the school to ask whether it had any long- term needs, Steve Freedman was ready with a serious, well-thought-out plan for rebuilding his facility and transforming it for learning. The funder, a Reform Jew with little knowledge of day school education, was captivated and made a large capital gift. It would be foolhardy to suggest that Hillel could have managed its transformation without extraordinary financial help. But it would be equally unreasonable to attribute the school's financial success solely to luck. Its leadership had a compelling vision to share with donors and has positioned Hillel as an asset in the community by working assiduously to contribute to the health of the wider Jewish community. It helps too that the school is run as both a responsible business enterprise and an institution with a strong Jewish mission. No wonder funders regard Hillel as a good bet.

The Benefits of a Hillel Education

With all of its considerable strengths, Hillel still contends with its short-coming. Its leadership is well aware of the disparity between offerings in general and Jewish studies. Not only do the latter lag in their adoption of twenty-first-century learning techniques, but the commitments to developing Jewish literacy are far weaker within the parent body. As is true in most other community day schools, parents tend to send their children for social and ethnic reasons, not necessarily for religious motives. The comparatively lower priority parents place on Jewish religious education and Judaic literacy limits what the school can hope to achieve. That's not to say that Jewish content and commitment are absent from the school. Anyone walking around its impressive building cannot but be struck by the ubiquity of graphic acknowledgment of Hebrew, Israel, and Jewish wisdom. Parents clearly want their children to be imbued with a strong connection to the Jewish people and the local Jewish community, and from all the reports, Hillel succeeds in doing so. Still, it is noteworthy how few complaints there are about deficiencies on the Judaic side compared with ongoing parental concerns about the ability of the school, for all its experimentation, to provide the strongest general studies preparation despite the enormous investment of time, energy, and funds in doing precisely that.

It's hard to gauge longer-term school outcomes, but for the short term, Hillel seems to succeed admirably on a number of fronts. Its alumni do well at the local community Jewish day high school whose school head compares them favorably to products of private schools. He sees no disadvantage to Hillel students in his school because they have been exposed to project-based learning. The Hillel alumni seem no less rigorous. Their Hebrew level also tends to be high. In short, their transition from middle to high school appears to be seamless.

It is common for parents whose children have finished at Hillel to refer to the strong connection their children feel to the Jewish people and Israel and the enduring bonds of friendship with former Hillel classmates among graduates currently in their twenties and thirties. Some parents speak proudly about their adult children who date only Jews and mark the range of Jewish holidays, even as they note that the same alumni do not attend synagogue often. It's impossible to know how these same alumni will behave once they have children and whether Hillel graduates in its pluralistic, community day school format will differ from earlier graduates from the Conservative (Schechter) version of Hillel. It remains to be seen too whether the current population of student from Orthodox homes engage in traditional Jewish practice when they are adults.

Hillel does not rest on its laurels. Steve Freedman makes a point of meeting with graduating eighth graders to learn about what was positive and negative about their Hillel experience. What can improve? Are Judaism and Israel important to them? If so, why? Hillel has hired an outside firm to administer a parent survey every other year, and it also surveys its teachers regularly. The school's leadership is continually monitoring and trying to learn how to improve.

Perhaps most notable, Hillel has managed with great success to attract families who might not under other circumstances have enrolled their children in a Jewish day school. By developing a general education program of high distinction capable of holding its own with the best private and public schools in its area, Hillel has overcome parental resistance. As such, it serves as a model for how Jewish day schools might address one of their most critical challenges: making the case to parents that a Jewish day school education offers excellence in general studies even as it nurtures the next generation of committed Jews.

CONNECTIONS AND EXCEPTIONS

Toward the end of the last century, during the great expansion of the non-Orthodox day school sector, funders of day school education were hopeful that

Jewish day schools would appeal to liberal Jewish families whose children might otherwise lose interest in leading engaged Jewish lives or marrying other Jews. Those hopes didn't fully materialize. Families never really shed their ambivalence about how worthwhile the schools' Jewish offerings were, and they questioned whether day school education was worth the high tuition costs. They were skeptical about the quality of general education at day schools, particularly compared to what was on offer at strong public schools, let alone rival independent schools.

Like Brandeis Marin (chapter 3), Detroit's Hillel Day School continues to make the case that day school education can be attractive to families that ordinarily might not consider enrolling their children. More than any other schools in our sample, these two schools appeal to families fitting this profile. Brandeis Marin has engaged vigorously with one dimension of this challenge, developing an approach to Jewish education that can be meaningful to Jews ambivalent about their Jewishness and even to families that don't identify as Jewish. Hillel has tackled the other aspect of this challenge by creating a learning environment that embodies the best in education today. Its physical facilities and educational approaches have become models for peer institutions across the continent.

No doubt, Hillel has been fortunate to be the beneficiary of significant philanthropic support from local families that appreciate the critical contribution it makes to Detroit's Jewish community, much as TanenbaumCHAT (chapter 7) has been similarly fortunate in recent years. But as was the case at TanenbaumCHAT, the largesse received was no casual windfall: it came about as a result of a clear and well-articulated plan setting forth what the school aimed to accomplish in the short and medium terms. It developed a plan to embrace students and their families in a warm, active Jewish community while offering a strong academic program in a genuinely attractive learning environment—a bold plan to compete academically and socially with the best public and private schools in its immediate area. It is widely perceived as having accomplished these twin goals.

Hillel's achievements have hinged on two things above all. First, its school leadership is transparent and communicative about its efforts to take a long-established institution (and especially its parents and board members) on a journey of discovery and reinvention. As head of school, Steve Freedman defined his role as "communicator in chief," a function also embraced by the principals at Hillel Torah (chapter 1) and the Rav Teitz Mesivta (chapter 6), two schools operating in completely different contexts. Second, the school has invested heavily in continuous teacher learning. In this respect, Hillel most resembles the Pressman Academy (chapter 4) in doubling down on what it takes to persuade its staff to embrace approaches to teaching and learning that radically depart from their own school experiences and, often, their own professional preparation. This work never stops nor, in fact, does the task of communicating to parents the critical importance for their own children of embracing new pedagogies.

The School as a Gateway

Brandeis Marin, San Rafael, California

A close look at Brandeis Marin offers an opportunity to peer into one of several possible futures for day school education in North America. Located just north of San Francisco and serving a population with low levels of Jewish affiliation, the school has grown while competitors have declined or disappeared. Led by a head of school who has nurtured a compelling vision for how day schools can appeal to Jewish families of all types, as well as to non-Jewish families, the school has become known as a place that enables those who were scarred by their own experience of Jewish education to join a joyous community even if the school's Jewish culture was not what drew them in the first place. The school offers an intriguing study of how, even when limited time is available, Jewish and Hebrew education can be as serious and as interesting as the rest of the curriculum when anchored by a goal that students should not be pushed to believe in anything in particular but are encouraged and enabled to think critically.

Seated in the wood-paneled sanctuary of a Reform temple one Thursday morning, the entire student body of the Brandeis Marin day school participated in a special *Tefila* service.[1] As is the case at every once-a-week prayer service, parents are invited to attend; on this spring day, larger numbers were present because the service was intertwined with presentations by the seventh graders about their Tzedakah project.

As children and parents settled into their seats, two teachers strummed on guitars and harmoniously sang "This Land Is Your Land," Woody Guthrie's anthem. The seventh graders sat on the stage facing the rest of the school. One by one they came to the microphone to speak about their Tzedakah project, including how they researched a Jewish value and then acted on it to improve the world. They reported on funds raised to support an organization dedicated to furthering the value they had chosen.

After a few such presentations, a transition to Tefila began, with different pairs of students leading passages from the liturgy and connecting the prayer they were leading to their projects. The assembled student body, led by the two musicians, sang "Modeh Ani," thanking God for helping them begin a new day. Next up were two boys who said something about their project and then launched into "Ma Tovu" ("How Goodly Are the Tents of Jacob") in Hebrew and English, again joined by the assembled student body. Another two students then stepped up to introduce Borchu, a call to prayer, followed by three students who spoke about what they had learned about having a positive impact on the world. This segued into the Sh'ma, the Jewish credo affirming belief in the oneness of God.

Next, two students explained how there still are people suffering in the world and how we can't wait for a Nachshon—the follow-me role model who was the first to jump into the Sea of Reeds as the waters parted in the Exodus account —to solve our problems; rather it is incumbent on all to take action. And that, in turn, led into "Mi kamocha" ("Who Is Like You, God?") and then Bob Marley's "Redemption Song."

Two more students introduced the eighteen benedictions, saying: "*Amida* means resistance. Standing up for something. We all need to stand up." They lead the Amida up to the Kedusha, which the whole gathering sang, again without musical accompaniment. And then the assembled student body skipped to the very end of the Amida, singing Oseh Shalom, a prayer for peace. The formal Tefila concluded with the singing of the "Star Spangled Banner "and then "Hatikva," Israel's national anthem. Another student explained how *hatikva* means "hope," a basic element of her Tzedakah project.

At times during the service, the students' efforts to connect their commentaries to particular prayers came across as a bit forced, but the theme of doing good in the world and helping those less fortunate came through with sincerity. Musically, this was an uplifting experience, a "greatest-hits" selection of Tefila melodies and more, which the assembled students and some parents sang with gusto. One might note how little of the actual liturgy was included, but it also is the case that in a number of community day schools similar to Brandeis Marin, there aren't any Tefila services at all. Also noteworthy was the large number of students who played an active role in the service, a normal occurrence actively encouraged by the school to give every child the experience of standing before the entire student body and speaking about something meaningful to him or her.

Throughout the proceedings, the dominant motif was on universalizing the messages of the prayer service. Beginning with Guthrie's paean to America and inclusiveness (America belongs "to you and me") through the transformation of the Amida, a prayer of supplication, into a call for resistance, the service implicitly communicated a worldview, if not political orientation, only tangentially connected to the prayers' literal meaning. And then the Tzedakah projects of students further reinforced the theme of universalization: few were in support of a Jewish, as opposed to a nonsectarian, cause. Still, the Sh'ma was recited and "Hatikva" sung, both speaking to parochial Jewish concerns.

The entire service, then, was carefully designed to communicate a set of messages. The emphasis was on responsibility to the world at large, even as a commitment to Israel was nonnegotiable. Students were exposed intentionally to some of the high points of the morning service so they would acquire some familiarity with the Jewish liturgy, but singing in a spirited fashion was also valued as a way of keeping students engaged. Tefila, a difficult aspect of day school education in most settings, was kept brief and occurs only once a week.

Tzedakah also is articulated in a universalized fashion. In official literature, it is defined as social justice work, explained as follows: "Students research issues of vital importance, such as poverty, human rights, education, global warming, health care, animal extinction, and substance abuse."[2] Whether consciously or not, this listing reflects a particular ideological understanding of what social justice issues are. These causes also are couched in nonsectarian terms. Not surprisingly, only two out of the dozen seventh graders took on a specifically Jewish cause.

On a more subtle level, the prayer service also was designed to resonate with the school's diverse student body. Nearly two-thirds of the students have one non-Jewish parent; one-tenth are not Jewish by any standard, with the remaining 25 percent offspring of two Jewish parents. Bridging those differences is a challenge Brandeis Marin has embraced, as was evident during the prayer service. The two teachers leading the musical portions were not Jewish, nor were some of the students who led a prayer. Though a small number of other Jewish day schools, mainly with much smaller enrollments, admit non-Jews primarily to help share the financial burden of maintaining a private school, Brandeis Marin regards its diversity as a matter of principle. The school's leadership—and the faculty who lauded this aspect of the school —are convinced that diversity of student backgrounds enhances the educational experience offered by Brandeis Marin. It also is a fact of life in Marin County that any day school has to acknowledge.

Brandeis Marin, California | 71

The Marin Setting

Marin County is located in the North Bay across the Golden Gate Bridge from San Francisco. The most recent demographic study of Jews in Marin makes it abundantly clear that this is a frontier where for the most part, Jews are not strongly connected to Jewish religious or communal life. Two-thirds of adults report they rarely or never participate in a Friday night Shabbat meal, more than half state they do not fast at all on Yom Kippur, and 40 percent sometimes or never participate in a Passover Seder. Nor are Marin Jews on the whole active in nonreligious spheres of Jewish life: over 80 percent do not belong to a Jewish organization; just shy of two-thirds feel "only a little" or "not at all" connected to the Bay Area Jewish community; nearly a third claim never to attend Jewish cultural events; and nearly half volunteered for organizations that are not specifically Jewish, while only 4 percent claimed they volunteered for a Jewish cause. Of those who are married or otherwise are in a coupled state, 54 percent are living with a Jew and 46 percent with someone who is not Jewish.[3]

The point of highlighting these findings is to contextualize the environment in which Brandeis Marin is located. There are few Orthodox Jews living in the county: only 2 percent of Jews in Marin self-identify as Orthodox. The self-identified Conservative populace constitutes 17 percent. These are usually thought of as the most natural constituents for a Jewish day school, and they are relatively few in number. Moreover, the high intermarriage rates in the county may further dampen enthusiasm for a Jewish day school education because intermarried parents do not enroll their children in Jewish educational programs to the same degree as in-married parents do.[4]

Political ideology may also add to the challenge. Two-thirds of Marin County's Jews self-identify as liberal or very liberal. This may lead them to eschew private schools in favor of public education. And even if they are open to sending their children to an independent school, they may be convinced that an ethnically diverse student population will best prepare their children for participation in American society as adults.

Added to this is the school's location in the Bay Area, home to the Boycott, Divestment, Sanctions (BDS) movement. Even among Jews in Marin, fewer than half are prepared to affirm they are more sympathetic to Israel's Jews than to Palestinians, though 49 percent claim they are sympathetic to both Israeli Jews and Palestinians and only 7 percent are more sympathetic to Palestinians. These ideological positions are not unimportant considerations when contemplating whether to send a child to a school that deliberately connects its students to Israel and features a two-week trip for eighth graders as the capstone of studies.

And yet in this environment, Brandeis Marin's enrollment is slowly growing. In the first four years since it hired a new head of school, Brandeis Marin grew by thirty students, nearly 20 percent. It has benefited from circumstances in its immediate environment, such as the closing of a Jewish day school in the East Bay, nearby enough for a few families to transfer their children to Brandeis Marin. Several independent schools in Marin County also have suffered setbacks, which has brought the Jewish school more inquiries from parents in those failing private schools. Though public elementary schools have a good reputation, they tend to be overcrowded. Parents who feel their children need special attention therefore are receptive to a small private school such as Brandeis Marin. Public middle schools do not enjoy as high a reputation, and this too has benefited Brandeis Marin. Uncharacteristically for a Jewish day school, there is an influx of new students in the middle school grades, a blessing to be sure but one that also requires the school to integrate students who have received very little Jewish education prior to enrolling at Brandeis Marin.

Brandeis Marin has also benefited from severing its formal ties to its sister school, the Brandeis School of San Francisco, founded in 1963. Fifteen years later, it opened a satellite school in Marin County. A single board and administration governed both schools, and periodically students attended special programs together, principally an eighth-grade Israel trip. In 2014, the board voted to become completely independent and hired a new head of school, Peg Sandel, to chart a new course. The driving concern behind the rupture was the difference in markets each served. As a report on the severed ties put it, "In San Francisco, parents have more concerns about the public schools and thus applied to BHDS [Brandeis Hillel Day School] in greater numbers. . . . In Marin, with a smaller Jewish population and a reputation for strong public schools, the Jewish day school needed to find a way to stand out in the strong public school landscape."[5]

The Vision of Peg Sandel

Brandeis Marin also made its own good fortune by hiring an educator with a specific vision tailored to the needs of her environment. Having earned a doctorate in Jewish studies and with experience in different educational settings throughout the Bay Area, including as head of Jewish studies at the Jewish Community High School of the Bay, Peg Sandel is acutely attuned to the market her school serves. For many parents, the Jewish studies component is more of an afterthought that anything else. What motivates many parents to explore what Brandeis Marin offers are its academic strengths in general studies, coupled with the special attention children receive, plus the warm, enveloping atmosphere the school cultivates. These features of the school will be described shortly. First, we focus on the market the school serves.

On a morning when one of us was visiting the school, a meeting was held for prospective parents considering whether to enroll their child for the coming school year. The eighteen visitors were given an orientation, introduced to key administrative and teaching personnel, taken on a guided tour of the facilities with stops in classrooms, and then gathered for a Q&A opportunity. Questions were raised about a variety of issues, but not a single one was posed about the Jewish studies or Hebrew program—with the exception of a parent who asked whether her daughter could be exempt from taking Hebrew because she would enter in grade 5.

Interviews with parents who have enrolled their children at the school confirm the low priority many accorded to Jewish studies when choosing a school. In some cases, they had placed their child in the early childhood program at the Jewish Community Center, which abuts Brandeis Marin. Someone at the preschool suggested they check out the day school. Not having any sense of what a Jewish day school was, they were skeptical. But the warmth of the school and the openness of personnel to their every question won them over. In some cases, parents transferred their children in fourth grade from a public or private school because they were looking for more personalized attention. Word of mouth also has played a role in persuading some non-Jewish families to take a look—and then were attracted by the small school atmosphere and warmth of Brandeis Marin.

That's not to say the Hebrew and Jewish studies dimension of Brandeis Marin plays no role in the consideration of parents. Some transferred their children from a neighboring day school that had closed or from another day school because they appreciate Brandeis Marin's Jewish studies offerings. A minority of families has created what one parent described as a "Jewish bubble" by gathering for Shabbat dinners in each other's homes on Friday nights and keeping kosher. Others come with a commitment to expose their children to the Hebrew language, an element valued especially by Israeli-born parents. And others, of course, are committed to a more intensive Jewish education that only a day school can offer. Peg Sandel estimates that these collectively constitute 40 percent of the parent body.

For the roughly 60 percent placing little priority on the school's Jewish mission, some possess very little Jewish knowledge; a few families have expressed resentment over the school's closings on Jewish holidays, days when they work. (The school offers day care on those days for an additional fee.) Nevertheless, the goal is for the school to serve optimally as a gateway to Jewish life. For many, change occurs over time as they get to know the school. Parents come to appreciate the good values it promotes as Jewish values. The school's emphasis on civic engagement and ethical behavior, the absence of bullying, let alone drugs, and other unwelcome intrusions into the lives of their children are framed as part of a Jewish ethos that attracts families once they learn more. Even Tefila, potentially the most Jewish religious aspect of the school, is described by parents, including Gentile ones, as an opportunity for their children to relate to God and connect with their own spiritual yearnings. As for Hebrew, it is valued as another foreign language, and for Christians it is the language of the Old Testament. There's nothing threatening about the school's Jewishness.

To the contrary, the school is completely neutral about the level of Jewishness that families practice. At one point, it issued rules prohibiting students from bringing nonkosher foods to school for lunch. Those guidelines were dropped, but officially the school urges parents not to send their children to school with pork or seafood lunches. Similarly, boys are not required to wear a head covering during Tefila or Jewish studies. Some children celebrate a bar or bat mitzvah, but in recent years, most, including those with Jewish parents, do not. The school takes no position on this, though it does run a program to place the bar and bat mitzvah on parents' radar. The one rule the school tries to enforce is to discourage families from celebrating birthday parties on Shabbat, so as not to exclude children whose families observe the day more traditionally. Parents are also asked not to serve pepperoni pizza, which is not kosher, at birthday parties.

Peg Sandel is acutely aware of the many Jewish parents who come to the school with a great deal of ambivalence, if not hostility, to Jewish rituals and parochial concerns. She likes to quote a local rabbi who describes himself as a bellhop: people come to him to unload their baggage. So too at the school, parents tend to have questions about whether the school teaches creationism or indoctrinates children with all kinds of Jewish rules and observances and also engages in endless "God talk." The first task in meeting with prospective parents, then, is to put them at ease, and that is done by conveying to parents that the school accepts them exactly as they are: whatever they do at home is perfectly fine. And, second, as Sandel puts it, she demonstrates how "core Jewish values emphasized at Brandeis Marin have universal resonance."

One non-Jewish couple described their first encounters with Peg Sandel as follows. She talked about education at Brandeis Marin as a "family journey." She made clear there is no Jewish agenda to make their child believe anything specific but rather to learn how to question and then come up with their own ideas. The parents came away persuaded of the school's genuinely open-minded perspective about the world.

That is not to say the school is without norms. To the contrary, it defines its mission as inculcating good values, which it regards as Jewish values. Inclusion, for example, is strongly valued. Of all the schools we visited, this is the only one with multiple signs affirming, "Another Jew for LGBT Equality" and "Trans Jews Belong Here." The inclusion of non-Jews as active Tefila leaders, a policy few synagogues of any denomination are prepared to permit, offers another example of the school's modeling of inclusion. "Boundaries hurt and have unintended consequences," Peg Sandel remarks. "Why hurt kids who want to participate and lead? It brings joy to see kids find meaning in the Jewish tradition even if it is not theirs." And as previously noted in connection with the Tedakah project, social justice is a key value that the school stresses. Brandeis Marin adds the critically important fillip that in fact these are Jewish values. Sandel is convinced her school is able to increase its enrollment, especially in the middle school grades when attrition is common in other community day schools, precisely because it articulates the value of day school education in universal rather than parochial terms.

Managing Growth

To make the school financially feasible, the administration has worked to increase the student body, with a goal of enrolling two hundred students. As at many other schools, key personnel monitor retention rates and recruitment carefully. Simultaneously, several countervailing considerations place pressure on the school to manage growth carefully. Maintaining relatively small classes not exceeding twenty students is a priority because it enhances the learning experiences of students and also is an important selling point for the school: Brandeis Marin is a small school that pays great attention to every student. In the lower school, an assistant teacher pitches in, and classes often are divided for more intense interaction with teachers and their assistants. Teachers also work with a single student at a time, as do some administrators. With the introduction of levels based on Hebrew proficiency as early as the lower grades, it has become common to see a handful or ten students working with a Hebrew-language teacher.

The school does turn away some children in order to maintain the right mix. It enrolls students with learning needs—academic, behavioral, or social —but is careful about creating a balance so that all students will have their needs met. It also strives for gender balance. No one has taken an official position about limiting the proportion of non-Jewish students, though a board member has been outspoken in his concern about reaching what he calls "a tipping point."

Not least among enrollment concerns, although Brandeis Marin has been successful in attracting new students, the process of integrating them and their families is not a small task. In the 2019–20 school year, 53 new students entered out of 186 in total. This means that over a quarter of the students were new to the school that year. Unlike many other day schools, this is not solely a matter of integrating students in kindergarten or grade 1, but on many grade levels. For example, ten new students enrolled in grade 4, and many new students enrolled in the middle school. Over the past three years, between 60 and 70 percent of students were new to the school.

Not surprisingly, when teachers and administrators were asked about the larger challenges the school faces, most referred to concerns about maintaining the school's culture even as so many new students are enrolled. All staff members and some parents are enlisted in this effort. Teachers speak about their additional roles explaining to students what they encounter that may be foreign to them. Here is what one teacher said: "Of course I celebrate diversity. But we are also part of the real world. It's a challenge to all of us to explain why we as a school don't celebrate Halloween or Valentine's Day. Many kids celebrate Halloween at home, and interfaith families celebrate Christmas. The school explains that here we celebrate Jewish values, but what you do at home is great."

The challenge is particularly acute when it comes to Jewish studies and Hebrew. How much time should be devoted to preparation for Jewish holidays that may be very familiar to veteran students but quite unknown to many newcomers? How does one make up for four years of Hebrew study when a student enters in grade 5 with no prior knowledge? From grade 6 and up, the school offers students a choice of studying Hebrew or Spanish, but some newcomers opt for the former even if they have no prior knowledge of Hebrew. These are practical concerns as the school remains open to enrolling new students at multiple grade levels.

Making the Case

Peg Sandel's so-called elevator speech to prospective parents offers important insights into how she positions Brandeis Marin. At a gathering for parents considering where to send their children, she stresses the school's project-based learning (PBL) approach. As an example, she cites a middle school math class in which students design a doughnut box as part of an exercise to learn about volume. PBL allows teachers to scale a project, she notes; by this she means they can increase or decrease the level of challenge to students. Students design volume for more or less complex numbers and sizes of doughnuts. Though all students are engaged in the same project, some are taking on more difficult challenges.

During the same pitch for the school, Sandel stresses how students are exposed to multiple perspectives in every subject area. Even in math, they learn how to articulate different ways of solving the same problem. Classes in literature and social studies encourage students to interpret. And for students with a more material way of making meaning, the makerspace offers an important outlet for interpretation and personal expression.

Next, she speaks about the school's aim to build a community of kindness. As an example, the fifth-grade leadership program brings older students into contact with younger ones to help the latter resolve issues. The school's insistence on kindness is grounded in the belief that students must learn to appreciate multiple perspectives. And capping these descriptions of what Brandeis Marin offers, Sandel speaks with passion about the culture of collaboration: "Children learn best in small groups how to collaborate, communicate and appreciate different perspectives." In fact, she explains, since we know so little at present about future workplace needs over the coming decades, the habits of mind and knowledge acquisition developed at Brandeis Marin are intended to prepare students for an evolving new era. All of these approaches, she notes, are part of being a Jewish day school: "Judaism has valued these ideals for thousands of years." They are explicit or implicit in Jewish teachings. In the Jewish tradition, asking questions is integral to problem solving.

This brief introduction to the Brandeis Marin approach imparts several important messages to parents looking into the school as an option for their children. It begins by stressing the school's strongly progressive educational approach. This is not a place of rote learning. It also is a place where learning experiences are curated depending on the abilities and needs of students. And here, students learn to respect each other and diverse viewpoints. Implicitly, she is telling parents they need not worry about bullying or other hurtful behavior children may encounter in larger schools. *We have the backs of your children*, she is saying. They will work collaboratively. And then to emphasize the point, she defines the Jewish dimension in the most universal of terms: it's about learning to ask questions and developing certain habits of the mind. Right off, she puts parents at ease about how the Jewishness of the school will be handled with a light touch.

In private conversation, she explains that years of experience with parents have taught her to be sensitive to the many Jewish parents who feel themselves to be judged in Jewish institutions or have suffered from poor experiences with rabbis or other Jewish teachers. Her educational approach aims to communicate acceptance of parents as they are, avoids using insider Jewish language that may be off-putting to some Jewish and Gentile parents and provides a "meaningful, relevant, and compelling" version of Judaism.

We've already noted the culminating presentations by students of their Tzedakah projects. During another visit, we also witnessed the initial stages of that initiative when parents of seventh graders gather to learn about the project. The messages Peg Sandel delivered at that meeting illustrate how the school helps parents plan for the children's puberty milestone. The meeting's agenda was about what, if anything, families will do to celebrate their child's bar or bat mitzvah. Peg makes clear that the school will do nothing to impose its views on families. Rather, the purpose of the meeting is to provide options to families. Peg acknowledges there are families in which parents have spoken of the vacuous experiences they had at their own bar or bat mitzvah. Peg expresses directly that her purpose at their meeting is to help parents consider how their family might imagine a meaningful milestone year.

To spur their thinking, Peg introduces ideas from biblical and rabbinic texts, and also an excerpt from John Dewey. She especially emphasized a rabbinic text from Midrash Rabbah, a rabbinic text from late antiquity about how parents are no longer responsible for their children's sins once the latter attain the age of thirteen. This text was met with a fair amount of pushback from parents who found it too cavalier about how much twelve- or thirteen-year-olds still require supervision and guidance. In response, Sandel and some parents suggested metaphors about helping children by gradually taking their "training wheels" off over the course of the year, helping parents "let go" of their children a bit more, and bringing the values of the school and home into sync.

Sandel's primary messages were for families to think of the year as a new beginning, not a culmination, and also a time when communal rituals help create memories. This last notion was quite alien to some. A Jewish parent who had recently immigrated to the United States confessed her ignorance about what happens at a bar mitzvah. And a non-Jewish parent raising his child as a Jew spoke glowingly about how the local Reform rabbi involves the non-Jewish relatives in synagogue rituals during a bat or bar mitzvah.

Though families celebrate the milestone in their own way—or not at all—the school requires every student to engage in a Tzedakah project. Citing "Jewish values," Sandel spoke about students who raise money for an organization combating gun violence, climate change, inequality, and a range of other causes.

Parents who opt to enroll their children at Brandeis Marin, then, are gently encouraged, mainly through what their children bring home from school, to see Jewishness as something positive. Sandel sees many parents scarred by their own experience of Jewish education. They're often brought to the day school by their non-Jewish partner. Interactions with parents therefore are carefully modulated so as not to awaken negative attitudes about Jewishness. Rather, the goal is to help parents discover something that's joyous and positive. The school deliberately strives to repair the harm done by previous generations.

As for students, Sandel aspires for them not to say, "I've finished now," but rather that they want to pursue more Jewish content after they leave Brandeis Marin. Day school education for her is not meant to use the limited time available to fill up kids with sufficient fuel to carry them out into the world. The goal is to leave them hungry for more.

General Studies at Brandeis Marin

In pursuit of her goals, Sandel has the good fortune of working with a staff almost entirely of her own choosing. True, some teachers and administrators have been with the school for decades. But for the most part, she has put together a leadership team that fits the culture the school seeks to nurture.

Sandel has raised morale among the staff by fostering collaboration among teachers. For example, when science teachers focus on the dynamics of projectiles, their social studies counterparts discuss walled cities and how medieval walls were assaulted at times of warfare. Design lab classes also focused simultaneously on projectiles. These collaborations did not happen by chance but were raised during faculty meetings or with supervisors. Nor are the collaborations limited to general studies teachers. Jewish studies faculty went out of their way to express pleasure over how they have never before felt as valued and central to the education at the school as in recent years.

The school's investment in continuing professional education for all faculty has helped greatly too. Most teachers, for example, have spent some of the summer months at programs run by the Buck Institute about ways to introduce project-based learning with the goal of setting "conditions for teachers to implement great projects for all students." Others have been involved in responsive classroom workshops designed to foster high-level academics in a setting that also includes "positive community, effective management, and developmental awareness." Similar to several other day schools we examine in this book, Brandeis Marin has become more deliberate about helping students integrate academic learning with social and emotional growth. Time is spent teaching techniques for managing emotions, working collaboratively, and building responsibility toward fellow students.

Teachers interviewed remarked on the impact these training courses have had on their approaches in the classroom. A middle school history teacher relates how he teaches his classes on the Renaissance to sixth graders: students write and perform a skit that incorporates answers to certain questions posed and do a major project on Renaissance art and architecture using online resources. The teacher sees his role as circulating around the classroom to offer guidance and suggestions to students who require help. For the most part, he notes, "Students love the project and knew what to do." A science teacher who has been in the school for a long period finds the PBL approach more likely to aid students to internalize new information. After they have spent time in the seventh grade learning about research skills, students take responsibility to research a science project. Under the teacher's guidance, they work in teams to conduct their research.

The progressive educational approach is on display when visiting classrooms. For example, an eighth-grade English class begins with a quick online quiz about Act III of Macbeth, which "goes live" soon after the start of the class. It's multiple choice, and kids get to see instantly how they've done. The pace moves quickly. By the time they finish, there's a new task on the board. The teacher gives them seven minutes to write their responses to the following questions: "Do you believe in ghosts or the power to summon them?" "Do you know anyone who does?" This is a tightly managed, intense operation, with some extremely bright kids in the room. In a later conversation, one provides a detailed explanation of the political background to Macbeth. After the class ends, the English teacher expresses her pride at the high level of the class and her feeling that at times it is almost like teaching a college course.

In a seventh-grade design class, students literally run to class. The room is a kind of Aladdin's cave: students handle tools for cutting, soldering, and gluing. A laser cutting machine and 3D printers are available for their use, and plastic boxes of accessories and spare parts sit on one side of the room; on the other side, traditional tools are available to students. The level of informality is high, and students call the teacher by his first name. Without any formal announcement, students simply pick up their work in progress and get started on cardboard animatronics models. The teacher has prepared a model to which they may refer, but otherwise his interactions tend to be with students who work self-sufficiently.

A sixth-grade literature class opens with students devoting the first ten minutes to journaling about a book they are reading together, *The Giver*. "What is fair and what is equal?" they are asked to address. Then students share with their classmates what they have written. Students speak about the necessity of everyone having equal opportunities, even as they realize that life plays out differently despite the level ground. They struggle with the impact of competition and the unfairness of not everyone having the same intelligence and skills. The teacher is completely in command of the students. She needs only to raise her hand, and they all fall silent. The last part of the class is devoted to writing with "precision of language."

A seventh-grade math class designed for students who struggle a bit with the subject matter is devoted on this particular day to working on ratios and proportions. Privately, the teacher expresses great pride in moving children who had been "terrified" of math and convinced they never could solve problems to feeling comfortable puzzling out answers to questions. In fact, he prefers the term *puzzles* to *math problems* because he wants students to see the exercise as a puzzle to be solved. Though this is not an advanced class, these students, he reports, are on level for their grade and have overcome their anxiety about doing math problems.

This last point is important for appreciating the respect in the school for diverse learning styles and abilities. Peg Sandel expresses her acute awareness that 20 percent of students are wired differently and learn differently. She feels an obligation to keep all students connected to the Jewish community. Even students who can't reach quite as high academically are important at the school. She sees this as part of the Jewish imperative the school must enact. All kinds of one-on-one support are offered. Not only do teachers sit with individual students; even some administrative staffers spend part of their time working with individual students.

That said, academic achievement is highly valued in the school. Dr. Sandel is committed to outdoing public school education and competing with the best local independent schools. The school is especially proud of the high attainments of students in math, where, for example, students graduate from eighth grade with an advanced-level knowledge of geometry and also in creative writing and the sciences. Compared to students in other private schools, those at Brandeis Marin score in the 80th percentile on standardized tests.

Still, there remains a tension in the school between its progressive educational ideals, which call for project-based learning and responsive learning classrooms, on the one hand, and covering material and measuring learning through the use of metrics, on the other hand. It's a tension many schools—Jewish day schools, and also public and independent ones—face.

The Judaic Studies Curriculum

The Jewish and Hebrew studies components of Brandeis Marin are limited to two class sessions a day, with some additional time devoted during assemblies, schoolwide activities around Jewish holidays, and special programming. Most weeks, there is one Hebrew class each day and four Jewish studies classes plus Tefila on Thursday mornings. Some weeks, these numbers are reversed to focus on an impending holiday.

With such limited time available for Jewish studies, the administration works to make every class session count. Hence, the teaching staff lives with a pressure to create a clear spiral of learning from kindergarten through eighth grade. A second consideration, though, also shapes the Jewish studies curriculum: how to offer a Jewish studies program that is not too heavily "religious" in orientation, while simultaneously introducing students to key Jewish concepts. The nature of the dilemma was illustrated by one teacher who noted that one cannot ask students about their Passover Seder because half the students in any class would not have had one. (To add to the complexity, the same teacher related that Gentile parents in the school organized a Seder for their children because they were curious about what happens at such gatherings. Some of the non-Jewish children and adults read the four questions; a Hindu person cooked a brisket).

Unique circumstances have prompted school administrators to craft their own curricula in both Jewish studies and Hebrew to address the school's distinctive needs. The driving forces determining the curricula are Dr. Sandel and Merav Steinberger, dean of Hebrew and Jewish studies, with assistance from other staff and teachers.

Hebrew Bible, especially the Torah, is the primary focus of Jewish studies classes. In the lower grades, students are introduced to biblical texts and a limited number of rabbinic *midrashim*, interpretations and amplifications of the text. By grade 5, students are introduced to biblical exegetes such as Rashi. And in middle school, they are exposed to selected texts excerpted from the Mishna, Talmud, and Jewish Codes in the context of discussions of values. Classes do not work their way systematically through a book of the Torah or any other Jewish work; rather, students are exposed to texts chosen for their relevance or other noteworthy importance. Ultimately the goal is to encourage students to make their own meaning of the texts. Merav Steinberger says she wants students to know there are multiple ways to understand the text and that "they too are part of a line of interpreters. Like Rashi, you too can explain. You are part of the chain."

Brandeis Marin has participated in the Standards and Benchmarks Program currently sponsored by the Legacy Heritage Foundation to help schools identify their own priorities for Tanakh (Hebrew Bible) study. The school chose standards 2 (interpreting the text through rabbinic commentary) and 8 (developing a love of the text and embracing it to inform values). A specialist in the Standards and Benchmarks project continues to work with teachers on implementation.

The same project also informs the program for fifth graders to celebrate their receiving a Hebrew Bible (Hagigat HaTanakh). Focusing on leadership as the overall theme, the project asks students to write their own *drash*, commentary, on a biblical text. Implicitly, the exercise is meant to inform their values and further their thinking about the nature of leadership. It also is designed to provide students with a sense of ownership, of feeling the Bible is part of their heritage and not foreign to them.

By middle school, Jewish studies classes are heavily focused on discussion and other means to foster critical thinking, and that is also true in approaches to biblical texts. This approach to study is very much in keeping with modes of general studies: that students learn collaboratively and critically. The latter in particular also means the school does not promote a normative form of Jewishness. Consistent with what the school tells parents, the curriculum, Sandel notes, is primarily focused on critical thinking: "Our job is not to get the students to believe in anything particular. Our job is to get them to think critically."

Perhaps, paradigmatically, an eighth-grade class discussion highlights this approach to study. Students focused on a text from the Book of Genesis that describes a brief exchange between Rachel and Jacob in which the former expressed her exasperation over her inability to conceive. "What was she actually saying to Jacob?" the teacher asked. "What did Jacob imply in his answer when he expressed his own limitations? Can you relate to the dilemmas these figures lived with by citing examples of jealousy or feeling that your life is unjust?"

As is evident from the last question, the purpose of the discussion was to help students empathize with the biblical figures. The ensuing discussion was about what the account means to them. Students spoke of the biblical figures' jealousy, envy, shame, anger, and frustration. A student asked whether God made Rachel infertile. Another wondered whether expecting God to intervene is unrealistic. One student empathized with Jacob's sense of impotence that he cannot help Rachel, while another empathized with God. The easy back-and-forth in the class exhibited the confidence with which students spoke up, their lack of self-consciousness, and their willingness to open themselves to the emotions presented in the biblical account.

In a follow-up conversation with the class, it became clear that some of themes discussed in Jewish studies classes appear in literature and social studies classes—and connections are drawn by students and teachers. One student cited discussions in a literature class about *The Lord of the Flies* and noted how the theme of deception runs through the book, just as it does in the biblical account of Jacob's deception when he fooled his father into thinking that he was Essau asking for a blessing. Other students related examples of classes in Jewish studies about current events that then were amplified in social studies discussions.

Though Bible is central to the Jewish studies curriculum, it is hardly its sole component. Classes are also devoted to preparing students for Jewish holidays, explaining prayers found in the Siddur, and discussing current events and Israel. Antisemitic incidents at home and abroad have been the focus of many conversations. That was especially the case in the wake of shooting attacks on Jews attending synagogue services. Similarly, when important news comes out of Israel, time is devoted to helping students understand situations. In middle school, students participate in the online program JCAT, the Jewish Court of All Time. In conjunction with students at other schools, sixth graders learned to cite one project, about the MS *St. Louis* incident of the late 1930s (when a shipload of Jewish refugees fleeing Nazi Central Europe were refused entry by the United States and various Central and South American countries). All of these topics must somehow be addressed during four class sessions devoted to Jewish studies per week, not a simple task.

One additional component of Jewish studies classes warrants attention: that in the second grade, students begin to engage in Hevruta-style learning, working in pairs to address challenging questions. In addition to initiating students into a classical rabbinic mode of study, this approach introduces them to the virtues of learning partnerships. Ultimately, too, the goal is to employ Jewish studies as still another avenue for character development.

Weekly Tefila and holiday preparations round out the Jewish studies program.[6] The school administration is well aware of some parental resistance to the inclusion of Tefila. That resistance is addressed by highlighting how Tefila is an important community-building exercise and also enables every student to build self-confidence by speaking before the assembled student body. Tefila is regarded as integral to the Jewish studies curriculum because, as Merav Steinberger explained, "it is a skill the kids will need to feel at home wherever they go [in Jewish settings]." This is why the administration settled on a *siddur* (prayer book) produced by the Solomon Schechter School of Boston after examining dozens of alternatives. It included the key prayers—the *matbea*, as it is called in rabbinic parlance. Brandeis Marin seeks to impart knowledge to students about the basics of prayer, even if they are not religiously inclined. Similarly, students learn how to recite the kiddush on Shabbat and Jewish holidays, even if their own families celebrate neither.

In preparation for upcoming Jewish holidays, Jewish studies and other classes devote attention to learning about the rituals associated with the festivals. For example, in the week leading up to Purim, students were instructed how to take turns reading one or two sentences of the *Megila* (the Scroll of Esther). Students also work in the design lab to create games and booths that will be employed during the Purim carnival. The entire effort is designed as a schoolwide PBL exercise, with students drawing on material from many different classes and disciplines. In class, students prepare *mishloach manot*, gifts of food traditionally exchanged with family and friends on the holiday. Parents respond positively, even though most never encountered this ritual practice before. With their children stimulated to think about giving as a value and no judgment rendered about the quality of each gift, it is little wonder that parents are positively inclined toward this Purim tradition.

So too the meaning of the holiday is framed in such a way that no one would object. Purim is primarily treated as a celebration of triumph over religious bigotry. Class discussions are framed in both Jewish particularistic terms—the evils of antisemitism—and universal ones—as examples of how intolerance of any sort is evil.

Hebrew Language

Hebrew-language instruction constitutes the second area of Jewish focus in the school. For many years, Brandeis Marin had employed the Tal Am curriculum, but jettisoned it in recent years because it was too heavily focused on religious texts. (Ironically, other day schools criticize this same curriculum as deficient in its incorporation of religious texts.) Moreover, the school has determined its key focus of Hebrew-language study will be on spoken proficiency. In grades K through 2, the curriculum used is Chalav U'devash, with strong support for reading and writing progress. Grades 3 to 5 employ Rak B'ivrit, and the middle school uses Bishvil Ha'ivrit. All of these packaged curricula are augmented because teachers found them to contain too many errors and archaic Hebrew terms that are no longer currently used on the Israeli street.

Hebrew instruction has been transformed with the introduction of leveling as early as the third grade. Now there are three levels in each grade to accommodate different student abilities. In the middle school, moreover, students who are fluent because they have an Israeli parent enjoy a very high level of Hebrew-language instruction that focuses especially on reading and writing. (These students converse at home with their parents in Hebrew and often spend part of their summers in Israel; they are weaker in reading and writing, hence the emphasis of their classes.) The Hebrew teaching staff also offers a good deal of individualized attention, especially for students entering the school at higher grade levels who have a major task of catching up.

The school offers the choice to middle schoolers to take Hebrew or Spanish. Rather than lose students to Spanish, Hebrew teachers work extra hard to ensure their classes are stimulating and enjoyable. (A slight majority of students continue with Hebrew rather than opt for Spanish.) But it is not only pride that drives these efforts. Merav Steinberger and her Hebrew staff are also committed to Hebrew as the heritage language of the Jews. They believe in the principle of Hebrew as a central feature of a Jewish education.

The emphasis on conversational Hebrew was on display in a fifth-grade Hebrew class. The group engages in an exercise requiring each student to speak in Hebrew with another classmate. It's all interactive and seems to engage every student as an active participant. Later during the same class period, students went online with the assignment to identify items described in Hebrew that match each other. This involved some blended learning using the medium of Bishvil Ha'ivrit. In the advanced middle school class, the focus was on watching news from around the world in Hebrew. Students spoke comfortably to each other and the teacher in Hebrew, and time also was set aside to write about what they had just watched. A parent of one of these advanced-level students expressed confidence in her child's ability to integrate into Israeli schools once the family returns to Israel. Other Israeli parents report in some instances their children speak fluent Hebrew with their relatives and friends in Israel.

During interviews, students expressed appreciation for their Hebrew-language teachers, something one does not always hear in Jewish day schools:

STUDENT I

My dad is from Israel. My brother's fluent, but we speak English in the house. But I have a little bit of a hard time with Hebrew. But here, all the Hebrew teachers are just so kind. And they always want to make sure that you know what you're doing and you know what you're getting into. . . . So they teach you about Israel and most of them have lived there for a while, and so they talk to you and they tell you about everything, and they try and get you into the whole culture instead of just language.

STUDENT 2

I'd say the Hebrew teachers are different from any other teachers because with Hebrew, you can go to any teacher. With other subjects, the teachers don't know exactly what you're doing. Like a couple years ago, I had no idea what I was doing and I couldn't find my Hebrew teacher. I just went up to a[nother] teacher and she taught me half of what I know right now. So yeah, that's really nice.

To be sure, it was not unusual for an observer to spot students fading out in Hebrew classes or unexpected to hear students struggle with simple grammar. It appeared that much individualized attention and sincere interest on the part of Hebrew teachers seemed to be winning over students who might have been struggling.

How Students Assess Jewish Studies

Though it constitutes but a small fraction of the school day, Jewish studies, including Hebrew language, loom large in the experience of Brandeis Marin students. The school endeavors to elevate Jewish studies so that it is as challenging as general studies. This means in some instances downplaying expectations about how much middle schoolers learn about Jewish studies and focusing instead on how well classes stimulate them to think critically. Interviews with middle school students in grades 6 to 8 surfaced a fascinating outcome of the different approaches to general studies and Jewish studies classes: many students find Jewish studies classes more stimulating than general studies classes.

Here is how two eighth graders put it: "I feel like the JS class is a lot more discussional. For most of my other classes we just have to listen to the teacher talk, but in the JS class we can actually have discussions and . . . debates." Echoing these ideas, the other student said, "Well, I think at Brandeis no teacher is ever just talking at you; but specifically in JS usually [the teacher] will talk for about five minutes and then everyone will talk. It can get kind of rowdy, but it's really interesting because all your ideas just are like flowing and you don't feel held back or feel like you're going to make some mistake about what you're going to say. Because in everything that you say there's some kind of meaning that you can get. So I think it's really fun." Variations on this theme occurred in discussions with over forty middle school students. One student, in fact, added a key element: what he liked especially is that "there is no wrong answer in JS classes," a questionable assertion, though one supported unanimously by an entire class of eighth graders when it was mildly challenged by a visiting observer.

Interviews with students in grades 6 to 8 brought to the fore how students bring material from Jewish studies classes to interactions outside the school. Some spoke about conversations they have with friends attending other schools. Here are the comments of two students:

I have some friends who don't go to Jewish schools, and . . . when I see them, I tell them about what we learned and about the Jewish [stuff], like what we do. They're really interested because they don't really know a lot about it. They get to know a lot when I tell them things that we do in Jewish Studies class. It's also interesting for me to hear what they think about it too. (An eighth grader)

When I talk to my friends outside the school about school, I tell them it feels like home and sort of like a second home for me. When I go home, and I bet that's like a lot of people, you feel a lot better. You feel like when something hurts, when you fall down, you automatically feel better. And I feel like it's the same here. I come here, I enter, it's all cold outside and I come here, I'm like, "Finally, I got here." I feel like everyone is so kind. I'm friends with everyone and it's really peaceful compared to other schools. (A sixth grader who entered the school two years earlier)

During interviews, students were asked whether they ever discuss material learned in Jewish studies classes with family members. The range of responses to this question was noteworthy, as the following excerpts reveal:

My parents, when I get home every day, they ask me, What's an interesting thing that you did in school today?" A lot of the times I bring up what I did in JS class because we do a lot of theoretical examination of the Torah. I think that it's really interesting coming from a philosophical point of view instead of kind of seeing it literally. My parents are from Israel. My mom kind of guides my learning process. It kind of leads into a deeper conversation.

I talk with my grandparents about the topic of JS [classes]. My grandfather's Orthodox, so he is very into all the stuff about what we do in JS. Often, I'll actually show him. I tell him how we've interpreted what we've read and how it can be perceived. He loves learning about it. We always have this big exchange between us. I think it's really important.

Well, my father grew up in a fairly Jewish household, but my mother did not at all. So, she'll ask questions all the time about what we're learning specifically in JS class. It's just really fun for me to be able to tell her the stories, and then she'll point out all these things that I didn't even realize and we'll have really long discussions about that. So it's really interesting to see her take on these Jewish stories when, as a child, she didn't really get that same education.

I'm a Christian. Christianity and Judaism have some similarities, but they are very different. So I discussed this amazing topic in a class, and I talked to my family. . . . We get to share their Christian views and our Christian views and I tell them what we discussed. So I think that allows us to dig deeper and study the Bible more and more.

We culled these excerpts from interviews with four dozen middle school students, running over forty pages. These comments are representative of views expressed by nearly every student who spoke up. Skeptics might wonder whether the positive assessments of Jewish studies classes stemmed from a desire to please the interviewer or the school and whether those positive feelings will last—all fair questions. Still, these views are noteworthy in the context of what we learned about parents at Brandeis Marin, many of whom carry with them decidedly ambivalent views about their own Jewish educational experiences. It would appear, then, that the school's strategy of delivering a Jewish studies program rich in thought-provoking and values-oriented discussion seems to resonate well with students.

What Parents Say

The unusual profile of the parent body at Brandeis Marin and what is reported about the ambivalence of many parents about the Jewishness of the school begs for some exploration of how parents speak about their family's experiences at the school. The sheer range of backgrounds itself—not an unimportant consideration of school administrators—warrants notice. Some are self-described defectors from Orthodox day school education that in at least one case ran from kindergarten through college; others are Chabad families. In some families, one or both parents are Israeli-born. In a sizable number of families, one spouse was not born Jewish but has converted to Judaism. Noting her own life's journey, one staff member marveled at the examples of some of her colleagues who were born into Christian families, often with serious religious commitments, but life took them on a journey to Judaism, one that may even serve as a model for some parents in the school. "None of us could have imagined we'd end up here, raising Jewish children and helping to educate other people's Jewish children," one remarked in wonderment.

During interviews with roughly twenty parents representing a cross-section of these various types, the obvious question came up about what interviewees liked about the school. Most frequently cited was the attention to the learning needs of each student and the warm atmosphere, which results in their children enjoying coming to school.

A parent spoke about her appreciation for how comfortable her children are with non-Jews because they befriend them in classes. As an example, she described her young son asking her about why people celebrate Christmas. Though offering a Jewish education, the school simultaneously lets in the wider world, this parent noted. She spoke also about the thoughtful way the school goes about considering what is taught and how it will be communicated. Especially valuable in her view is the middle school's discussion- rather than text-oriented approach to Jewish study. This, in her view, enables students to find their own way as Jews rather than get hung up on memorization of texts and which commentator said what. Another parent confesses that the presence of intermarried families and non-Jewish ones "hearten" him. "It's not all despair about Jewish life. This is uplifting about the future of Jewish life" in the United States.

A Jewish parent who received a minimal Jewish education while growing up expresses great satisfaction that his daughter is getting a deeper Jewish education than he received. He also notes that due to the school's impact on his daughter, his own negative views of Judaism have softened. More than that, he now feels a greater responsibility to support Jewish institutions. This parent also describes how another child of his was initially unreceptive to Tefila but now "she loves it." His Israeli-born wife speaks of her own journey toward "a more positive attitude toward religion. Jewish content is presented in a way I can appreciate. It is not imposed. I can see a lot of value in Jewish ways. . . . I have more religion in my life now than ever before—and than all my Israeli family combined." Her once-secular Jewish husband has taken to building a Sukkah every year and marks Jewish holidays, such as Shavuot and Simchat Torah, that his own family ignored while he grew up.

An intermarried couple report that they stumbled on to Brandeis Marin because a friend suggested they check it out. What sold them was the eloquence and confidence with which eighth graders spoke, said the mother: "They were confident and unafraid to engage with adults. They displayed critical and creative thinking." The father who was raised Christian regards the Jewish studies program as his favorite topic in the school: "You can get good academic studies in every school, but here you get to discuss your religion, how to live your life, your history." The school, in this Christian parent's view, discusses situations in the Torah creatively: "Students are required to consider themselves in a situation [described in the Torah], to interact with people having conflicting ideas, to place themselves in the middle of stories, and to understand what happened in the past. Kids are encouraged to question everything. What kids contribute is treated as important."

What also impresses this Christian parent is Tefila because every student gets to speak before the entire school and share ideas and interpretations of the parasha (weekly Torah portion). They engage in "fearless discourse. It's engrained in students to stand in front of a hundred people, an important life skill. This becomes easy for them. They are also not afraid to question." By way of conclusion, this parent remarks that the school "doesn't teach people what to think but how to think. Brandeis Marin should be a model for a certain population." He adds that their son's uncle was so impressed with the boy's creative way of thinking and well-rounded devotion to music, sports, and extracurricular activities that he enrolled his own son at Brandeis Marin.

Some non-Jewish parents commented on the easy, relatively smooth integration of their children into the school and their appreciation of the staff's attentiveness to each child's needs. Interestingly, they expressed special appreciation for the Jewish studies classes, noting their children enjoy those classes because they enable them to reflect on their own beliefs and spiritual yearnings. True, a parent acknowledges, non-Jewish children have to catch up on specifically Jewish references to holidays, terminology, and cultural touchstones, but at the same time, every student can relate to discussions about human responsibilities to the environment and place in nature. All students also share common values. When, for example, Tefila is held in the nearby woods, all students feel a connection to nature. This parent also noted that his own attendance at Tefila has awakened in him long-suppressed spiritual yearnings. "The version of Judaism taught at the school is a very nice experience," he adds.

These laudatory comments notwithstanding, some parents also noted irritation about aspects of the school. Some, for example, raised questions about teachers "assuming the role of political activists" who promote causes. Said one parent, "Jewish teachers are teaching *their* values, not just articulating views to address diversity. They want to secularize the Jewish conversation."

Others voiced concern that classes are so focused on how texts speak to us today that students develop little appreciation for the vastly different cultures in which those texts were produced. The focus of so much discussion on the present—"How does this text speak to you?" students are routinely asked in middle school—overwhelms any effort to understand how people in past eras thought about life's big questions and moral dilemmas.

Some parents, including board members, are troubled that in some years, the majority of students do not celebrate a bar or bat mitzvah in a religious setting. In the 2019–20 school year, an estimated two-thirds of seventh graders were not planning this celebration in a religious setting. "What message does this send about the priorities of the school?" they ask. One can interpret the emphasis on the milestone year, however nonjudgmental and unthreatening it is, as an effort by Peg Sandel to focus more parental attention on choosing a way to mark the milestone in a communal setting.

That almost all seventh-grade Tzedakah projects support nonsectarian organizations rather than Jewish ones has also raised some eyebrows. During the previous year, only two of the twelve projects raised money for specifically Jewish causes.

Still other parents express concern about whether the school will reach a tipping point if it admits too many non-Jews. Will that lead to a dilution of the school's Jewish mission? Others wonder about the school's policy of offering non-Jews the same scholarship funding as is made to Jewish families. Yet in a school so committed to diversity and inclusion, how can it be otherwise?

Like many other day schools, Brandeis Marin navigates between competing, if not incompatible, parental concerns. For parents who stay the course, its assets outweigh its deficits. Not least of those assets is that it is actually the more Judaically intensive school in its immediate geographic area. Most parents are pleased by the support their children receive as they progress through the school, support that comes from the administrative and teaching staff and from fellow students. Parents too are in sync with the school's inclusiveness—its openness to Jewish families of all types and non-Jewish families. Also important to its success, the school communicates a message of broad acceptance. Its norms are framed in terms valued by the parent body, and it sets forth no Jewish norms of behavior or religious observance. Brandeis Marin understands the Jewish population it serves and the broader culture of its environment. Whether its approach would be a good match in other settings remains to be seen. At the least, it offers a fascinating and thoughtful model of Jewish day school education worth watching.

CONNECTIONS AND EXCEPTIONS

Brandeis Marin is an unusual day school in many ways. First, the Jewish profile of its student body is different from that of the majority of other day schools: fewer than a quarter of students are being raised by two Jewish parents, and about 10 percent are not Jewish in any sense. By comparison, at the Akiva School (chapter 5), a similarly pluralistic institution, about three-quarters come from homes where both parents identify as Jewish. Second, while most other schools tend to experience enrollment attrition in middle school, Brandeis Marin has benefited from an influx of transfer students in grades 6, 7, and 8. In fact, while enrollments at community day schools across the United States have seen a slight decline over the past five years, enrollment at Brandeis Marin has grown by nearly 20 percent during that period. As noted, at the time of our study, about a quarter of the students were new to the school that year.

These features complicate the work of delivering an appropriately differentiated curriculum, especially in the middle school, and of cultivating a stable school culture that is authentic and at the same time fully inclusive in Jewish terms. How the school has approached these challenges—less extreme forms of which face all community day schools—makes the school such an instructive case and a possible model for others.

Like some of the other especially dynamic schools in our sample, the school's response to these challenges begins with the leadership of its head of school. Peg Sandel has an unusually clear sense of what her school is trying to accomplish, and with particular adroitness she articulates a vision for day school education in a universal language that resonates with parents. Prospective parents find the educational vision she articulates compelling, and once their children enroll, they discover the school functions as a "repair shop," enabling them to mend the lasting harm done to them by their own Jewish education. We noted a similar phenomenon at the Pressman Academy and Akiva School (chapters 4 and 5). This is not a case of bait and switch. The first concern of parents is their children's education, but in time they come to learn that there is something at the school for them too.

The school also provides a compelling example of how, when teachers are given opportunities to develop the appropriate skills, day schools can deliver a child-centered experience of active learning that rivals the best of their immediate competitors in both the public and private sectors. This is what a twenty-first-century day school education looks like. At Brandeis Marin, the responsive classroom, blended learning, STEM education, and makerspace are all employed actively, as is the case in one mix or another at all of the other elementary schools in our sample. These approaches and experiences empower children to take charge of their own learning to think critically about what they encounter across the entire curriculum, in Jewish and general studies.

It is perhaps jarring to observe day school educators at Brandeis Marin expressing the view that students should not be pushed to believe in anything particular when it comes to Jewish subject matter. Certainly no other school in our sample embraces such a neutral approach to Jewish commitments. But this orientation is one possible way to frame a pluralistic day school education. At Brandeis Marin it plays well with most families.

4

Nurturing Students' Reflectiveness and Wellness

The Pressman Academy, Los Angeles, California

The Pressman Academy calls for attention on many counts, most
distinctively for its special focus on meeting the social and emotional
needs of students. Class-based curriculum and extracurricular programing,
as well as staffing choices, are directed toward a goal of building student
resilience and collaboration. These goals supersede the obsessive
preoccupation at other schools with getting graduates into the finest
high schools and then America's top colleges. Pressman's priorities flow
from a larger countercultural ethos that is strikingly discordant with the
school's location just on the edge of Beverly Hills, one of Los Angeles's
glitziest neighborhoods. This ethos is traceable to a set of well-honed
Jewish and educational values that derive in turn from the school's home
within a venerable Conservative synagogue community. The chapter
demonstrates how these values find expression in outcomes ranging
from unusually intensive investment in professional development for
teachers, to a strong commitment to Hebrew-language instruction,
and to choices about how to develop the school's campus.

Located in the densely populated Jewish neighborhood of Pico-Robertson in
West Los Angeles and just a stone's throw from the wealthy enclave of Beverly Hills, the Pressman Academy might have become a somewhat glitzy private school catering to Jewish high society. In fact, this school, which enrolls
around 450 students from early childhood through grade 8, is something
very different. Its quarters are modest, with most classes meeting in a utili-
tarian school building and others, mainly for middle schoolers, held in spaces
within the adjacent synagogue building. For most of its more than thirty
years, its sports activities were confined to the school building's small out-
door rooftop, though in September 2019 it inaugurated a newly constructed
structure housing a gym. It focuses on a high-quality general studies and Judaica education but especially prides itself on creating an environment that
nurtures children who care for and respect one another. It also has not given

in to the obsessive preoccupation with getting graduates into the finest high schools as part of the race to place alumni ultimately at America's elite universities (though its graduates can and do get into prestigious high schools and colleges). Pressman's priorities may well explain the unusually high proportion of children and grandchildren of rabbis, educators, Jewish communal professionals, and professors enrolled in the school. Indeed, one of the most frequently voiced claims made within the school by parents, teachers, and community leaders is about Pressman's emphasis on decency, serious study, and well-thought-out values.

Pressman is a neighborhood school in the sense that it draws most of its students almost entirely from families residing within a three-mile radius. Though some parents drive to drop off and pick up their children, a good number walk with them to school, itself a countercultural activity in Los Angeles. Living in close proximity to many other Pressman families means that both students and parents tend to regard their Pressman peer groups as their Jewish community. Uncharacteristically for a Schechter day school, a fair number of students spend part of the Jewish Sabbath and holidays hanging out together in the same synagogue or each other's homes.

Temple Beth Am formally founded and continues to oversee Pressman Academy. This arrangement is not common among Jewish day schools around the country, but in greater Los Angeles, the linkage between school and shul (synagogue) is more widespread. At least eight congregations, both Conservative and Reform, run their own day schools for reasons having to do with the history of busing in Los Angeles and the perceived inferior quality of the public school system.[1]

Beth Am is not bashful about its ties to the Conservative movement and tries to shape Pressman Academy to follow suit. The intertwining of the synagogue with the school is most dramatically evident spatially. Not only are the school and synagogue buildings adjacent to each other, but the synagogue's facilities are constantly in use by Pressman students every school day. The rabbis of Beth Am, moreover, play a role in the school: the senior rabbi sets religious policy for the school (which we note is named after a previous senior rabbi of Beth Am, Jacob Pressman), and a rabbi in the congregations works with parents who enroll their children in the school as part of his portfolio. The head of school is an employee of the synagogue and accountable to the synagogue board. Even fundraising for the school is run jointly by the synagogue's executive director and the head of school.

As is the case with other day schools housed at synagogues, membership in the congregation—with a price tag of $4,000 above school tuition—is a prerequisite for enrolling children in the academy. As a result, Beth Am gains between fifty and eighty member families each year who join in order to enroll their children in the school. This does not mean that all the parents regard Beth Am as their home synagogue. Just under one-fifth of students come from homes primarily affiliated with nearby Orthodox synagogues. The families of another 15 percent are either secular, belong to a Reform temple, or attend the independent Ikar congregation. The other two-thirds, though, are not only formally affiliated with Beth Am but also attend with some regularity.

A further level of diversity is added by the varied subethnic backgrounds of parents. Many are American born, but others come from Iran or other Middle Eastern countries via Israel. Some are religiously Orthodox Israelis, and others are secularists from Israel. Religious affiliation or nonaffiliation and ethnic differences are all part of the pluralistic environment of Pressman.

The school's own cultural identity revolves around three cardinal educational emphases. First, Pressman prides itself on its strong commitment to Hebrew-language education. Beginning in its early childhood program and through the lower school years, Pressman offers what it advertises as immersive Hebrew learning. Second, the school has defined its own approach to high-quality education in the form of a progressive education that stresses cooperative learning experiences, with students working together as partners in developing projects. Especially in the middle school, classes are far less likely to feature frontal teaching; instead, students work cooperatively on project-based learning. And third, the school invests heavily in personnel and curricula promoting social and emotional learning. Helping students to understand themselves and their own emotional reactions while providing support as they learn to navigate social interactions with classmates and others are high priorities at Pressman. These educational emphases largely explain why parents, especially those with no connection to Conservative Judaism, have opted to enroll their children in the Pressman Academy.

Charting the Course from the Top

With a staff consisting of some teachers who have been at the school for several decades and a historical and ideological connection with the same synagogue, there are strong pressures at Pressman to stay its course. But no school is static, and in fact the board does not want Pressman to remain as it always was. When Erica Rothblum was hired as the new head of school in 2014, the board charged her to make changes in some key areas. Her strength and experience as an educator had been in general studies, and that is the primary area where she has left her mark.

Rothblum is an active user of student data to measure how students are doing in reading, math, and writing skills. As she and the staff identify areas of weakness, they have addressed issues by adopting new curricula in math and language arts. When Rothblum was hired, parents called the science program "abysmal." Under her leadership, the school also has introduced a far more robust program of STEAM (science, technology, engineering, the arts, and mathematics) classes by hiring new teachers (and letting others go) and creating a new makerspace. Rothblum reports that "students love the STEAM classes because they are learning these subjects in new ways." She is also gratified that with the improvements, parent satisfaction has risen. If anything, these positive advances have whetted Rothblum's appetite to address other areas of educational weakness. The teaching of math in the last years of the lower school attracted her attention during the year when we visited the school. New curricula and teacher training were instituted to address that area.

Each year, together with the board, she sets goals for the coming school year to address specific challenges. But as is true of all school administrators, her time is divided between "the important and the urgent." Day-to-day issues get in the way of working on the big-picture issues. She describes her day as divided equally between putting out fires and instituting structural changes.

Undergirding her efforts is a particular set of beliefs about what Pressman should aspire to accomplish. As students progress through the school, their learning is increasingly accomplished through teamwork and project-based learning. This is particularly evident in middle school classes, which rarely are primarily frontal in orientation. Rather, teachers serve as consultants to students working in pairs or small groups to define their own projects. Interestingly, few classes have adopted a flipped learning model, even though technology is employed in classes. (Flipped learning reverses the traditional way of learning and measuring student competence by delivering instructional content, usually online, outside the classroom; in the classroom, students demonstrate their mastery of the material by completing exercises —that is, doing what in the past would have been considered the domain of homework.) The predominant use of computers is to search for information, not to serve as the delivery system for curricular content.

More broadly, Pressman's leadership takes a cautious, if not skeptical, approach to the new technologies that have posed challenges at so many schools. Educators at Pressman are acutely aware of how unsettled parents are about the question of technology use. At what age should students be given their own smartphone? (One-third of ten-year-olds at Pressman have their own phones.) How much time ought children to spend on smartphones and other devices? And how might parents set limits on such use, especially if their children's classmates have fewer constraints placed on them? Pressman is beginning to distinguish itself by addressing these matters from a Jewish perspective. Drawing on the wisdom of Jewish tradition, it tries to tap sensibilities and wisdom that might help families navigate these challenges. This is not some tactical move designed to make the school more appealing in a competitive marketplace. The school's embrace of the challenge seems genuinely in tune with its historical values.

The course it has chosen is to enable students to use tablets in classes but with strict controls over what they can access in school. The school requires middle school students to acquire iPads for use during classes and distributes them to older students in the lower school on a selective basis. But technology does not drive classes. Judging from iPad agreements posted on classroom doors, there is a fair amount of monitoring of how students employ the new technology during the school day. The agreement states among other things, "I will not use my iPad without teacher permission, and I will put my iPad under my desk when not using it." Smartphones are not allowed in classrooms and are confiscated if they are brought to school. The IT team blocks students from using games and other unauthorized Internet content while at school. As to students' use of technology outside school, Pressman works with parents who are unsure of what is appropriate and how to enforce guidelines for their children.

Also basic to Pressman's approach is a strong commitment to helping students develop the interpersonal and self-awareness skills necessary to succeed in a fast-changing society. Rothblum speaks eloquently about how impossible it is to know in advance what skills and knowledge her students will need when they will be of age to enter the labor force in the future. For this reason, she has invested serious time and resources in programs to cultivate resilience in her students and help them manage their own emotions when confronting new challenges. Parents, in her experience, often are focused on the present needs of their children. Rothblum is convinced that the school must prepare students for an unknowable future by helping them develop coping capacities. The best way to do that is by helping each student to "know thyself," a value Rothblum has elevated in the school's approach.

Investing in Social and Emotional Learning

Toward that end, Pressman has invested heavily in programming to help students and their parents with social and emotional issues. The director of student services has been at Pressman for twenty-three years, albeit in different capacities. She is acutely aware of how many more children at the school are diagnosed with some type of learning or emotional issue than in the past. Rather than leave parents and children to fend for themselves, the school offers counseling, guidance on where to find therapists, and other forms of help. Her department, for example, helps parents whose children have been diagnosed with a learning disability. And she also works with teachers on what individual children need from the school—for example, whether their work requirements should be modified or whether other accommodations are required. She also works with case managers who help students speak up and become better advocates for what they need. All this requires a significant staff. In addition to the director, the school employs two full-time school counselors for the lower and middle schools, one each, and also part-time learning specialists—with the assistance of outside consultants. (Some of these personnel are provided through a program offered to Jewish day schools by the education department of the Los Angeles Jewish Federation.)

The office of student services also works with a Boston-based program, B'yadeinu (In Our Hands), to assess its own efforts and strengthen its support services. The office measures how well its interventions have worked, sets benchmarks for more effective action, and continues to measure how well it addresses the learning needs of students. With the help of B'yadeinu, it also determines whether to ask parents to withdraw their child from the school and how best to manage such meetings.

Pressman also employs a director of wellness who views a major part of her role as teaching students to self-regulate their emotional responses and providing support to their parents. "Parents," she asserts, "feel overwhelmed. They don't know how to parent and want the school to do it for them. But at the same time, many parents are overbearing in order to ensure their children will obtain what the parents think they need." She teaches classes devoted to resilience and emotional self-management, using texts from Jewish sources to convey these messages.

For students in all grades, Pressman has had a once-a-week program, called Council. Students sit in a circle and talk about their lives. The goal is to develop communication skills. A sample discussion may be about a time each student felt included or excluded. This is an opportunity for students to develop skills in expressing their thoughts and feelings among peers, and to help them develop empathy for challenges others encounter. In addition, two counselors and a social worker meet with classes to teach interpersonal skills, communication, how to regulate emotions, and negotiating questions of identity, puberty, healthy choices, and Jewish relationships. The wellness head pays special attention to preparing eighth graders for the challenges they will encounter when they enter high school the following year.

In the 2019–20 school year, this was further systemized through the adoption of a new curriculum on life skills for the entire school. SEE Learning —Social, Emotional and Ethical Learning, a curriculum developed at Emory University—is incorporated at weekly gatherings from kindergarten to grade 8 (with a half-hour devoted to the material up to grade 5 and an hour for middle school students). The multipronged goals are to cultivate "ethical intelligence," particularly compassion; offer attention training to help students keep themselves focused on their work; systems thinking to help students navigate in different settings and monitor their own emotional responses; and resilience training to face setbacks. All of these are to be accomplished through a student-focused pedagogy that encourages children to reflect on their own values and goals. A Jewish dimension is added by the school to this generic curriculum. At the time of the High Holy Days, for example, the four steps of *teshuva* (repentance) were added to the discussion; forgiveness loomed large too, including forgiving others and forgiving oneself.

To help build a sense of responsibility toward others, the school has divided the entire student body into "families" of twelve to fifteen students from all grades. Once a month, these student families meet for a class session to engage in play and conversation facilitated by a teacher. Middle school students assume the role of older sibling taking younger students under their wing. It's an interesting model in how to cut across grades and break down the insularity students feel within each grade level. Instead, all students interact with older and younger schoolmates, with a dose of "elder brother or sister" support to help all students forge new bonds.

Pressman also runs an annual three-day retreat for middle school students early in the school year. The entire middle school faculty attends during the daytime. The goal is to help students, especially those who have just enrolled in the school, to interact and bond with classmates. Though the purpose here is to help students integrate into their own grades, as opposed to the family program. which cuts across grades, the goal is not so different: the school works to develop social ties among students.

Why does Pressman make such a huge investment in this auxiliary staff and devote time to various programs focused on nonacademic topics? Simply put, new ways of thinking about child development and the diverse ways people learn and what students require in order to flourish all have heightened awareness that there is no point investing solely in academics without caring also for students' social and emotional needs. Parents have come to expect such investments because, as staff at Pressman and many other day schools comment, there is more widespread awareness of learning and psychological challenges besetting today's students. Day schools have become attuned to these needs, as have other schools, including colleges and universities, all of which have expanded their health and emotional learning services departments.

In addition, staff members at Pressman have commented on the shifting needs of day school parents. They observe major differences between parents of current high school students, middle school students, and children enrolled in early childhood programs. In the perception of school personnel, parents of younger children come across as overwhelmed by the rapidity of change. They tend to feel less in control and certainly feel more uncertain of what their children will need to flourish as adults in the rapidly changing economy. Day schools are feeling the added stress that parents bring to the school setting and are ratcheting up their efforts to offer support to families and their children. If anything, school personnel worry that they may be lagging behind rapid changes and need to provide more emotional support to family units.

Pressman is hardly unique in this regard. Its heavy investments in social and emotional learning illustrate a major area of change undertaken by many Jewish day schools—and other kinds of educational institutions, both public and private—to address issues that were ignored even a few decades ago. These efforts, though, come at a price: day schools are paying salaries to an entire staff of people who were absent from schools as recently as twenty years ago. That financial price is part of the reason that enrollment fees have risen, often to the dismay of parents saddled with heavy tuition costs. And yet, many parents also expect day schools to offer these services.

To Erica Rothblum, moreover, these efforts are essential to the culture of Pressman. She is convinced that for all their concern about academic excellence, parents are equally drawn to the school by its ability to nurture *menschen*, well-rounded and grounded human beings who exhibit concern and respect for others. This is a major selling point for the school and sets it apart from some of its competitors. It also offers a viable countercultural alternative to the more materialistic aspirations of the surrounding culture by helping students develop empathy, value other human beings, and build a support system to help each other navigate through often difficult middle school years.

In a message to her entire community on the eve of Thanksgiving 2019, Rothblum underscored her commitment to nurturing a particular kind of person. Noting the nastiness of discourse gripping American society—and pointedly noting this was hardly limited to political issues—she committed Pressman to building the character of its students in a countercultural direction: "When I think about the kinds of people I want Pressman to produce, kindness tops the list. . . . So let's be authentic, let's be explicit, let's narrate, and let's model. Let's build a community that talks the talk *and* walks the walk. We may be up against some pretty weighty cultural forces, but I do believe that if we are intentional in our parenting and our educating, we can prevail."

Pressman, along with most of the other day schools presented in this book, supports social and emotional learning personnel because they see these staff people as critically important aids to students and also because their efforts create a supportive, nurturing environment that sets their schools apart and attracts some families that might not have had a strong commitment to Jewish day schools but are attracted by the warm ambience and attention paid to each child's development.

The Four Pillars of Education

Social and emotional learning is but one facet of Pressman. The school also prides itself on its academic strengths. These include a strong commitment to teaching modern Hebrew, Jewish studies classes designed to foster thinking and creativity, and STEAM classes and cross-curricula learning bridging Jewish and general studies learning.

Hebrew Immersion
Perhaps the best way to capture some of the unique features of this school is by bringing readers into classroom settings. We begin with Hebrew-language

instruction, a feature at every grade level. One of the more energetic classes on display is a kindergarten class taught by a long-time teacher with nearly fifty years of classroom experience. Along with an assistant teacher, she leads the twenty students in the class through a nonstop hour of improvised singing. Employing children's melodies and other songs from different contexts, she adapts the music to drill students on the letters of the Hebrew alphabet and the vocabulary for colors, the days of the week, the seasons of the year, the months of the Jewish calendar, and numbers—all in Hebrew. The teacher and children sing with gusto, and the teacher's enthusiasm is infectious. She speaks solely in Hebrew and ask students to respond as well in Hebrew. How much they understand is impossible to know, but certainly the class exposes students to a remarkable range of Hebrew vocabulary and secondarily to sentence formation.

In the lower school, all Jewish studies classes were conducted in Hebrew until the 2019–20 school year. A third-grade class, for example, featured students acting out the relationship between Lot and Abraham as recounted in the Book of Genesis. Two students assumed the primary roles while the other students asked them questions. The entire discussion was conducted in Hebrew. These classes bring great pride to the school, which regards its immersive Hebrew studies as a selling point and distinctive feature.

In recent years, that immersive approach did not apply for students in middle school. For one thing, whereas all Jewish studies classes in the lower school were conducted more or less in the Hebrew language (*ivrit b'ivrit*), Hebrew was spoken in the middle school only during classes devoted to that language, not during any other Jewish studies classes. For another, the approach to teaching Hebrew embarked on a radically different course beginning in grade 6. In the lower school, Jewish studies classes revolved around, albeit not rigidly, a printed curriculum, TaL AM, and more recently its digital and interaction online iteration, TaL AM. The hallmarks of that curriculum, developed in Montreal and Israel for diaspora Jewish schools, is to teach Hebrew as a heritage language. This means that Hebrew is intertwined with the study of sacred texts, Jewish holidays, Israeli songs, and aspects of Jewish culture. The goal is both to teach modern Israeli Hebrew and help students form a strong connection to Jewish life through an integrated Jewish studies curriculum.

But the TaL AM curriculum runs only through grade 5, and at that point, schools must shift to a different way of studying Hebrew. By the 2019–20 school year, Pressman decided to shift away from TaL AM in the fourth grade due to dissatisfaction with its Jewish studies components. In part, the decision was prompted by a desire to develop its own Jewish studies curriculum to fit the needs of its student body. Even in the lower grades where TaL AM continues to be used, its curriculum is supplemented by texts chosen by the school's own teaching staff, especially those trained in a different method of Hebrew learning developed by Hebrew at the Center.

Hebrew at the Center is a U.S.-based program guided by the proficiency approach, an entirely different method and philosophy from that of TaL AM. The proficiency approach stresses what students can do with their language skills: how well and accurately they communicate, especially in spoken Hebrew. It tracks students by their ability to use language, and it measures their abilities frequently. In grades 4 and 5, students are placed in Hebrew classes appropriate for their level of proficiency. Teachers adapt different curricula for each level and also teach Hebrew to smaller classes. According to the head of Judaica at the school, students are much happier in these leveled classes; some, he claims, now regard Hebrew classes as their favorite. Especially appealing are classes that bring Israeli settings to life, where foods, music, and dancing are part of the learning experience. And in leveled classes, students who have greater difficulty learning the language feel less frustrated because the curriculum is keyed to their abilities.

By adopting the proficiency approach and dropping any requirement that Hebrew must be used as the language of communication in Jewish studies classes beyond grade 3, the school has shifted dramatically. Not least, it would be a stretch to describe Hebrew learning from grades 4 to 8 as a Hebrew immersion environment.

Pressman is switching its approach to Hebrew so drastically because many students are unable to function in an ivrit b'ivrit classroom environment when the subject matter becomes more sophisticated and abstract. In the higher grades of the lower school, students are already balking at responding in Hebrew, due in part to the disconnect between students' conceptual abilities as they mature and the level of their language sophistication. It also is connected to the heightened self-consciousness of students as they approach their puberty years: they don't want to fumble around searching for words and potentially embarrass themselves in front of their peers. A few Hebrew teachers at Pressman put matters starkly: in their estimation, a fair number of middle school students are well below grade level in their communication skills. And teachers are convinced that immersion begins to backfire for students with weaker language abilities, who feel frustrated and resentful.

None of this is unique to Pressman students. One study reported that middle school students regress in their knowledge of the Hebrew language at many Jewish day schools. A proportion of students spoke Hebrew better in grade 4 than they did in grade 8, some Hebrew teachers report. And so, as at Pressman, ivrit b'ivrit often is cast aside as a method of middle school instruction. Communication in Hebrew is relegated to Hebrew classes. Moreover, the enterprise of teaching Hebrew is seen as highly problematic by many students and their parents.[2]

Still, as is the case in many other day schools, for a select group of students at Pressman—those with a facility for languages or a strong commitment to learning Hebrew or children of Israeli parents who hear Hebrew at home—Hebrew classes continue to be conducted on a high level. For such students, Pressman offers impressively sophisticated classes. Here are two examples.

A seventh-grade Hebrew class began one day with the teacher projecting a photograph on the classroom interactive whiteboard. In the photograph, a girl aged perhaps five is hugging her teddy bear, seemingly bereft of company, while a man—presumably her father—is seated next to her, completely absorbed in his laptop while listening intently through headphones and quite oblivious of the girl next to him. Students were asked first to write a paragraph on what they saw in the photograph and then relate their answer orally, all in Hebrew. On the few occasions when a student interjected an English word, the teacher gently offered the Hebrew equivalent and prodded the student to get back to conversing in Hebrew. The rest of the class hour was conducted entirely in a high-level Hebrew. The purpose was to prepare students for class presentations focused on explaining how an Israeli invention operates—for example, cell phone components, the WAZE navigation system, or a solar water heater. Certainly, explaining advanced technology in any foreign language is not a simple matter. But the teacher did not leave it at that. She also prepared students to discuss their responses to each class presentation. The goal was to develop a constructive way of framing responses, including questions and gentle commentary, directed to the presenters. Throughout the class session, the teacher spoke a sophisticated, modern Israeli Hebrew, and from all the evidence, students were able to follow. This class consisted of the strongest Hebrew-language students, constituting nearly half the grade.

An eighth-grade class in Hebrew offered another example of high-level learning. Here too the class began with an image projected onto a screen. In this case, students were asked to take turns making up a story based on what they saw, with each student speaking fluently, albeit in American-inflected

Hebrew. Next came an exercise in which recent work submitted by students was "graded" by the class using an elaborate notation system. The point was to catch grammatical and spelling errors as a means of improving their own and their classmates' work, thereby upgrading their own competence through progressive refinement. The class concluded with a flourish, the playing of a poem or song by the Israeli rock musician Shalom Hanoch. Many students knew it by heart and sang with gusto. The entire class, it should be noted, was designed by the teacher rather than taken from a packaged curriculum. In total, it was an impressive tour de force of pacing, clever pedagogy, warmth, and intellectual stimulation.

At its best, then, Pressman offers students with the requisite abilities and interest a strong Hebrew-language education from early childhood through grade 8. As in most other Jewish day schools, only a portion of the student population is able to take full advantage of the highest-level offerings. But serious Hebrew learning is there for the taking.

Jewish Studies

The shift away from TaL AM has also necessitated developing a new curriculum for Jewish studies, especially in the lower grades. To complicate matters, with students in the same class at different levels when they read Hebrew texts, assignments may differ within the same classroom. These are challenges Pressman has eagerly embraced because they create opportunities for Jewish studies teachers to assume a greater role in developing curriculum and enable the school to tailor teaching to the needs of specific groups of students. This illustrates again the commitment of the school to develop its own curricula and create materials that are uniquely its own, another expression of Pressman's countercultural ethos.

As this process has unfolded, several directions have come into focus. First, students are now exposed to classical Jewish texts at an earlier age and more intensively than before. Second, Israel has assumed a more prominent place in the curriculum. And third, the school relies less on teachers of Hebrew (usually native Israelis) to teach Jewish studies classes. A cadre of American-born teachers has been hired to staff Jewish studies classes. And fourth, the new system has opened opportunities to address a persistent complaint of parents that their children were not exposed to the weekly Torah reading. Under the new system, time is allocated for precisely that purpose.

Significantly, these curricular changes are also aligned with Pressman's commitment to social and emotional learning. The new system has opened opportunities to explore Jewish teachings, such as honoring one's parents. In the higher grades, students are paired to study Hevruta, a way to foster greater student independence in pursuit of the meaning of Jewish texts. It also helps students develop listening skills because each student must attend carefully to what a study partner is saying. Even emphases on resilience and learning dispositions are filtered through Jewish studies classes.

Other changes in the Jewish studies curriculum have included new ways to teach Talmud. The focus, employing curricula developed in Israel, is on helping students understand the structure of Talmudic discourse. Once they grasp how the text operates, they are able to work independently on deciphering new texts on their own. Some students also participate in what is called Moot Beit Din, a parallel to moot court but based on debating the uses of Jewish texts to address a case of Jewish law. Pressman is proud to have won citywide Moot Beit Din contests in recent years.

Jewish studies classes have evolved at Pressman to stress Hebrew, textual skills, leadership, and independent inquiry. What has remained a constant is the commitment to devote 40 percent of the school day to Jewish subject matter. Significantly, Pressman sends a high proportion of its graduates to Jewish day high schools, including Modern Orthodox ones. This has placed pressure on the school to prepare its students to engage in Jewish studies at a high level. From all the reports, Pressman students are valued at local Jewish high schools for their independent thinking and leadership qualities, even as they have no difficulty handling Hebrew and Jewish studies classes.

General Studies

As noted previously, Pressman has embraced project-based learning, especially for middle school students. The complexities of this kind of approach came into focus in following eighth graders over the course of their day. For their humanities course, students were learning about the amendments to the U.S. Constitution. In pairs, students were assigned an amendment and then had to research why the amendment was enacted, what it means today, and whether it has gone too far; the exercise also includes a call to action and a debate about pros and cons of maintaining the amendment. On the day we tracked them, students were working on podcasts about their chosen amendment. A small subgroup was situated in a makeshift recording studio held in the small chapel of Beth Am synagogue. The task for various small groups was to integrate a recoded interview into their podcast. In one group, a boy read the script from his tablet. His partner was recording on his tablet, connected to a high-quality mic set up in a box soundproofed with egg cartons. The teacher showed them how to splice the material together. Thus, while mastering the content of the constitutional amendment and its implications, students also were learning technical skills. When the recording was completed, they returned to the chapel to edit their sound effects. Other pairs of students in the chapel were working on their own podcasts. Fellow students checked in with each other to see how they were doing and settled into a pew at the back to work on their own piece in relaxed fashion. Overall, there was a sense of the work coming to a climax as students put together different components of their project.

Sounds of recorded segments came from other parts of the room in this hive of activity, with each group of students busy on their own project. Analogizing this setting to a hive is not inappropriate: students were working in different corners of this sprawling space, in the nooks and crannies of the synagogue chapel. It's hard to see how their separate activities were connected to one another, yet there was a general framework holding this all together, under the direction of the humanities teacher.

While some students worked in pairs on their own, others reconnected with the teachers. One pair debriefed with the humanities teacher, while confessing a conflict between their personal views and some of the material they had gathered. They also discussed what they should base their case on and what action they were recommending. A few moments later, some other students come back to the teacher to check in. She helped them improve their work. At one point, she pushed the team member who was writing the script to express himself more clearly: "You already said that! . . . Good. That's much better now."

In a subsequent private conversation, the teacher explained that in project-based learning like this, meaningful performance is not delayed to the end. It's happening all of the time. All of the groups, for example, had been interviewing people in professions (lawyers, especially), many of whom they cold-called for interviews. On one day we observed, several girls were working on the issue of gender equality. They had scheduled a phone call with an attorney in Los Angeles who specializes in legal issues surrounding equal pay (and remarkably, this attorney and others make time to speak with Pressman students). The learning process occurs at every stage as the project unfolds.

One is left wondering whether it is more or less challenging to manage teaching and learning in these situations. The teacher must be prepared to let go. The students are dispersed across the building (a synagogue!), and it's difficult to track how focused they are or which team members pull their weight, though to keep the students accountable, the teacher requires students to complete a log at the end of classes that says what were they doing, what they accomplished, and what they were having difficulty with.

When the class is over, the teacher seems exhausted by the intensity of this exercise because she has to improvise constantly, offering suggestions to students about whom they might talk to in order to get different perspectives on their topics, drawing on her own personal network, and looking online for relevant information. For this kind of assignment, teaching does not mean coming to class with already prepared material. The artistry is in knowing where to find resources in response to the students' questions.

Yet for all the teacher's advice, this assignment clearly is a case of self-directed learning, with students helping each other figure out how to complete specific tasks that they might not otherwise have mastered. It is striking how little time over the course of this day, the students spend working by themselves. They always seem to be working with a peer or with a shared app.

The entire exercise also captures the distinctive, positive educational dimension of the Pressman experience. The setting is improvised because space is limited, and so much of the work is done in the synagogue's chapel. On the other side of a partition, one hears singing from an early childhood program, and on this side of the partition, a giant recording studio is improvised. Some might find it inappropriate that a sacred space is being put to profane use, and yet there is something normalizing about the students inhabiting this space so comfortably. As the class hour concludes, four boys are still sitting beneath a row of stained-glass windows deeply focused on their tablets, working on their scripts. This is a tableau in some ways of what their school represents, an informal mixing of an enriched general studies program within a Jewish religious setting, even as students sit comfortably engaged in their collaborative work.

In a second class that same day, students squeeze into a repurposed room in the synagogue building for a science "lab." Once again, the students are working in teams on a project: two large teams are constructing scale models of the proposed new middle school building Pressman is hoping to construct in the coming years (one that will eliminate the need to create science labs in synagogue classrooms). Another small group is off on the side writing up an explanatory text about what they're doing.

The challenge first is for students to understand how models work. Using the actual architectural plans proposed for the new building, students construct a model according to scale. They then wire the model with a functioning electrical circuitry so that every room lights up. The learning happens in various ways: students must engage in precision measurement, figure out how electrical circuits work, and problem-solve when things don't work. They also must work out a system for who will take on which role—who will read the architect's plans, measure to scale, build the walls, glue, solder and run wire, paint, and so on. Beyond the mechanics, the exercise also involves team-building work.

The teacher privately notes, "The great thing is that the kids come in and just start working." There is a certainly a buzz and smell of activity here. A couple of students are armed with soldering irons, which make a terrible odor. By this final stage, some of the activity looks like busywork. Some students are tasked with removing as much masking tape as possible from the model and instead are gluing the corners. Some kids really do just seem to be spectators, while most others step up to do what they're most interested in: measuring cut-to-scale pieces of cardboard, circuit wiring, painting the walls and floors. Two girls in a class otherwise made up of boys seem to be holding their own admirably. They are highly focused on soldering the circuits. It's hard to ignore how radically this science class differs from what might have been the norm a generation ago, for it combines different elements of STEAM education, project-based learning, student initiative, teamwork, hands-on learning, and a transformed role for teachers.

Cross-Curricular Studies

Integrating learning from general studies with Judaica is a challenge all Jewish day schools face. A former Pressman school head identified the complexities of holding dual curricula in balance while also helping students draw connections between the Jewish and general studies materials they are learning.

In the first class of the week for grade 8 students, the flexible interaction between different subject matters is on display. The room seems to be a Judaic studies classroom: a mix of materials in Hebrew and English hang from the walls, including a series of images related to different books of the Tanakh (Hebrew Bible); another wall is dedicated to different kinds of *brachot* (blessings), a Torah time line, and themes from the Mishna. In a telling indicator, it's not clear what's the front or the back of the classroom. The teacher (a substitute that day) asks if anyone has any "words of dedication" to start the class. Students proceed to dedicate the class in honor of someone who had a baby, a family that has moved out of its house, a friend who is going to be reading the entire Torah *parasha* next week, a family that was murdered. And then the students offer the blessing, thanking God for commanding the Jewish people to engage in matters of Torah (*l'asok bedivrei Torah*). It's not clear if the blessing is said then because it's the start of the week or the start of the day. And then with little ado, the class shifts gears to engage in a social studies project. The easy movement from Jewish religious subjects to personal reflections and then to a general studies project is striking.

Beyond this type of informal interaction between the school's Jewish and general studies missions, Pressman is still feeling its way toward cross-curricular studies, a goal the school has set for itself. In the realm of formal learning, we observed how on the occasion of a Jewish new moon (Rosh Hodesh), a science teacher met with third graders to discuss the phases of the moon. A fifth-grade class devoted to explaining what the United Nations does also learned about the role of the U.N. in the founding of Israel. More generally, project-based learning, a method favored in many classes, facilitates integration because it enables teachers to tailor assignments.

Yet even what appear to be straight Jewish studies classes draw on external sources. An eighth-grade class studying Kohelet (Ecclesiastes) was shown a clip from the TV show *The Good Place* as a lead-in to a discussion about the purpose of life. Moving back and forth from excerpted statements taken from Kohelet to the TV clip, the teacher elicited student reactions to similarities and differences in approach to the same human dilemmas, such as the meaning of life, the importance of wealth, the suffering of good people, and the seeming flourishing of those who are evil. The discussion ranged from experiences students had during the just-completed Christmas vacation break to Talmudic formulations. Meanwhile, the classroom walls are festooned with "essential questions": In what ways has Jewish law guided my life? How have Jewish rituals helped me through milestones and transitions? How will Jewish law and ritual be part of my life in the future?

How such integration is accomplished varies considerably at Pressman, as it does in other Jewish day schools. The school's educational leaders concede they have a long way to go to bring about a maximal amount of integration and that with separate Jewish studies, Hebrew-language, and general studies teachers, the challenge is great. Still, it remains a value cited in Pressman's school philosophy as a goal—"integration between Jewish and secular, Hebrew and General Studies." And there is evidence in classrooms and outside that the school is working to bridge the different cultures and subject matters to which students are exposed.

Addressing Religious and Ethnic Diversity

Although Pressman is under the auspices of a Conservative synagogue with a strong commitment to its denomination, the homes from which students come vary a good deal in their approach to religious practices. That holds true for students from homes identified with Beth Am. In addition, one-third of families are not Conservative Jews. The school touts this diversity as one of its strengths. At times, though, tensions over religious practices surface. As an example, some parents who have a more flexible approach to Jewish dietary practices have chafed at the school's insistence that any food served at birthday parties or during school events must come from a restaurant under kosher certification. Some parents have lobbied unsuccessfully to include vegan food stores that lack such supervision as an option. On the other end of the spectrum, when LGBT issues have been discussed with students in the more welcoming approach one generally finds in the Conservative movement, some traditionalist parents complained about the school's decision to discuss fraught issues of sexuality. The school's requirement that all students learn Torah trope so they can read in the synagogue also has caused some dismay among Orthodox parents who did not want their daughters to aspire to read Torah when that is impossible in their synagogue. As the Pressman leadership explains it, these types of tensions arise but also are managed with a fair degree of success by the school.

Like many (if not most) other Jewish day schools, Pressman also struggles to find a compelling way to help students find meaning in daily prayer. Younger children generally enjoy Tefila (prayer) because singing is fun. But as children progress toward middle school, daily prayer becomes more of a burden. Indeed, some educators wonder how realistic it is to expect pre- and early teens to relate to a deity they cannot see, repeating the same Hebrew prayers day in and day out. Pressman addresses the challenge in a number of ways. First, the school rabbi speaks openly with students about their responsibility to develop a relationship with God. This may seem like an obvious pedagogical goal, but in fact "God talk" is not common in many Jewish day schools —or for that matter in most synagogues. At Pressman, the school rabbi (not the same as the rabbis of Beth Am) takes a different tack. He encourages students to reflect on what God means in their lives. During interviews, students invoke similar language about their efforts to relate to God, suggesting that the challenge the rabbi presents is taken to heart by at least some students.

To keep students focused on Tefila rather than private conversations, teachers are present, including general studies teachers who may not be Jewish. Teachers play a role as monitors, keeping an eye out for student talking and distractions, and in some cases separating students. Such policing tends to subdue acting out but hardly leads to engagement with the prayer services.

And so the staff tries other approaches. Alumni of Pressman, for example, have been brought back to the school to speak about how they now connect to Tefila, even if they were tuning out while in the school. Tefila also takes different forms depending on the day of the week, at least in middle school. On Tuesdays, middle school students may select from a Parasha play, yoga, mindfulness, Tehilim study (Psalms), a Sephardic Tefila, a boys' or a girls' minyan, among other options. Fridays offer a Kabbalat Shabbat service focused on the Sabbath beginning later that day. On Wednesdays, speakers come to the school. And on Mondays and Thursdays when the Torah is read, the services follow a traditional course. Illustrative of the overall approach is what the school offers on Fridays to its elementary school students: it varies Tefila from a schoolwide gathering to a traditional service, to a creative Kabbalat Shabbat where students focus on a particular part of the Sabbath liturgy and design their own hands-on activity to an enhanced program, combining a fifteen-minute service with a guest of honor who tells a story or explains a ritual. In brief, the Tefila program addresses the challenges of prayer head-on and varies what students do each day. Here too the range of religious outlooks represented in the parent body has at times led to lobbying by parents for more of this or less of that, an area of tension the school navigates.

Diversity at Pressman is not only a religious issue. The school also draws students from a range of ethnic backgrounds. One-third of families are Sephardi, mainly Jews of Persian background and also Israelis. Pressman's leadership is aware of the Ashkenazi-normative approach in the school and is working on modifying it. One way the school addresses the diversity issue is in Jewish life cycle classes. Students learn about Jewish ritual practices around life cycle milestones and how those rituals take different form among Jewish subethnic groups. Teachers invite parents of different backgrounds to speak about their own family's customs: invitees have included a Sephardic Jewish parent who organizes a henna ceremony, a Jew by choice, and parents of different Ashkenazi backgrounds. In one class on wedding rituals, students assumed roles as bride and groom in a Sephardic-style ceremony. Students also are exposed to different ways of singing the Torah trope in Jewish communities from around the globe.

There are also fault lines over matters of political ideology—more so over Israeli than American policies. Most families identify with the American Israel Public Affairs Committee (AIPAC), a nonsectarian lobby supporting pro-Israel policies, but a minority does not. A point of contention arose when some parents protested the school's posting of maps not showing the green line delimiting where Israel's border was before the outbreak of the Six-Day War and the territories conquered during that war. The matter was resolved by using new maps, though the school recognizes this as an issue requiring further work. Pressman sends its sixth-grade class on a trip to Israel, and thus far, that has not prompted protests by parents, perhaps because regardless of policy differences, there is a consensus within the parent body over the desirability of Pressman students developing a relationship to Israel.

Affordability Anxieties

Pressman also faces a more intractable problem that besets many day schools: Are the costs associated with its education so steep that young families will opt not to enroll their children? The most obvious challenge comes in the form of considerable tuition costs, all the more burdensome for families with a number of children. In dollar terms, tuition and fees for children in elementary school are over $25,000 and middle school tuition costs several thousand dollars more. On top of that, parents must take out membership in Beth Am, which costs them an additional $4,000. That most non-Orthodox Jewish day schools in the area charge even steeper fees (over 20 percent more) is only a modest consolation. Rising tuition costs, moreover, have emboldened some parents to make demands of the school. The rationale seems to be along the following lines: if the school continues to raise tuition, parents ought to have a greater voice in how their dollars are spent. Several veteran teachers not only note the willingness of parents to throw around their weight but also express worry about the growing influence of parents and the school's catering to them.

In addition to rising tuition costs, Pressman must contend with an inflated housing market. It's no secret that housing costs in California have skyrocketed, and that is particularly true in the Pico-Roberson section of Los Angeles. As a neighborhood school, Pressman relies heavily on families living near the school, if only because in other areas of Greater Los Angeles, other day schools are available. (We note, too, that teachers cannot afford housing in the neighborhood, which adds a teacher retention and recruitment element to this challenge.) Leaders in the school and synagogue express great trepidation that younger families will be priced out of living in the neighborhood and will lack the wherewithal to pay the school's tuition.

To be sure, Pressman has developed assistance plans to help families with tuition fees. Forty percent of students receive some form of tuition assistance compared to 8 to 10 percent at private schools. To get a sense of the dimensions of the challenge, we need only note that the majority of tuition assistance given out by Pressman goes to families earning between $250,000 and $400,000 a year. Families earning less than $250,000 a year receive even more assistance. And so the school must juggle the imperatives of meeting its budget while offering assistance to families unable to shoulder the entire tuition amounts. The affordability crisis is hardly unique to this school. It is one that day schools across the country face, regardless of denominational identification.

"A Special Sense of Community"

Yet for all the financial costs, parents continue to value the school. During interviews, they speak of the warm, *heimish* (homey, cozy, warm) vibe of the school. "It felt like Camp Ramah to us," reported one mother of three Pressman students.[3] In her experience, the Early Childhood Center (ECC) already brings families together and helps them feel welcome. "The school fosters a family-type atmosphere," remarks another parent. Parents single out teachers who develop a direct relationship with their children as a key ingredient in Pressman's appeal.

Though some parents hover anxiously over their children (and perhaps are overinvolved with how their children are doing), the overall goal of parents seems congruent with the self-defined mission of the school. Most are less concerned with high-flying academics and expensive extracurricular opportunities and appreciate how the school nurtures their children and embraces them in a warm communal setting. Modern Orthodox Jews enroll their children because they value the way Jewish life is taught. One such parent remarked, "If I send my children to an Orthodox day school, they will learn Halacha [Jewish law]. At Pressman, they will learn to love it."

A wide swath of parents also values the Jewish mission of the school. Symptomatically, an unusually large proportion of parents send their children to a Jewish day high school. Two-thirds of eighth graders at Pressman go on to a Jewish high school, a fact that must be placed in the broader context of a significant dropout rate in the middle school years. When she arrived at Pressman, Erica Rothblum was surprised by the importance parents ascribe to the Jewish studies offerings at day high schools and communicated how important it was to them that their children would be prepared at Pressman to do well in Jewish day high schools.

None of this is to diminish Pressman's strong academic programs. We have noted how student performance on standardized tests is monitored carefully, how the school continually upgrades its curricula in STEAM and the language arts, and how both Hebrew-language and Jewish studies curricula have been revised to address student needs and abilities. If anything, Pressman's board and educational leadership worry that the achievements of its students are not sufficiently broadcast. In 2019, the school hired a marketing specialist to get word out about its academic strengths.

Still, what remains most vivid to visitors is the countercultural model Pressman represents. Interestingly, several teachers with experience working in other Jewish day schools noted what they regard as a major distinguishing feature of the community that has grown around the school: parents at Pressman, several teachers remarked, tend to be "more down to earth." Pressman, in turn, intentionally downplays glitz. When faced with the choice of building an ECC or a new middle school building, it opted for the latter, even though the relatively spare facilities of the ECC might not impress potential families. And even when it has embarked on a construction effort, it intentionally went for a simpler design so as not to change the ambience of the school. "Keep it modest" was the watchword of the construction effort, so as not to lose the population that looks for a low-key rather than ostentatious atmosphere. "Our people are here for the community and *menschlichkeit* [decency and integrity], not the glitz of the building," observes a board member. "People come here in spite of the facilities. We are the antiestablishment, not label oriented." Significantly, when asked to reflect on which of her accomplishments at the school's helm she regarded with greatest pride, Erica Rothblum, without hesitation, spoke about the role Pressman has deliberately assumed to nurture reflectiveness and wellness among its students, aspects of character building that ultimately will enable them to thrive as citizens and Jews in a challenging world.

In some respects, Pressman Academy is a throwback to an earlier age. A few decades ago, the most common non-Orthodox day schools in the United States were part of the Solomon Schechter network. Today, numerically, those schools have been overtaken by community day schools whose explicitly pluralistic orientation seems more in tune with the times. Indeed, some Conservative day schools—such as Detroit Hillel (chapter 2)—recreated themselves as community day schools. Others simply closed.

Pressman has not taken these paths. Though constitutionally and organizationally it remains an arm of a Conservative congregation (and requires all families to pay membership dues to the congregation), it is a fully inclusive institution, attracting students from observant Orthodox homes to secular, non-observant, and unaffiliated families. While this congregational-based model is quite common in Los Angeles, it is unique among our sample of schools. The arrangements limit Pressman's independence and necessitate complex planning for using physical space in the synagogue, but it also weaves student experiences into the fabric of congregational life. Undoubtedly students' comfort in the synagogue space and with Jewish rituals are enhanced by their constant presence in the shul's precincts.

The school's geographic proximity to upscale American society accentuates its countercultural ethos. This ethos is immediately evident in the physical environment at the school, one that lacks the kinds of impressive facilities that draw families to Hillel Detroit, for example, and to some extent Darchei Torah (chapter 9). More profound, this spirit is reflected in the priority Pressman places on meeting the evolving social and emotional needs of students and their families. To be sure, all the schools we studied are occupied with this task: it is perhaps one of the ways in which Jewish day schools today differ most radically from their earlier counterparts. Pressman has invested more in social, emotional, and ethical learning than any other school in our sample. The sheer numbers of personnel it deploys to address these challenges are noteworthy, as are the array of settings where work occurs through its social, emotional, and ethical learning program; its student council; and the family counseling it offers. All of this takes place in a school where the majority of students don't have exceptional learning or social-emotional needs. Nonetheless, Pressman is committed to cultivating resilience in students and to enable them to flourish.

Another noteworthy feature of the school is its commitment to helping students attain proficiency in modern spoken Hebrew. For a long time, this was reflected in the adoption of ivrit b'ivrit (Judaic studies taught in Hebrew) across the grades. In recent years, as has happened at Hillel Torah (chapter 1), for example, and at other schools, it has separated responsibility in the higher grades for teaching Hebrew from Judaic studies instruction. In the middle school, Pressman employs a Hebrew proficiency approach. While Hillel Torah sustains its commitment to strong Hebrew outcomes by investing heavily in bringing *shlichim* from Israel to the school, Pressman has doubled down on the professional development of existing Hebrew-language instructors. This approach is fully consistent with the school's unpretentious ethos.

5

Doing More with Less

Akiva School, Nashville, Tennessee

Akiva School is the smallest of the nine schools described in this book, with fewer than eighty students at the time of the study. It is also the only school in our sample that serves as the sole Jewish day school in the city where it is located. Studying a school shaped by these circumstances brings into view the ways in which Jewish day schools can function as both anchors and compasses for the broader Jewish community, not only for the families whose children attend the school. Required to serve all children interested in some form of day school education, Akiva reveals how a socioeconomically and religiously diverse population of Jewish students can form a genuine community through the use of ritual, seriousness about Jewish learning (aiming for the highest common denominator), inspirational leadership, and the willingness of families to compromise so that this unusual community can function peacefully and productively. This school's story reveals also how hard it is to shift deep-seated prejudices about what populations, in the broadest terms, day schools serve.

An innocuous announcement over the school PA system reveals something significant: "Michael, please come to the office to pick up a package from your mother." In a small school where just two children share the same first name, there's no need to use family names to catch the students' attention. Like being called down for supper at home, it would be incongruous and unnecessary to use someone's full name.

This is the reality at Akiva School, the only Jewish day school serving the Jewish community of Nashville, Tennessee. With just seventy-eight students between kindergarten and sixth grade, there are many occasions when this place seems more like a family home than a school. In fact, almost everything that happens at Akiva seems to be shaped by the school's small size and its geographic circumstances.

From an early stage in this project, we recognized that to properly appreciate the contemporary Jewish day school, we must include in our sample at least one school that is the only Jewish day school in the city where it's located. Such schools often face acute financial and educational challenges. They may have no direct competitors in the Jewish sector, but they have access to a limited fundraising base. They typically enroll a small student population with no opportunities for economies of scale. At the same time, they must serve unusually diverse populations; they don't have the luxury of recommending to parents that the day school down the street would be a better fit for their family.

We estimate that there are at least thirty schools of this kind in North America. Most serve fewer than one hundred students. Akiva, founded in 1954, is one of the oldest. How this community day school transcends the acute challenges created by its size and geographic circumstances makes vivid what day schools promise children, families, and especially communities. Smallness, it seems, amplifies both the challenges and the promise of day school education.

A School for Everyone

Akiva was established by the rabbi of Nashville's only Orthodox synagogue, Congregation Sheikh Israel. It operated for forty-five years out of the synagogue's first floor and was constituted as an Orthodox day school delivering a dual curriculum of Judaic and general studies with half of the day devoted to each, as happens at the great majority of Orthodox schools. For most of this period, it attracted about seventy children, mainly from traditionally observant families. In a Jewish community where the majority of affiliated families were members of what at that time was Nashville's one Reform congregation, Akiva was perceived as a "shtetl school," in the words of those who were involved with the school at that time; it had little appeal beyond the more traditionalist segments of the community. The school's enrollment grew as high as 120 students when busing and interracial school integration were introduced to the city in the 1970s, and a fair number of Jewish families fled the public schools. It also benefited from an influx to the city of émigrés from the former Soviet Union. When those two waves were spent, enrollment slipped back again to somewhere between seventy and ninety students.

Throughout much of this period, about a quarter of the school's budget was provided by the local Jewish Federation. However, at some point in the 1990s, Federation leadership pressed Aviva's founder to open the school to the children of interfaith families and include non-Orthodox faculty to teach

Hebrew and Judaic studies. The Federation had aspirations for the school to be a more inclusive institution. Thanks to the generosity of one donor, there was now an opportunity to construct a purpose-built school on the grounds of the community's campus, a 42-acre property already home to the Jewish Community Center and Federation. Federation leaders proposed that this move should coincide with reestablishing the school as a community day school, one that better reflected the composition and character of the Nashville Jewish community.

All of these changes led to a change in the school's leadership. Akiva was reborn, and its rebirth came with high hopes that it would appeal to a wider swathe of local families. The new facility was designed to accommodate 120 students from kindergarten to sixth grade.

In many respects, Akiva today reflects the vision that animated the school's move to the community campus. The size of the student population has not changed, but the student population is more diverse than ever before. In 2019, students came from families with an unusual mix of religious affiliations: 31 percent identified as Orthodox, 19 percent as Conservative, 21 percent as Reform, and 29 percent did not identify with any Jewish denomination. About one in ten were being raised in homes where one parent did not identify as Jewish. About one in five were being raised by at least one person of color. In socioeconomic terms, there was great diversity too: the homes of 41 percent of the students were in Title 1 areas, meaning they are eligible for free school meals. Half of all families at the school were receiving some form of financial aid. Other students lived in what can only be characterized as mansions in some of Nashville's most prosperous neighborhoods. A couple of students live on farms. As one of the faculty put it, "Kids see very different lifestyles when they do playdates."

The challenge for the school's leadership is to enable students and their parents—for all their diversity—to find and form a singular and meaningful community in this place. Most of North America's community day schools do not serve such a wide spectrum of Jewish families. Typically—as at Hillel Detroit and Brandeis Marin, the other community elementary schools we've studied—the communities they serve are entirely non-Orthodox. When there is an Orthodox day school within commuting distance, Orthodox families usually take up that option (the case at Hillel in Detroit). And when there isn't an Orthodox school nearby, Orthodox families simply make their homes elsewhere (the case at Brandeis Marin). This is what is so striking about Akiva: it has found a way to enable both Orthodox and non-Orthodox families to feel at home, to enable children whose Jewish lives are very different one from the other to worship and learn Torah together, and to celebrate days of significance in the Jewish calendar. By force of circumstance (a circumstance it shares with other schools in places where there is only one day school option), the school has found a way to serve the entire Jewish community.

Building Community

School community members say that Nashville is not like most other places in America: an unusual number of Jewish families who are synagogue members are affiliated with more than one congregation (for example, Reform and Conservative or Conservative and Orthodox), and people in the area are perfectly comfortable attending programs in synagogues other than their own. They point also to the example provided by the community's rabbis who are welcomed to speak from one another's pulpits, and some of whom are known to study regularly together despite their denominational differences. All of the community's rabbis' children are currently attending the school, something that parents and board members celebrate.

These phenomena are noteworthy and no doubt create a certain inclusive atmosphere, but they tell only part of the story. While denominational boundaries might not be as stark in Nashville as they are in other places (a phenomenon noted by a recent demographic study of the community), the forging of a genuine community in the school has not come about by chance. We identify four factors that have made a difference to this outcome in recent years: the use of ritual, a kind of highest-common-denominator ethos in the school, strong modeling by the school's leadership, and ultimately a willingness to help make the school's Jewish vision work among the families who have bought in. These are the four basic elements that enable Akiva to function as a site of meaningful community for children and adults despite the diversity of its members.

Ritual

Formally defined by *Merriam-Webster's Collegiate Dictionary*, ritual is "a sequence of activities involving gestures, words, and objects, performed in a sequestered place, and performed according to set sequence." In schools, when enacted with regularity (whether daily or yearly), ritual activities can be powerful experiences for socializing children into shared beliefs, values, and commitments.

What is to be done when beliefs and commitments are not universally shared by members of the school community, as is frequently the case in community day schools? How, for example, might school leaders approach the task of daily prayer, an almost universally challenging component of the day school experience even in places when all involved subscribe to the same denominational commitments? In schools that serve older students, the solution is to offer a choice of prayer experiences so that all students can find their own place. Alternatively—as at TanenbaumCHAT (chapter 7)—a different possibility is not to require students to pray at school each day. Neither of these are options at Akiva where the oldest students are only twelve years old, where there are not enough students to form ideologically distinct sub communities, and where to do so would be an anathema to the school's communitarian ethos.

The solution has been, first, to construct school Tefila from those prayers that are part of the service at synagogues of all denominations—selections and songs with which all can identify. Second, students receive *siddurim* (prayer books) that include the various denominational forms of the most common prayers. Finally, and perhaps the most powerful move, has been to integrate prayer with a daily assembly that enables all members of the school community to learn together, share news, and celebrate one another's successes. This daily experience woven from spiritual, social, communal, and civic threads helps bind these young people. Tefila has become one part of what holds this community together, not something that divides it.

It's early September, almost a month since the school year started in the southern United States. With the school day having commenced at 7:55 a.m., by 8:00, some seventy children from kindergarten to sixth grade are gathered for Tefila and assembly in a carpeted multipurpose room escorted by their teachers. At the front of the room is a glass-faced *aron kodesh* (the ark housing Torah scrolls). On one wall, the school anthem is displayed on a large banner. On the opposite side of the room, large windows look out on a grassy yard. As is the case most days, movable chairs are organized in arcing rows facing the front.

The students take the Pledge of Allegiance and next sing the "Hatikvah," Israel's national anthem. They then launch into a lively rendition of the school's anthem, the final words of which are, "We learn from one another, We take care of each other, *Kol am Yisrael, Anachnu mishpacha* [we, the Jewish people, are all one family]." Before the start of Tefila, the head of school talks with the students about Hurricane Dorian, which had just hit the Bahamas. She shares some images of the hurricane's destruction. Some of the students have spent time on the island and—as happens most days—the talk becomes a conversation, with students of all ages and grade levels contributing. When the discussion is complete, the sports teacher shares news about the school's track team's performance over the past weekend. Students who participate in an extracurricular *chesed* (social action) group—Kids4Kids—also stand up to report on a new fundraising initiative they're launching. Finally, the head of school transitions to leading the students in singing a popular selection of prayers from the *shacharit* (morning) service, beginning with "Mah Tovu" ("How Goodly Are Your Tents, Jacob"). Most students join in without a siddur (prayer book) in their hands, while others follow along using siddurim of various shapes and sizes that they've retrieved from the cupboards lining one of the walls. Wrapping up after twenty minutes with an upbeat rendition of "Oseh Shalom Bimromav" ("He Who Makes Peace in His High Places"), the students then file out to their different classes chattering about their affairs.

Whatever the day of the week or the time of the year, this is how all Akiva students start their day. It would be a stretch to describe what happens as a formal prayer service or a means by which students learn synagogue skills, an aspiration often used to justify the daily grind of day school Tefila. More accurately, this is a ritualized experience that draws on prayer, song, and story to create a sense of shared commitment and community. Taking up about two and a half hours a week, this exercise doesn't seem to stir up the low-key resistances that often accompany prayer in school. Instead, it is a powerful means by which students gain an appreciation for the publicly stated values in which the Akiva community is grounded: *limmud* (learning), *kavod* (respect), *klal yirael* (connection to the Jewish people), and *kehila* (global community).

Providing an additional and notably different vantage point on the role of ritual at the school, our visits to Akiva coincided with a further ritualized event that takes place only once a year and helps forge a sense of historical community for students and adults as well. This is the school's Yom HaShoah (Holocaust Memorial Day) ceremony, which occurs toward the end of the spring each year.

Grade by the grade, the students, all wearing white tops, head out from the school building into the glare of the sun along a path that leads through the Jewish Community Center parking lot toward a wooded corner of the campus. The students are joined by about twenty parents and other adults who have come to participate in this event. Sixth-grade students—the oldest in the school—are stationed along the pathway. When a group reaches them, a student stands on a chair and tells a personally researched story about a heroic individual in the Holocaust. One tells, for example, about Nicholas Winton, the moving force behind the Kindertransport from Germany to the United Kingdom. Another tells the story of Maximilian Kolbe, a Franciscan friar who volunteered to die in place of another person at Auschwitz. Some students are confidently capable of commanding the crowd's attention and invite questions when they've finished their presentation. A painfully shy girl can barely be heard telling her story, but with so few students in her grade, she hasn't had the luxury of opting out. The group gathered around her, and especially the adults, express appreciation when she meekly finishes.

Gradually the crowd winds its way up to the community's Holocaust memorial, twelve tall headstones on which are inscribed the names of Holocaust victims. Standing in the shade of the tall trees, three students begin to play string instruments. Their peers from the sixth grade then lead a short ceremony, reading poetry, singing songs, and reciting traditional memorial prayers. One of the students fluently reads the El Moleh prayer, beseeching God to watch over the dead, in a strong southern-inflected accent. A student from each grade steps forward to light a candle while the string trio continues to play. As the ceremony comes to an end, the eight sixth graders hook arms for a final recital of the "Hatikvah."

This unusually powerful ritual brings together a multigenerational community that evidently takes pride in the competence of the young participants. The contrast between the peaceful setting and the violent events being remembered is especially jarring. It surely is not lost on a few of the older participants that these young people represent a Jewish future the Nazis tried to extinguish. The fact that the event's format is the same every year contributes to its power too. The youngest students understand little at first, but over the years, they learn what to expect. By the time they make it to the highest grade, they are leading the event. And when they do so, it is an opportunity for them to learn about an important moment in the Jewish past and to take responsibility to step up and teach others, whatever their anxieties about public speaking. In front of a small and supportive crowd, the most bashful young people must find their voice, which many parents celebrate.

These two very different rituals provide a glimpse of how the diverse families that come to Akiva are enabled to form an authentic community. Shared experiences provide occasions for emotional release. No less important, they intentionally provide opportunities for learning. And foregrounding learning is how Akiva's leadership builds community.

Aiming for the Highest Common Denominator

In diverse Jewish school communities, there is a tendency to adopt a lowest-common-denominator stance when it comes to the Jewish dimensions of school life. The thinking goes something like this: When there are no other day school options, the more engaged families are going to come to the school anyway. It's more strategic, therefore, to reduce the intensity of the Jewish program to make it as palatable as possible to those who might otherwise go elsewhere. If people want more, they can always provide it for their own children on their own time. If they want less, they'll stay away altogether. This is the thinking that contributes, for example, to an increasing number of schools cutting back their Hebrew programs or making them optional in the higher grades alongside choices of learning Spanish and Mandarin.

A different ethos is at work at Akiva, even if at first glance, the school looks very much like other community day schools that offer eight hours a week of Hebrew and Judaic studies, about 20 percent of the program. Akiva's ethos is closely identified with its current head of school. Daniella Pressner has been at the school in various capacities for more than a decade and has played a significant role in shaping its educational spirit. She is driven by high expectations of her young students and her teachers. Pressner is of the view that parents who may not lead intensive Jewish lives outside school might well be confused or unsettled by a serious approach to Jewish and Hebrew education at school, but they won't be turned off. Seriousness is not about quantity; it's about quality. Parents won't be angry, she says, if they see that the Jewish programs are pursued with the same rigor and creativity as other areas of the curriculum. If they see that their children are happy, are developing Jewish textual skills, and can communicate at intermediate or advanced-level Hebrew, they're not going to be upset, even if these outcomes were not important to them when they first enrolled at the school.

Conversations with current parents, including those who are decidedly untraditional, indicate that they have not been disappointed by the school's seriousness about its Jewish mission. On the contrary, some attribute their children's success in general education once they graduate from Akiva to the content and quality of the Jewish studies program. In a striking example, the mother of two children who had moved on from Akiva to hypercompetitive private schools was convinced that one of her children was so successful in high school Chinese, Latin, and German because of the "textual deciphering" and communicative language skills she had learned in Judaic studies at Akiva. Serious Jewish education does not need to be experienced as oppressive or alienating. Another parent, an active member of one of Nashville's Reform temples (there are now two in the city), expressed it like this: "Capital J Jewish is going to turn people off." But that isn't the kind of school Akiva is, a place, she admits, where she and her husband had never originally expected to enroll their children. In her husband's words, the trick is that Akiva has found "an odd, quirky, goofy balance . . . it's Jewish enough for the Orthodox and not too Jewish for the non-Orthodox."

These reflections probably underestimate the craft involved in enabling parents with diverse commitments to feel equally comfortable at the school. As one could say about a great many things at the school, the secret is to do more with less. Within the few hours a week set aside for Judaic studies, the faculty approach this work with intensity and seriousness and aim for a highest common denominator. One can observe how that happens in sixth-grade Jewish studies with Daniella.

Nine children sit around one large table. They have Chumashim (texts of the Pentateuch), binders, and computer tablets in front of them. The topic is leadership, the theme of the sixth-grade Judaic studies program, and the class text is the first chapter of Dvarim (Deuteronomy), the beginning of Moses's long final speech to the Israelites. The staggering variety of abilities in this small group is quickly clear. A couple of students joined the school the previous year with no prior Judaic studies experience. One student is being home-schooled and comes to Akiva just for Jewish studies, in which he evidently excels. Yet another student is the child of one of the community's rabbis and demonstrates sophisticated textual skills.

Over the course of forty-five minutes, the class swings from occasions when the whole group wrestles with big abstract questions to close reading of the biblical text in Hebrew. Some of those big questions include: How do people gain trust? What is a reputation? Why do people need to be known? The textual analysis, led mostly by the teacher, focuses on how the Hebrew suffixes in this particular passage reveal the nature of Moses's relationship with the Jewish people.

Daniella distributes verses from different parts of the Tanakh with the charge that in pairs—"chavrutot"—the students figure out whether the pasuk (their assigned verse) is stating a problem or a solution, a high-order question. Students are expected to report their conclusions back to the rest of the class. Surprisingly, given the mix of students, the verses are only in Hebrew. They've been formatted to indicate their grammatical root, a move that invites students to piece together the meaning for themselves. The students are also free to use Google Translate or dictionaries. Some pairs barely complete the translation in the allotted time, while others are encouraged to check on a biblical commentary that might support or contradict their conclusion, something they seem able to do.

The amount of Hebrew being used is unexpected in a class consisting of students with such mixed abilities. There is no question that some of the students really struggle. Yet some of these same students catch fire when invited to wrestle with the conceptual questions. James, a young man who spends an inordinate amount of time yawning, presents a fascinating case in point. His Hebrew is very limited, and he seems far away for much of the time, but he's right in the zone when it comes to the question of "What do powerful people need to be successful?" Quickly, he demonstrates that he's grasped the core concepts of the class. "They should get help!" he concludes.

This class offers an exquisite example of the balance that Pressner seeks to attain. She aims high while giving all students a chance to excel. She uses traditional language to talk about Hebrew concepts while she invites students to employ critical thinking skills. She exudes seriousness while facilitating a warm, joyful atmosphere, aided immensely by the intimacy of having all students sit around the same table. At times this feels like a graduate school seminar, but before wrapping up the class, we're back in elementary school when she has the class join in a breathing exercise before they run to recess. It is as if this exercise helps students acclimate from the rarified atmosphere of the last forty-five minutes.

How Leadership Models the Values

In a school with just nineteen educational and administrative staff, every member of the team is able and even expected to make a decisive contribution to school life. Most staff members end up wearing numerous hats during the course of the day. And yet in such a small community, the head of school probably plays a more significant role than in larger institutions. She leads a lean administrative team, plays an active role in shaping almost every major event that happens at school, teaches every day, and spends a good deal of time in other teachers' classrooms in a mentoring role. She probably interacts with every staff member and student during the course of a typical week.

In considering what enables Akiva's diverse families to form a community, Pressner's role looms large. It's inescapable and is grounded in a paradox.

Pressner is unapologetically Orthodox. The wife of the rabbi at Sherith Israel, she covers her hair in the style of many modern Orthodox women. When she talks to the students, parents, and donors, her language is infused with traditional Jewish concepts. In her spare time, such as it is, she is training to be a Maharat (the liberal Orthodox equivalent of a woman rabbi). The Jewish life she leads outside school is undoubtedly different from that of the great majority of families at the school.

At the same time, she is deeply committed to the inclusive community Akiva has become. She bristles when a family doesn't enroll because they perceive Akiva to be an Orthodox school, a hangover from its history. She takes great pride that her own children are students at the school. Spending time in the school, one comes to appreciate her role in sustaining this community. She is ready to tell parents when they're being close-minded about some aspect of school life. That might be when parents tell her they don't want their child to talk about God or participate in Tefila or when another parent, this time a traditionalist, wants to withdraw her child from the Yom HaShoah ceremony because it involves playing musical instruments during the Omer (a period of the year when some Orthodox Jews don't listen to live music). She is fiercely committed to giving children opportunities to be informed and to make choices for themselves.

The values that fuel this passion are less about pluralism as an abstract concept. As she puts it, "Pluralism isn't a topic of conversation"; it is more about a commitment to *klal yisrael* (the Jewish people), to building a community that includes all parents raising their children as Jews whatever their commitments or beliefs. There is more. This passion seems to come from a profound faith in other people, from refusing to be judgmental about others. As one of the faculty expresses it, "She believes so strongly in every single person. She always pulls out the positive in every situation. Everyone knows that. Students and faculty."

Pressner's personal example, the values she models in her life, are as important as the specific activities in which she engages in order to sustain the community. Interviewees note both her deep seriousness about Jewish learning and her investment in creative arts. (She's a graduate of twelve years of day school education. She had a double major in college in religious studies and dance, a source of pride for her. She also completed some of the day school sector's senior leadership programs at Harvard and at the Day School Leadership Institute.) Interviewees comment on both her religious demeanor and her modernity. In fact, given how much the school's culture is intertwined with her persona and her deeply felt principles, one wonders what will happen should she decide to move on. That will be a challenging transition for the school.

Readiness to Compromise

Despite all we have highlighted that contributes to the unusually diverse Jewish community at Akiva, many more Jewish families prefer to stay away from the school than enroll their children. In fact, at nonsectarian private schools in Nashville, there probably are more Jewish children per grade than at Akiva. Board members report how some non-Orthodox or secular families assume that if Orthodox families are happy with the school, they couldn't be happy there and therefore stay away.

If Akiva functions as a community, then, it is because it is a self-selecting one. It is made up of families who have chosen to be there, and in choosing to come, some have had to compromise on important considerations. A religiously Orthodox mother reports that she and her husband came to check out the school when weighing whether to relocate from the Northeast for a job opportunity in Nashville. Touring the school, she says, they were struck by the kindness of the students they met during the course of their visit. They recognized that the Jewish education at the school was certainly less intensive than what they were used to, and yet, she explained, "You can supplement Mishna and Gemara at home; you can't supplement kindness." Visiting the school tipped their decision to relocate.

Other families make different compromises. In Nashville, a good deal of social cachet is associated with the school where one's child is enrolled. The rabbi at one of the Reform congregations explains that in a city where social integration comes through one's children's school, especially for stay-at-home mothers, the members of her congregation who come to Akiva are risking "social ostracization." It was a "no-brainer" that her own children would attend the school; the existence of a Jewish day school in Nashville was a decisive factor for her and her husband in their decision to move to the city, but for her congregants, many of whom are already resistant to paying for Sunday school, signing up for a day school education is a radically countercultural commitment. For these families, especially those who were raised in Nashville, there must be something especially compelling at Akiva to compensate for the social networking they will forgo.

Having made compromises of one kind or another to enroll in the school, parents relate to one another and to the school with a special spirit. Those who don't keep kosher at home are prepared to sign up for school lunches or provide their children with meat-free lunches from home, a policy that can be source of contention in other non-Orthodox day schools. It's rare that families hold birthday parties on Shabbat, thereby enabling all students to attend (a norm that many other Jewish day schools struggle to enforce). Finally, in a most unusual instance, the parents in one grade, having established a custom of going out to dinner as a group each month (something we've never come across in other day schools), are willing to meet each time at one of Nashville's tiny number of kosher-certified restaurants so that all are able to take part. Having opted in, parents seem genuinely ready to make this unusual school community work.

Size Is Everything

It's tempting to attribute this unusually cooperative culture, at least in part, to the school's small size and the intimate community it has fostered. In a school made up of fewer than eighty students and fifty families, so much that is distinctive about Akiva is traceable to its size. Two phenomena in particular loom large: everyone is known, and everyone is responsible.[1]

Being Known

We've already noted the presence in the school of recently arrived transplants in Nashville. A significant minority of parents in the school were not raised in the city. In fact, recruiting long-established Nashville families has proven a perennial challenge in a community where strong social pressures are exerted to send children to prestigious independent schools. For those who have relocated to Nashville from elsewhere and have even a passing interest in Jewish life, there is no better way to find one's feet in the city than by enrolling one's children in the school. This was a story we were told over and over again: parents arrived in Nashville knowing no one, and within hours, they'd been contacted by other parents whose children were in the same grades as theirs. As one mother put it when reminiscing about her family's arrival in town, "Thank goodness for the village." In this kind of environment where families are so closely knit and everyone knows everyone else, it's not surprising that those who join this community are ready to help make it work for others, no matter how different their Jewish or socioeconomic circumstances. If families schedule a birthday party on Shabbat, they know full well which families they're excluding.

For students, being known so well has more far-reaching implications. When the average class includes eleven students, everyone's strengths and weaknesses are readily known by their teachers and also by their peers. During a day shadowing one of the grades, we noticed how while many of the students convey a palpable sense of self-confidence, those more vocal students also make space for quieter and slower students to formulate their ideas. This, it seems, has not come about by chance. These are learned social behaviors that are absolutely essential when students with diverse educational strengths and needs are knitted together so closely.

Further ensuring that students don't fall through the cracks, all members of the educational team meet as a group twice a week while their colleagues in administration run elective options for students. These meetings not only ensure that challenges are identified fast and addressed in a coordinated fashion, they also become brainstorming sessions for faculty to explore opportunities suggested by student curiosity. Smallness allows a certain nimbleness in this respect, and over the years, these meetings have resulted in the curriculum across the grades being developed in unexpected directions.

In social terms, smallness is both a challenge and a blessing. As one of the teachers expressed it, classmates are to a large degree like brothers and sisters; when there are fights, they are much more intense. If students are left out, they're really left out; there aren't any other children in the class with whom to play. These are situations to which teachers need to be especially alert, and so the twice-weekly faculty meetings are helpful and necessary. Even when all students in a grade get on reasonably well with one another, there's no question that social horizons can feel quite limited by the end of seven years. The mother of two alumni reported how some students compensate: her daughters formed close friendships with children in the grades immediately above and below their own. These friends are people with whom her daughters continue to be close more than a few years after graduation. If classmates are like siblings, then those children in adjacent grades are like extended family.

Being Responsible
Before making a first visit to the school, we had been more than a little skeptical about how rich the educational experience could be in an environment with so few students and so few teachers. We especially wondered

how well students coped with the transition to much larger schools after sixth grade.

What we learned is that when it comes to access to resources, the students evidently don't miss out. This is a school with its own vegetable garden (maintained by the students), green screen technology with which to produce sophisticated videos, access to a wide variety of sports facilities at the adjacent JCC, and a makerspace, which is at the heart of an extensive STEAM (science, technology, engineering, the arts, and mathematics) program. In fact, the school recently gained accreditation as a Cognia STEAM-certified school, an achievement that it now widely publicizes as "the only Jewish day school in the world, and the only elementary school in Nashville" to have gained this particular recognition. Maintaining competitive sport teams is more of a challenge when there aren't enough students to make up representative grade-level teams. As a result, the school has focused on track and field, where individual students can compete instead. When it comes to the educational experiences on offer, size has not been a disadvantage.

In fact, what we heard from parents, teachers, and—most decidedly—alumni was how smallness was an advantage and a special appeal in coming to the school. Parents told us how shy children were able to find their voices and in the family-like environment at Akiva gained the confidence and the skills to excel when they graduated to much larger settings. Alumni told us that because there were relatively few of them in each grade, they were showered with opportunities to act as leaders. If, for example, they wanted to launch a new lunchtime club, they could, as long as they could persuade their fellow students to take part. Across the board, interviewees noted that students left the school with a strong sense of themselves as young Jews and a confidence and ability to communicate with others. In the words of one father, "They leave with an unflappable pride in their Judaism. They don't duck from it. They're not overzealous. They're just proud to be Jewish."

To explore these matters further, we made a point of talking to educators in the schools to which Akiva students most commonly transfer for middle school and high school. We discovered that far from being overwhelmed by the transition to much larger environments, Akiva graduates tend to stand out in their aptitude for leadership and their strong textual skills. "They are boys of high character," the director of admissions at a competitive boys' prep school reported. In his view, Akiva students have an advantage in transitioning to his school because of the opportunities they have enjoyed to engage in leadership and character-building programs. He found, for example, that Akiva alumni gravitate to the mock trial and debate teams in his school, something that gives them an experience of traveling the country and whets their appetite for applying to colleges beyond the Southeast.

During the course of one of our visits, we had a chance to observe an extracurricular program in which many of these features come together. A few years earlier, following a discussion during an assembly about the devastation caused by Hurricane Maria, the students were given a charge: "Over the course of this day, let us know if you think you want to do something." As Pressner subsequently described it, "That day, eight students from four grades decided they wanted to use their power productively." They formed Kids4Kids, an extracurricular student-led group with the goal to help children around the world. This was in 2017. Three years later, after raising funds to help rebuild an orphanage in Puerto Rico and partnering with other local schools to convert plastic Crayola markers into fuel, this year's group, made up as in previous years of new members from across the grades, was focused on gathering clothes and toys for children at a Nashville-area school where 75 percent of the students were immigrants or refugees.

Outside one can hear the laughter and cries that make up the usual sounds of recess. Here, in the school's modest-sized boardroom, five students, a group of third to fifth graders, are gathered around the table in earnest conversation with a couple of teachers. This is a working lunch. Close your eyes and it's easy to imagine yourself listening to a group of adult activists figuring out strategies for catching people's attention, determining which committee members are responsible for what, and confirming who's responsible for which follow-up tasks.

The group is confident that members of the school community will generously contribute shoes, clothing, and toys from home once they get their attention; the challenge they're wrestling with today is how to get people's attention. A member of the group, this year's chair, had made an announcement in assembly earlier that week, but that was "only heard by kids." They have to make sure that parents know what they're doing. Bouncing around ideas in fairly free-form fashion, one member of the group, a fourth grader, is dutifully noting on her laptop all of the suggestions they float. They wonder how effective it will be to hand out flyers at pickup time. But parents don't always give these handouts a lot of attention. One member of the group suggests using paperclips to attach flyers to people's shoes. The group giggles at the surreal suggestion. After a few more ideas are suggested, one of the teachers prompts the students to vote on what they're going to do.

Akiva School, Nashville | 137

The flyers have it!

The chair, a fifth grader, checks with his colleague that he got everything down. He proposes they start a Google Doc with the ideas they want to include in the flyer. The teacher suggests that when they meet next week, they can lock this down. All seem aware and excited that the time to swing into action is fast approaching.

This was a remarkable episode, not least because of the young age of those playing an active part in shaping decisions. It looks a lot like young people trying out adult roles and behaviors, but this is not simply a case of young children playing house or office. This is not pretend play. The students' choices have consequences beyond this room primarily because the school has made resources available to enable them to act on the decisions they make. The students have power. They're also not left to muddle through by themselves. Through subtle prompting and modeling, the teachers who join them help improve their effectiveness; they ensure that decisions get made and that each time the group meets, it moves forward. This is educating with a very light touch. Consistent with what was observed in many of the classrooms, the teacher here was educating by suggestion more than by instruction: recommending a course of action or resource, floating a possibility, reminding the group of something it had previously examined or intended.

Teaching in this fashion—if *teaching* is the right word—does not come easily. Indeed, just as for parents who choose the school, those who elect to work at Akiva with its small faculty are very much a self-selecting community. Like the students, they also need to be prepared to be both known and responsible. Without a senior educational team, Pressner has no deputies or division heads; the faculty therefore functions as a flat structure in which the entire staff is expected to step up. There are lead teachers in particular specialist areas, such as math, STEAM, and English language arts, but once faculty find their feet, they're expected to stretch beyond their immediate specialty.

The veteran members of the team evidently like it that way. Echoing the alumni, they celebrate being given "plenty of leadership opportunities." As a case in point, the first-grade general studies teacher during her seven years in the school has been the lead for English language arts and currently serves as lead for math while also coordinating scheduling and some professional development. The director of admissions and outreach, who was everywhere on the days we visited, manages logistics for special events in the school, functions as director of operations, and coordinates after-school offerings.

The fact that faculty members play so many different roles means that they have the capacity to be quite flexible in the ways they shape the curriculum. They're not locked in by a narrow set of skills. They can and are encouraged to take their lead from the students to follow their passions or the things they're most curious about. That can result in exploring unexpected topics during the course of the year, which recently included sound effects, windmills, and birdhouses. This inquisitive spirit is celebrated in what the school calls "Curiosity!" an evening event that has supplanted the science fair. As we've noted before, the message conveyed is that in a small school, children have a chance to leave their mark on the curriculum. Students have an opportunity, as the school's website puts it, to be curious and to wonder.

Community Significance

A full appreciation of Akiva is not possible without looking more closely at the school's role within the Nashville Jewish community—that is, beyond the lives of those who inhabit the building every day. Paradoxically, this small school appears to play an especially large role in the fortunes of the Jewish community as a whole.

First, it serves as a kind of glue that holds people in this city. To be clear, Akiva is not what one might call an education destination—a school to which people relocate from another parts of the country. It does enable those who already have good reason to consider moving to Nashville to weigh such a possibility seriously. For families that want to lead an intensive Jewish life and want their children to receive a rich Jewish education, Akiva makes Nashville a viable option. Over the years, the school has been a decisive factor in bringing Jewish professionals to the city, including the community's rabbis, Federation leaders, and faculty members at Akiva and at Vanderbilt University. If the school did not exist and wasn't such an appealing place to educate children, these people might not have come to the city. Many interviewees made that clear when reflecting on their own decisions to relocate to Nashville. Without the school, a variety of local Jewish institutions would have struggled to recruit high-quality leadership.

This dynamic is at the heart of the school's fundraising strategy. Tuition is currently $12,850. Given that a significant number of families are not paying full tuition, the school has to raise almost half its budget ($600,000) each year. This balance comes in part from the Federation and from an extensive network of individual donors. Many of those donors have been mobilized by an unusually effective volunteer fundraiser, a generous donor to the school himself. He reports that about 80 percent of donations to the school come from people without children or grandchildren in the school. Many of these donors would never dream of enrolling their own children in the school, but they realize that Jewish life in Nashville would be impoverished if the community did not support a Jewish day school. They appreciate that the school benefits more than just those it enrolls.

This same sentiment accounts for why more than half of the current members of the board have not sent their own children to the school. Instead, these are dispassionate individuals with a keen appreciation of the school's significance for Jewish life in Nashville. This was not always the case. Until about a decade ago, shortly after the school had moved to the community campus, the board was composed almost entirely of parents. In an effort to make the school more appealing to their peers, the board had kept tuition costs artificially low, which left the school with an unsustainable debt. The school's professional leadership turned to the local Federation for help and worked hard to bring in a new cadre of leaders to get the school on a firm footing. Recounting how things played out, the board chair from that time tells of how tuition was raised by 50 percent from one year to the next, but not one family left the school. As he argued at the time, people won't take a product seriously if they're being asked to pay peanuts for it. It wasn't as if they priced themselves out of the market. Tuition was still substantially lower than in the local private schools. Today, the school continues to pay the Federation for financial management services, and the school's financial situation is sound. Thanks to the help of the Grinspoon Foundation's Life and Legacy Program, the school has secured a sizable number of legacy gift promises, again from local donors without an immediate connection to the school. Once these gifts are realized and the school's endowment fund grows, there will be much less pressure to secure donations each year.

Drawing people to Nashville, the school makes a tangible contribution to the broader well-being of the community, as it does in helping absorb new Jewish families to Nashville. We noted earlier the role played by the school village in that respect. Akiva functions as an anchor, securing Nashville's Jewish community, enabling it to weather the sociodemographic storms that challenge many small communities. What's more intangible is the school's contribution to local Jewish life, including its ethos of blurring boundaries. Much earlier in this chapter, we noted how interviewees argued that the school's inclusive culture reflects the weakness of denominational boundaries in the community. After spending time in classrooms and at school rituals, we suspect that the school in fact helps shape that community culture by modeling how diverse individuals can form a meaningful community. These are the values that alumni exhibit when they take on leadership roles in their high schools, on campuses, and then back in the community if they choose to return, which (reflecting an upturn in Nashville's economy) more of them are choosing to do. In this respect, the school is not just a physical anchor; it also serves as a spiritual compass for the community.

In a community where there is just one day school, it is much easier to discern Akiva's contribution. In congested marketplaces or contexts cluttered by other institutions, a day school's contributions may be harder to recognize. In Nashville, the contribution of the day school to the broader Jewish community looms unusually large.

Facing the Future

With so much to celebrate in terms of its contribution to children, families, and the local community, it is almost shocking that Akiva's enrollment numbers are still not much higher than when it was located on the first floor of the Orthodox synagogue. One could say that the school has been running hard in order to stand still. This is, without question, Akiva's primary and perennial challenge: how to persuade local Nashville families that the school is different from the one that operated out of a synagogue. These families still need to be convinced that Akiva is no longer an Orthodox school and is today a genuinely inclusive and child-centered institution, offering students a multitude of opportunities to learn and develop leadership skills.

Context is everything. As in many other cities in the United States, perhaps especially in the South, the prestige associated with competitive independent schooling looms large. That's why USN (the University School of Nashville) is known by the locals as JewSN. The lure of the institution is irresistible. And parents are fearful that if their children stay at Akiva until sixth grade, no matter the skills they acquire, they won't be able to transfer to one of those elite schools in seventh grade. "There is a scarcity mentality among those who were raised here," a parent explains. That's one of the reasons why not one current student at Akiva is the child of an alumna or alumnus. Newcomers to the city haven't been socialized yet into these local norms.

This, then, is the task for Akiva, and probably for non-Orthodox day schools everywhere. Revealed so vividly here because of the school's unusual circumstances, the challenge is to shift deeply set prejudices about the population, in the broadest terms, that day schools serve, what kinds of educational experiences they offer, and what values they model. Echoing Deborah Meier's influential book, *The Power of Their Ideas: Lessons for America from a Small School in Harlem*, this is the lesson for America from a small school in Nashville.[2]

CONNECTIONS AND EXCEPTIONS

At first sight, Akiva School's small size seem to overshadow all else in shaping the experience of its students. In reality, at least in classrooms, the school's smallness is not so unusual. As we have seen—for example at Brandeis Marin (chapter 3) and Pressman Academy (chapter 4)—there frequently are fewer than fifteen students in the day school classroom at any one time. In non-Orthodox settings especially, low teacher-student ratios are part of the value proposition of a day school education. This also seems to be part of the reason that many students from these schools move on to much larger institutions with the confidence and capacity to make a contribution to the school community.

If anything, Akiva's school size makes more of a difference in terms of teacher assignments: with a total administrative and teaching staff of just seventeen people, there are far fewer subject-area and educational specialists at the school than at all of the other schools we studied. There are, for example, no English as a Second Language or technology specialists here. To teach in a small school like this means being ready to wear numerous hats and to stretch into new domains of responsibility even later in one's career.

As the only day school option for hundreds of miles, Akiva draws an unusually diverse array of students. TanenbaumCHAT (chapter 7) is the only other school in our sample that enrolls students from a spectrum that runs from observant Orthodox families to the completely secular or nonobservant. This circumstance surely has a profound influence on the students' experience and on what the school contributes to the lives of families and the wider community.

Unlike TanenbaumCHAT, a high school where prayer is optional, Akiva has developed a mandatory policy about prayer that nonetheless is inclusive of everyone. Also, unlike TanenbaumCHAT, which is almost twenty times larger, Akiva does not have the luxury of streaming students for Judaic studies. It has developed a highest-common-denominator approach that seeks to engage all students where they're at and where their parents want them to be. As a consequence, students and their parents come away from this experience with an intense appreciation for the value of *ahavat yisrael*—Jewish peoplehood. At home, families lead very different Jewish lives, but at school they make space for one another's values. Requiring parents to step outside their comfort zones in this way, the school functions in a similar fashion to Brandeis Marin as a kind of corrective to parents' expectations of what a Jewish education involves and for whom it is relevant.

Akiva's unusual geographic circumstances help make clear how day schools contribute to the ecosystem of the wider Jewish community. As the only day school in Nashville, this contribution is especially vivid. But it is actually quite similar to other completely different schools: as an anchor for families who wouldn't otherwise choose to live in the city or neighborhood, it is similar both to Darchei Torah (and its ultraorthodox constituency) and Hillel Torah (and its Modern Orthodox constituency) (respectively, chapters 9 and 1). In serving as a home for families who might not otherwise have connected to the Jewish community, it plays a similar role to Brandeis Marin and Hillel Detroit. It is therefore not surprising that it has been successful in securing financial support from individuals whose own families don't attend the school but who recognize the school's contribution to the health of the local Jewish community's general ecosystem.

II

High Schools

Recentering the Centrist Orthodox Day School

Rav Teitz Mesivta Academy, Elizabeth, New Jersey

Rav Teitz Mesivta Academy in Elizabeth, New Jersey, offers a dramatic
example of a school in the midst of being turned around. One of the
oldest day schools in America, this Centrist Orthodox high school had
a less-than-stellar reputation for more than a decade. It is housed in a
decades-old facility and is challenged by a shrinking local community and
severely constrained finances. The charge to turn around this institution
has been translated over the course of a few years into a compelling
vision for student-centered day school education by a principal whose
own professional journey brings to life the special challenges and
rewards of educational leadership. This story is all the more dramatic
for being set against the backdrop of societal and cultural changes that
challenge the most robust providers of Yeshiva day school education.
This chapter suggests the hopeful possibility that leadership and a deep
commitment to doing what's best for children can beat even the most
challenging odds.

The Centrist Orthodox Yeshiva high school is an unusually challenging educational model. Students—boys between fourteen and eighteen years old—start their day early and end late, with only a few short breaks. The day runs at least from 8:00 a.m. to 5:00 p.m. In the winter, students don't see the sun; they commute to and from school in the dark.

Fueled by a deep commitment to *Limmud Torah* (Jewish textual literacy) and to *Derech Eretz* (a strong general education), this model is especially challenging for teens when the curriculum includes almost no scheduled time for sports or the arts. Most of the school day is devoted to verbal and mathematical reasoning, whether in Jewish or general studies classes. For many students, the subjects with greatest utility are relegated to the afternoon hours, after the morning *seder* (learning period) is complete.

For school administrators, the model poses a set of logistical or structural problems. With such a clear demarcation between the times of the day when Jewish and general studies are taught—*kodesh* (religious content) in the morning, *chol* (secular content) in the afternoon—they can make relatively few full-time hires. A rebbe who teaches during the morning seder session will need to look for additional work outside the school to supplement his part-time salary unless he plays some administrative or pastoral role in the school or is qualified to teach some component of the general studies curriculum.

Implementing this model is yet more challenging in an age when technology, in the form of ubiquitously available handheld devices, seems to relentlessly erode students' powers of concentration and their interest in the written word. In a Centrist Orthodox community that straddles the world of tradition and a contemporary social context where those at the edges of the community are lured by drugs, drink, and other socially undesirable behaviors, the yeshiva day school model is for a great many students alien at worst and challenging at best.

In this context, it is instructive to see how a small Centrist Orthodox school that for more than a decade had a less-than-stellar reputation, housed in a decades-old facility, situated in a shrinking local community, and with severely constrained financial resources is overcoming these challenges. If this small school can stay the course, improve itself, and offer students an educational experience that aspires to truly make a difference in their lives, then it constitutes an important case for the day school community as a whole. It offers an example of how leadership and a deep commitment to doing what's best for students can beat even the most challenging odds.

A Story of Finding and Losing the Way

Rav Teitz Mesivta Academy opened in 1955 as the high school section of the Jewish Educational Center of Elizabeth, New Jersey (JEC), an institution itself launched in 1941. In the years immediately before and after World War II, Elizabeth, located just south of Newark Airport, began to develop as a hub for Jewish life under the legendary leadership of Rabbi Pinchas Meir Teitz.

A *New York Times* obituary from 1995 tells Rabbi Teitz's story and the story of the school's founding:

Rabbi Teitz was a scion of a line of rabbis stretching back centuries. He was born in Latvia and trained in rabbinical seminaries in Lithuania. He arrived in the United States in 1933 for what he thought would be a year-long lecture tour. Instead, he stayed to marry Bessie Preil, daughter of Rabbi Elozor Mayer Preil, the rabbi of what was then a small Orthodox community in Elizabeth. He succeeded his father-in-law in the rabbinate upon Rabbi Preil's death in the 1930s.

Since then, the community, founded in 1881, has grown to some 5,000 people affiliated with five synagogues under one united rabbinate. Rabbi Teitz established that rabbinate and the family tradition is upheld by his son, Rabbi Elazar Mayer Teitz, who has been his associate since 1958.

The Jewish Educational Center he founded made Elizabeth the fourth American city, after New York, Boston, and Baltimore, to offer a full-range of Jewish and secular education. It consists of the elementary yeshiva, along with Mesivta Academy, a high school for boys, and Bruriah High School for girls. Together, they have more than 900 students.

When he founded the Jewish Educational Center, the preamble of its bylaws promised that it would become something for Jewish communities throughout the United States to emulate.

Almost twenty-five years later, by 2018, there were estimated to be about nineteen thousand students at more than seventy-five Centrist Orthodox schools like those of the JEC. However, the numbers at the Elizabeth schools associated with Rabbi Teitz's legacy have somewhat declined to just over 750 students in the three schools. While enrollment at Bruriah, the girls' high school, has remained strong, numbers at the *mesivta* (a term used to describe a Jewish high school for males) have fallen from a peak of more than 220 to just under 140 students over the four grades of high school.

It is not clear what accounts for this decline. The school has been squeezed by a population drift away from Elizabeth; Modern Orthodox families have moved to Bergen County, thirty miles north, and more comfortable families have relocated to other commuter communities in New Jersey. Elizabeth's main street, Elmora Avenue, where the school is located—and home to one of the nation's first kosher Dunkin' Donuts—possesses the unmistakable air of having seen better times. Today, a sizable minority of the student body no longer lives nearby; about a third come from Monsey, New York; Brooklyn; Staten Island; and the Jersey shore.

Jewish migration patterns are likely only part of this enrollment decline —perhaps the most benign part. Other factors have been at play on both a macro- and microscale. In macroterms, the last two decades have been challenging for the Centrist Orthodox day school sector. Across North America, the yeshiva day school marketplace has been polarizing between two broad populations. Religiously Orthodox families have started to turn their backs on expensive universities in favor of community colleges; they seek a more Yeshivish educational program with a greater emphasis on Torah learning and observance. Pulling in a different direction, families concerned about their children's potential access to quality higher education insist on strong academic courses in general studies and oppose its relegation to the afternoon hours. Some Centrist Orthodox schools have found it hard to resist the centrifugal pull of these market forces.

Individuals associated with Rav Teitz Mesivta suggest that in this polarizing environment, the mesivta's leadership "lost the plot." They did not skillfully navigate these competing pressures and offer a clear vision for what a *Torah Im Derech Eretz* education could be in contemporary America. As was the case with Elizabeth more generally, the school—both its faculty and facility—aged and got left behind. As the school became less appealing, its leadership was caught in a vicious cycle. Determined to fill seats, administrators admitted greater numbers of students who were not mission appropriate —for example, students who were not fully Shabbat observant or were not ready to participate in a minyan every morning. The school developed a reputation for admitting young people who couldn't get into other Jewish schools. Taking such measures to increase enrollment led still more of the students who were fully aligned with the school's mission to go elsewhere. In what is probably the most competitive day school market in America, the school slipped to the back of the field. And as we will see, it is hard work getting back to the front of the pack.

8:00 a.m.: A New Day

Fifteen minutes before school starts, a few of the high school students are already on the premises. A good number are wearing headphones in various shape and sizes. Many are playing on their phones. Some are reviewing science material ahead of an AP test later in the day.

The Mesivta Academy occupies the upper floor of a building it shares with the yeshiva elementary school. Its classrooms and offices, in a building that must be at least fifty years old, line the sides of a long L-shaped corridor. Large photos in the stairwells show happy students arm in arm with teachers on various special occasions. There are photographs of Israeli soldiers too (they might be alumni) and of students engaged in extracurricular sporting events—hockey and basketball, for example. The sports pictures wouldn't look out of place in most high schools in America. Students' work is not on display.

The boys are causally but neatly dressed, with polo shirts and multicolored long-sleeved shirts. They wear *kippot* in a variety of colors and cloth. Teachers are sporting conventional yeshiva dress: dark suits, white shirts, large black kippot. Crocheted kippot are no longer part of the landscape in this corner of Jewish America.

As 8:00 a.m. approaches, the corridor clears with boys making their way to minyan for morning prayers. The *bet knesset*, a long, narrow space not specifically designed as a worship space, is close to full by the time *davening* (the prayers) starts. Rebbeim, rabbis teaching Jewish studies, are dispersed across the room with their own small desks for *sefarim* (sacred books) and other accessories. The boys sit in regular lecture-room style chairs. The great majority are on time, but some drift in later. A small number are in no hurry at all to put on their *teffilin* (phylacteries). Those who don't are not urged by teachers or their friends to do so; they are left to sit quietly. There are more than a hundred people in the space, and most are davening in sync with the prayer leader, the *ba'al Tefila*. There is still a continuous flow of people in and out of the room. Evidently, a minority would prefer not to be here or at least not for the entirety of Tefila.

After *tachanun* (a daily supplication prayer), before *leyning* (Torah reading), there's a time-out for small groups, each of which gather around a rebbe to hear some words of prayer-related *musar* (religious inspiration) informed by a shared text, *Praying with Fire*, a small volume made up of five-minute reflections designed, according to its back cover, to "fine-tune attitudes and approaches to daily communicating with *Hashem* [God]."[1] Many students are not taking part. A fair number are occupied on their phones. Those who do seem to be involved are gradually drawn into animated discussion. This interlude is very much about opting in.

The service continues with leyning and some final prayers, and there are a few announcements about scheduling and program matters during the day. This is the height of AP season. The great majority of students head out to the breakfast room for fifteen minutes before the start of seder, the course of Talmud study. About twenty boys of different ages stay behind. They're treated to cupcakes and a *dvar torah* (a Jewish teaching). They spend five minutes a day on the same tractate of Talmud, one they'll complete in this fashion over the course of two years. It's a subtle demonstration of what can be accomplished if you're *kovea itim le'Torah* (if you make regular time for Torah), even with so few minutes available. Again, this is a case of giving students the choice to opt in.

Rav Teitz Mesivta Academy, Elizabeth, New Jersey | 151

The Road Back and Its Challenges

After a turbulent and even toxic period that lasted more than ten years and saw different configurations of leadership at the most senior levels of the Mesivta Academy, the school set out on a new educational path over the course of 2016, with the midyear promotion of Rabbi Ami Neuman from assistant principal to principal, and, financially, with the appointment a few months later of Rabbi Pinchas Shapiro as executive vice president. Neuman was a twelve-year veteran at the school who had started out as a rebbe and varsity hockey coach. He had served as student activities coordinator for more than ten years and then as assistant principal of Judaic studies for two and a half years. Shapiro had been the CEO of a private investment firm. He was a parent with a multigenerational family connection to the school.

Shapiro's task was clear: addressing a financial deficit that had ballooned dramatically by cutting about $300,000, or more than 25 percent, from the school's budget. Over the next two years, this resulted in downsizing the business office, the school's senior administration, and its marketing and development departments, not to mention postponing expenditures on furnishings and maintenance.

Neuman's task was much less well defined. He was expected to preserve the school's communal and educational legacy, and at the same time find a new way forward that would revive the school's fortunes. In effect, he was tasked with transforming what it meant to teach and to learn at the school while limited by acute financial constraints—essentially, that is, with one hand tied behind his back. Thus, while previously the school employed a principal and two assistant principals, in the current configuration, Neuman serves as principal, and Rabbi Noach Sauber served as assistant principal while continuing to function as both Mashgiach Ruhani (spiritual supervisor) and rebbe. In effect the two of them fulfill roles that were previously carried out by four people.

What makes the situation at the mesivta so gripping is that the charge to turn around this venerable institution has been translated over the past two years into a compelling vision for student-centered day school education by a principal whose own professional journey brings to life the special challenges and rewards of educational leadership. Moreover, his vision is being implemented in a context where there are acute financial and logistical constraints, all against the backdrop of societal and cultural changes that are challenging the most robust providers of yeshiva day school education.

9:15 a.m.: Gemara—The Reactor's Core

Ninth grade, Gemara. The top track of three in the grade. Thirteen students and an intense energetic rebbe. On a Monday, the students have a one-hour *shiur* (Talmudic lecture) before heading down to join the rest of the school for *a beis medrash style* seder.

Every boy has his own Gemara—no Steinzaltz or ArtScroll with English translations, just the traditional Aramaic volume. Every student has his own volume on which he writes notes or marks up the text with colored highlighters. Students place their phones on the desk at the front before the start of the lesson.

After a short chat about events of the weekend, the teacher asks students to take turns to review the text for the rest of the class, *Masechet kidushin* 31b. The topic is concerned with the scope of the laws of *kibud av v'em*, honoring one's parents. The students read the unpunctuated text fluently and translate with limited teacher prompting. When the teacher asks a particular student to continue, he says, "I'd prefer not." The teacher reacts, "I appreciate your honesty."

Over the course of the next sixty minutes, the topics covered include questions about the circumstances under which one can leave Eretz Yisrael, the Land of Israel (ordinarily forbidden, but what if it is to honor one's parents?); a debate about Maimonides' position on exceptions to this rule and a critique of his position and its application to parents' needs; how exactly one should quote things in one's father's name; and how to honor people after they die. Those are the bare bones of the issues raised by the text. They come to life in the anecdotes and stories inspired by the text. The teacher poses a series of philosophical questions: "How can you honor someone after they die? Do the dead know what's going on? Why would you take punishment in this world for the sins of your father?" The teacher also introduces a series of personalizing pivots, asking a boy whose father is a well-known rabbi, for example, if people listen to him because they know who his father is.

The pace is relentless, and the teacher is continually on the move, sometimes at the front of the class, sometimes sitting at an empty desk among the students, sometimes at the back. Figuratively and literally, this is not frontal teaching, it's wraparound teaching. Perhaps a law of educational physics is at work here: the more static the students, the more kinetic the teacher. If the students are pinned down in their seat desks, the teacher seems to compensate by being continuously on the move around the classroom, posing dilemmas to the students, sharing anecdotes and inspirational stories, investing great energy and creativity in holding students' interest.

Rav Teitz Mesivta Academy, Elizabeth, New Jersey | 153

It's actually exhausting, and not everyone wants to join in first thing on a Monday morning. One boy spends a good amount of time with his head on the desk (a pose more likely signaling disinterest than tiredness), another seems to have his mind in another place (perhaps the place where he left his packet of supplementary materials), and one boy is happy to pop out to make the teacher a cup of coffee. There's continuous traffic back and forth to the washroom. Keeping everyone's attention for the duration of the shiur seems next to impossible.

In many ways, this is the core of the yeshiva day school, the energy source that powers the whole enterprise. It is surely no coincidence that the first class of the week for all students is a Gemara shiur, the quintessential expression of Torah study, *Limmud Torah*, as traditionally understood. Meaning is made in the interaction of text, student, and teacher. An interactive whiteboard at the front of the room remains untouched throughout. Students have packets of supplementary texts and worksheets, but during this class, the heart of the matter is the text and the world that the teacher weaves around it.

Realigning the Center: Making Room for the Student

The school's educational philosophy as spelled out in the student handbook makes very plain the hierarchy of values that orient this yeshiva day school:

> Our goal at the Rav Teitz Mesivta Academy is to provide each student with the tools he will need to make his life an edifice worthy of the potential G-d has given him. Clearly, without Limudei Kodesh and the ability to learn Torah, we cannot acquire the knowledge and understanding to truly comprehend what HaShem wants of us and how we can best serve Him. Limudei Chol, whether as a means of preparing to earn a livelihood or of enhancing the world in which we live, serve as an important adjunct to the study of Torah. Our aim is to help our students acquire skills, knowledge and appreciation of the gifts HaShem has bestowed upon us.

This is a clearly stated commitment to Torah im Derech Eretz, both Torah and general education, but at the same time, it's clear which values have precedence. In this hierarchical and traditional universe, Rabbi Neuman seeks to introduce a new vision for the yeshiva day school. To say that this vision places the student at the center perhaps sounds too subversive, almost heretical. In the rabbi's own words, it is a vision of school where "students become teachers, where they're accountable and have ownership of the things they do." As he put it in a different conversation, "It's not meaningful unless the students are doing it." This concept, unexceptional in the great majority of American classrooms, challenges the ways in which classrooms at the mesivta, both Jewish and general studies, have traditionally functioned. It's a concept that's difficult for both teachers and students to internalize. As one of the veteran teachers complained, "I sense we rather run a camp than a school."

Before he became principal, Rabbi Neuman's teaching had already moved in this direction. Instead of teaching Gemara from the front of the classroom, he started to prepare source sheets for the students. He bought multiple copies of the Jastrow dictionary of Talmudic terms for the school. He told students that they would have to look up words in the text and learn prefixes. Students hated it and complained: "We pay your salary. Why don't you teach us?" they moaned.

In more recent times, the school has gone one step further: every day for first period and on Mondays straight after morning shiur, all students—all the tracks from all four grades—assemble for a *bes medresh* (yeshiva study hall) style of seder. When all come together in this way, the noise is so loud there is no possibility that a teacher can lecture to his students as he might in the classroom. Instead, guided by worksheets and using source packets, the students must study independently, in *chevrutot* (pairs) or in small groups. Some of the older students who have lived through this pedagogical transition lament the change. They complain about the lack of supervision in the *bes medresh*, about how difficult it is to concentrate amid the hubbub and about the awkward physical setup around long lunch tables. Some of these students also offer a more profound criticism that gets to the heart of what is implied by this educational shift: they argue that Gemara is about more than just understanding the words; it's about the close connection with the rebbe and the kind of intimate conversation that happens with him in the classroom. The students don't say it in so many words, but independent learners are, by definition, less dependent on their rebbeim.

Jarringly, Rabbi Neuman's strongest ally in introducing a more student-centered approach is the school's STEM teacher, a non-Jewish, female science educator who does not exactly fit the profile of a yeshiva day school educator. She says, "I don't teach content anymore." Her task instead is to help students learn how to use information rather than master facts. There is a pragmatic intent behind this reorientation: students have to be prepared to function, if not succeed, in the new economy, using the technology that supports it.

The factory model of education no longer makes sense in school or beyond. At the same time, this orientation seems to be about more than pragmatics: it's driven by principle and a sense of how students learn best. Echoing Rabbi Neuman almost word for word, she says, "Students learn best when they buy in and are doing things. Spewing information does not help me. The key is to figure things out." This educational principle has profound implications for the role of the teacher, especially in a hierarchical system. She adds that as a teacher, "I'm not important in what I say, but in what *they* (the students) do."

10:20 a.m.: Seder—An Irresistible Force Meets an Immovable Object

Seder brings all of the students from all four grades into the school canteen at the same time. The concept is that as in a regular advanced yeshiva, at certain times of day all students should learn the same material in the same place at the same time; there are few more powerful expressions of the collective ethos of Limmud Torah. Bringing students together to learn with and from one another is also very much in sync with the ethos of having students take ownership of their own learning.

Unfortunately, the physical facility doesn't help realize the goal of intimate and interactive student engagement with the content. More than fifty years after its construction, the school still does not have its own *bes medrash*; furnishing such a space is one of Rabbi Neuman's most immediate fundraising goals.[2] Today, at least, seder doesn't start straight after breakfast. On other days, the first few minutes are spent clearing away spillages and leftovers from the tables.

The boys sit around lunch tables on long benches that can seat five at a time. Until the teachers gather, almost every boy has a phone in hand, playing games or watching videos. A few are simply schmoozing with one other. Otherwise they're furiously absorbed in another reality altogether.

When seder gets under way with every boy in the room, the noise is deafening. This is the healthy sound of the bes medrash, of argument and animated conversation about the text. It also seems to be the sound of joking and off-topic conversation, of adolescents easily distracted. It's hard for boys to hear anyone other than those sitting immediately next to them or across the table.

In this hybrid world where the school attempts to recreate the experiences and norms of the yeshiva but still functions like school, the boys work from worksheets that prompt them to study the text. At the best moments, teachers step back and the boys figure out things for themselves, debating the meaning of a point in the text and its halachic implications. At these times, the noise in the room is productive noise. The challenge is to sustain such moments.

For some boys the noise is too much. They wear headphones to keep out the racket or they listen to music, which, they say, helps them concentrate.

When there are so many boys together at the same time, there isn't a protocol for handing over phones at the start of class. In regular classrooms, the usual procedure is for students to place their phone on the teacher's desk. If teachers find students with phones out during class, the device is confiscated until the end of the day. At seder, intercepting those who are making inappropriate use of their devices tends to be Rabbi Neuman's role since he is the only teacher without a shiur group of his own. In this bad cop role, it seems he often has to relieve students of the offending device.

At first glance, it looks as if there are plenty of reasons not to bring all of the boys together in this way. And yet doing so every day serves the goal of creating the feel of a yeshiva seder. The space is not really conducive to these ends, but in the short term, Rabbi Neuman is not willing to forgo his goal while he tries to woo a donor to help furnish a proper bet midrash.

Following the Ripples Outward

Committing to a student-centered approach requires building up a faculty that is prepared to cut loose from a style of "stand and deliver." Rabbi Sauber reports that while some teachers find this difficult, they're at least ready to be flexible. And when they see for themselves what a different kind of pedagogy can produce, they start exploring how to get onboard. Rabbi Neuman is optimistic. Quoting a Talmudic expression, he says, "*Ein domeh shmiah l'reiah*" (seeing these things for yourself far exceeds hearing about them). And yet it seems that there is still a long way to go to get the whole Jewish studies faculty on board. The skeptics are as likely to say that worksheets are an unserious cop-out as they are to suggest that they're suited to only the more advanced students. One way or the other, there's resistance.

Not everyone is ready or able to change. For example, Rabbi Sauber reports, "There's one rebbe who won't get out of his chair." As the school evolves, it is having to refresh its faculty after decades with hardly any turnover such that it had a reputation for fielding poorly performing teachers who were allowed to stay and went unsupervised. It is remarkable that until recently, Rabbi Neuman was one of the most recently hired. He expresses his goal succinctly: "It's not good enough to cover material. I want teachers who will engage the students on a deep, meaningful level while creating meaning-ful relationships."

On one of the days we visited the school, a teacher candidate was trying out for a new position. Those who observed the lesson reported that the can-didate was completely on top of his material, and to an exceptional degree. And yet they knew immediately that he was a not a fit for the school. Rabbi Sauber shared, "He was rejected not because he didn't master the material, but because he didn't engage the students."

Placing students at the center is not only about pedagogy but about main-taining positive, nurturing relationships between students and teachers, something that has been a strength of the school over the years. One of the most immediately visible features of the school is that the male *kodesh* faculty, those who teach sacred subject matter, without exception possess a distinctly Yeshivish profile; many do indeed live in Lakewood (an intensely religious, heavily Jewish town in New Jersey) and learned in yeshiva there. Their talk is inflected with Yiddishisms or distinctively blends Ashkenazi-accented He-brew with English, as is de rigueur in the yeshiva world. Their dress code of white shirts, black jackets, and black pants is absolutely at one with yeshiva norms. Their students, though, come from a different world. They talk and dress differently. No doubt, the norms in their homes are different too.

While it's clear that there is no problem with teachers talking with stu-dents about how they conduct their own lives or with their inviting students to their homes for shabbat, there is no tolerance in the school for teacher talk that could be construed as disparaging Modern Orthodoxy. By the same token, *kiruv* is off limits, or what a parent called "trying to convert anyone." Condescension on the part of a prospective teacher would rule him out as a potential hire. A handy test case in this respect is how the Lakewood men respond on Yom Haatzmaut. They have to be prepared to participate in a prayer service including Hallel, a classic expression of a religious Zionist ori-entation. As Rabbi Neuman explains: "They can't be here if they don't sub-scribe to the Modern Orthodox ethos."

Respect for students takes additional forms—for example, in the rare in-stances when a student comes out as gay. The guidance services head stated, "The approach to homosexuality has never been punitive here. Students who flaunt it or try to involve others, then it becomes an issue." The school has run programs about accepting classmates who are different. Referring to a current student who is gay, the guidance teacher describes how well sup-ported this student is by his classmates. A member of the faculty who hails from Lakewood says something very similar while acknowledging that the issue causes great inner conflict for him personally. It would be unacceptable, however, if other students related to this boy other than with the greatest of respect. "They don't say derogatory things to him." The school seems to have drawn firm lines that protect students. This position is consistent with an overall ethos of respect for all members of the school community.

11:52 a.m.: The Bomb Kasheh

The last class before lunch is *chumash* (Pentateuch) with a group of eighteen ninth graders. There are not enough seats in the room for everyone. A couple of boys don't seem to mind, perching on the windowsill. The teacher has an interactive whiteboard ready for use by the time the students enter the room. The first ten minutes are devoted to plans for the next day's *siyyum*, a party to mark the completion of *parashas vayiera*, the Torah portion the class has been studying for the last few months with accompanying exegetical commentaries.

There's good-natured banter about how to make sure certain absent-minded students don't forget to bring the treats they've committed to provide. The teacher commits to bringing a hotdog maker from home.

Eventually the teacher transitions to the content they need to cover before the siyyum. Of all the teachers the students encounter during the course of the morning, his use of English may be the most idiomatically Yeshivish. "So wait for the bomb kasheh I have for you!" he announces. What he means is that the students are expected to identify a severe difficulty in the text of the kind addressed by traditional exegetes and to which he wants the students to figure out a solution at home. The first task, and from a yeshiva perspective where sharp questions have special currency, the more important task is to figure out what the question is, what textual difficulty needs to be identified. Ironically, this teacher whose pedagogy and style most evoke the world of the yeshiva also makes more use of technology than his colleagues—including an interactive whiteboard, online study resources, and virtual classroom software. No one finds this incongruous.

Whatever it is—whether the good spirit created by talk of tomorrow's hotdogs, whether use of technology, or simply the Socratic question-and-answer style that leads the students on a hunt for a textual treasure whose location the teachers knows and wants others to uncover—the students without exception seem to have signed up for the ride. Each time the students take the next step and unpack a piece in the textual puzzle—one that starts with the message

Avraham received after the *akeida* (the binding of Isaac) that his cousin Milka had given birth to a child—the teacher makes sure that all stragglers are on the same page as everyone else. Eventually he rouses the class: "Who's got the bomb?! Come on, ask me a crazy bomb!"

One boy tries his luck. "Good question, but you have to tweak it," replies the teacher. Evidently the teacher has a very specific explosive bomb in mind. Eventually, to the relief of all concerned, a different boy nails the problem. "They don't call him the Raba'ish for nothing," celebrates the teacher with another inside baseball joke that turns the boy's name into a rabbinic acronym of the kind by which many medieval commentators are known. The teacher spells out the question for everyone in yeshiva singsong: "If Avraham had been told Rivka was born, why wasn't he more specific in his instructions to Eliezer about who he should bring back as a wife for Yitzchak?" It's a neat question, but one can't help thinking that without the buildup, it might not have grabbed the students' attention. Indeed one suspects that without the drama that the teacher generated over the course of the lesson as a whole, the students long ago would have stopped paying attention. Still, over the course of forty minutes, the teacher gave a masterful demonstration of how to keep students provoked and stimulated; he was acutely alert to the students' needs but not exactly student centered in the educational sense of the term.

Giving Students a Voice

The profundity of the shift being attempted at the school is in many ways less about what happens in the classroom than about what happens outside it, first, in the creation of opportunities for students' voices to be heard with genuineness and seriousness, and second, in the development of systems within the school that provide students with every possible opportunity to grow in positive ways. This is a profound realignment of the school's culture that few current or prospective parents hear about in parking lot chitchat or discern in the marketing copy about "student-centered learning, dynamic rebbeim and teachers, and our warm nurturing environment." The shift in educational orientation goes a lot deeper.

Take the way teachers talk about students. Every six weeks, the school convenes a faculty meeting to discuss the students and how they're doing, identifying those who have particular needs. This is standard practice in many schools. For years, these meetings followed an unhealthy dynamic. When a challenging student's name was raised, there would be groans around the room, and staff would jump in with complaints and concerns. The student's troubles were effectively magnified in this way but infrequently solved. Over the past two years, the meetings have followed a different protocol. Staff are not allowed to say anything negative about the students. Instead those who are having success with the student or are seeing positive changes are asked to share what's working for them. The focus is on growth and what is constructive. In a profound adjustment, the onus in these meetings is on teachers to figure out how to do better for the young man by building on instances of success rather than trying to ameliorate failure.

Another shift that parents may not know about are the focus groups in which every student participates toward the end of the school year. In these meetings, groups of six students at a time sit with Rabbi Neuman and Rabbi Sauber for forty minutes to address four questions: What positive experiences have they had in school during the year? What negative experiences have they had? What would they like to see more of? What would they like to see less of? These meetings are conducted in a friendly but serious manner. Students don't hold back, but they don't indulge in fantasies either. And the administration does get to learn the pressure points for students: for example, the rhythm of the test calendar, the rhythm of the school day, and how students experience "double periods" and the school's merit system, which makes it easier to lose points than to gain them. Issues such as these are treated seriously. Other topics that students raise provide a chance for the rabbis to talk with the students in a nondidactic manner about the values that lie behind some of the school's regulations that students find most onerous. It's fascinating, for example, after a long discussion about the students' complaints about the dress code to hear Rabbi Neuman share what is evidently a core principle for him: "Your task is to see how far you can push. That's how you grow. Our task is to maintain the structure and the parameters." It's a profoundly invitational way of indicating to students that they have a voice and that they should exercise it.

One higher-profile way in which students' voices are seriously heard is through student-teacher conferences, an innovation introduced during the past year. The structure is the same as parent-teacher conferences except that no parents are present. Ahead of the regular parent-teacher conferences, lessons are cancelled for half a day at a time, and while half of the student body goes off-site to engage in some form of *hesed* (benevolent) activity, the other half sits down for five- to seven-minute conferences with each of their teachers. As with the focus groups, the framework provides an opportunity for students' voices to be heard with intention and care and at the same time enables educators to get across messages to individual students that might be drowned out during the course of day-to-day activity at school.

It's too soon to know in what ways students' growth is enriched by opportunities such as these or more generally by the changing ways in which their teachers relate to them. In a sense, the positive and negative consequences of these adjustments are not yet known. As Rabbi Neuman expressed it wryly in an interview, "The thing is, the more students have a voice, the more students have a voice." It's possible that there is a point when you can have too much of a good thing.

12:30 p.m.: Out for Lunch

Because the school is relatively small, when the students are let out for lunch, it doesn't feel like an explosive release. After three and a half hours of Limmudei Kodesh, the students have thirty-five minutes for lunch before starting a four-and-a-half-hour program of general studies. Some head outside to play ball. Most drift out to the local main street where there are about half a dozen kosher establishments the boys are permitted to visit for lunch. The atmosphere is remarkably calm.

For a local person passing through Elmora Avenue at this time of day, there is nothing exceptional about this group of youngsters heading down the street, except that they're neatly dressed and not very rowdy. It's as if the energy that was compressed within the relatively confined space of the school building has dissipated in the open spaces outside. Certainly the folks working at Jerusalem Pizza are thrilled to have this business each day, and other customers make positive noises about the "nice group of boys" passing through.

What's unmistakable is that whether they're out on the street, in the store eating pizza, or back on the school premises, very few boys are not gripped in some way by what they're viewing on their phones. In most cases, they're viewing or playing some form of online game. At the time of our visit, the game absorbing an exorbitant amount attention is Fortnite, a Battle Royale game that had become a worldwide phenomenon. The change of gears couldn't be greater —from the verbal gymnastics of the text-based, norms-oriented kodesh classroom to this visually intense kill-or-be-killed fantasy where words are of no use at all. Online it's the survival of the fittest. It's no wonder that these young men find it so hard to tear themselves away from their screens when they're back in the classroom. This is a problem that seems to be becoming more and more acute.

Getting Personal

Rabbi Neuman is not the sole driver of the push toward a more learner-centered form of yeshiva education at the mesivta, but there is no question that he is its moving force. For someone who spent so many years as student activity coordinator, it's no wonder that his goal is for students to be active shapers of their own learning, responsible for their choices inside and outside the classroom.

Even with s'micha (rabbinic ordination) from Yeshiva University and a decade of service as a rebbe, his trajectory from hockey coach to school principal is an unconventional one. Spending time with him, it's evident that he wrestles with being the man in the principal's office, even if that office contains an unusual quantity of sports paraphernalia alongside traditional sefarim (sacred Jewish books) and volumes on educational leadership. He's a sports coach and informal educator at heart (he was a senior educator in summer camps for more than ten years), and yet on a day-to-day basis, he is the most senior figure in the school. He's the bad cop who has to confiscate boys' phones during seder. He's the person who ultimately has to call parents about especially challenging issues. He says of himself, "Sometimes I'm the cool hockey guy; the next day, the disciplinarian. This creates a tension." One suspects that it is not only a tension for him but also for students and parents, especially for those who have been associated with the school longest and knew him before he entered the principal's office. And yet walking down the corridor with him, as he playfully pulls boys to their feet when it's time for shiur to start, draping his arm around their shoulders as he walks them to class, there is no sense of contradiction between the authority he carries and the students' affection for him.

A small incident offers a clue to what drives Ami Neuman, the bedrock of what he's trying to accomplish in the school and what he wrestles with. Standing in the staff room at one point in the morning, through the window he sees a high school junior outside in the schoolyard. The student has attached himself to a middle school class whose teacher had taken them out to toast marshmallows as a treat. The high school student should be in his own class. Rabbi Neuman resists calling out to the student to reprimand him. Quizzed about his decision, he explains that he doesn't want students to feel they're being watched all of the time. It's counterproductive, he says, especially when most are aware that a system of closed-circuit cameras records everything that happens in the school's public spaces. He wants the students to make the right decisions from their own volition, not under compulsion. He wants them to figure out what's right and wrong.

To clarify, he recounts a story from his own high school days. He was on a school *Shabbaton* (Sabbath retreat). It was late on Friday night, and he had stayed up to schmooze with a veteran teacher. While talking, they saw through the window one of his fellow students smoking. The teacher didn't do anything to stop or reprimand the boy. At the time, Rabbi Neuman was in shock. This boy was out of line on so many counts: he was smoking on a school trip, it was past curfew time, *and* it was the Sabbath when smoking is forbidden. The teacher took the time to explain that had he reprimanded the boy, it would mean calling his parents and then, in all likelihood, suspension or expulsion from the school. The teacher asked rhetorically, How would that benefit the student?

This story from his past gets to the heart of Rabbi Neuman's mission as an educator: to enable young adults to grow without doing harm to themselves. There are so many ways they can ruin their chances in life by making bad decisions. The key, therefore, is to create an environment that prevents students from making harmful mistakes, or at least where they can learn from mistakes without being ruined by them. In a culture where, thanks to the ubiquity of social media, pranksters and jokers are continually on the lookout for ways of gaining attention and admiration, this task is all the more urgent. Gaining short-term attention can come at the cost of long-term well-being and self-respect.

This philosophy is reflected in the way Rabbi Neuman is prepared to cut deals with some of the kids who are perennially challenged by coming late to *shacharit* (morning services) or who come in and then either don't get around to putting on their teffilin or take no part in the service. Fighting these boys, forcing them to pray, as it were, would be self-defeating, pushing these young people still further away from the values the school holds dear. The trick is to steer students toward the right choices.

In another example of this ethos at work, at a senior staff meeting to plan an end-of-year school trip to Florida, the educators spend a great deal of time coming up with ways of keeping students occupied and distracted until the small hours of the morning so that at the end of the day's program, they'll want to go to sleep rather than get into trouble. In an age where students can summon Uber on their phones, they have the means to sneak out of a hotel wherever they're located. Better to finish the day as late as possible, so as to prevent such a temptation even being an option.

These principles don't mean that Rabbi Neuman is ready to forgive every student misdemeanor. The priority is to provide students with opportunities to succeed, but only if they're willing to make the most of those opportunities. Since Rabbi Neuman was appointed principal, the school has asked more than twenty students in the highest grades to leave. These students, with profiles and behaviors that never aligned with those of the school, had been admitted in an effort to help the school's monetary balance sheet. They had not aided the school's educational situation and had modeled problematic behaviors to their peers and juniors. Asking them to leave meant taking quite a substantial financial hit. From the perspective of the school's head of recruitment, however, letting those students go has sent an important message to prospective students about the school's seriousness. It has changed the buzz on the street about the school in a positive way. For Rabbi Neuman, this move had a different significance: the most immediate outcome of this step has been to reduce opportunities for students to be led astray by their peers, as painful as it is to let any student go. In this instance, the well-being of the student body as a whole outweighed the needs of these individual students, as important as those may have been.

2:31 p.m.: STEM—A Parallel Universe

Ninth grade. For the first time since morning seder in the breakfast room, the teacher is not front and center. In fact, other than conducting a short orientation to set up the class's work for the day and for the remaining classes until the end of term, in this particular STEM class the teacher does not address the group as a whole except to bid them farewell at the end of the session.

The class begins with the teacher offering students options for what they could do over the next few weeks until the end of the semester. Their options are thermal physics, studying an eclipse, and "battlebots," an exciting form of computer-aided design. This prompts a lot of excited talk, but the winning selection is never in question: building battlebots wins by a landslide.

It turns out that the students' preferred choice comes with financial implications. It will require finding a few thousand dollars that are not readily available to buy the necessary pieces of equipment. This is something the STEM teacher and Rabbi Neuman will need to figure out. With the school gaining a reputation for offering a high-quality STEM program and with the program delivering student-centered learning in a fashion that Rabbi Neuman sees as a model to other subject areas, in both Jewish and general studies, finding the money isn't in doubt. The question is, Where will it come from?

Rav Teitz Mesivta Academy, Elizabeth, New Jersey | 165

The students, meantime, quickly organize themselves into teams. They gather around computer screens looking at models of vehicles they'll be launching into battle against their fellow students. They watch video clips that explain the strengths and weaknesses of different options and begin to explore what it will take to build such machines. There's excited talk about potential upgrades to these machines that can surprise their opponents. The teacher and an assistant circulate among the groups, offering guidance and advice, but the students are almost completely self-sufficient. It's hard to find any of them off-task. There's an excited buzz in the class, unquestionably the noise of productive work. In fact, by the time the forty-minute class finishes, it's staggering how much each group has accomplished, with plans afoot to start building machines in the next class.

The class finishes at 3:11 p.m. with the boys heading to another classroom for mincha, the afternoon prayers. Each grade *davens* separately rather than bringing the whole school together at the same time. In an instructive contrast, through the classroom window it's noticeable that out on the main street, students from a local public school are heading home. At the mesivta, there are still more than two hours of classes to go before the end of the day.

Ein kemach, ein Torah—Putting Fuel in the Tank

Changing the direction of a sixty-year-old institution is hard enough. It's all the harder when money is in short supply. The Jewish Educational Center is well known for providing families with tuition assistance. Annual tuition plus extras stands between $21,000 and $22,000, and more than 55 percent of the students are on financial aid. This means that annually, the school needs to raise more than 20 percent of its budget from donations.

When the school's leadership was restructured, that triggered a further financial challenge. Some of the school's longest-standing donors felt disenfranchised by the personnel decisions that were taken at that time and have not been so willing to support the school. Then, by asking more than twenty students to leave—equivalent to about 15 percent of the student body—another revenue stream was reduced.

Under these circumstances, it is hardly surprising that in the course of observing the school's senior team go about its work over a number of days, many conversations inevitably led to talk about the mesivta's severely constrained finances. Finding a few thousand dollars more for the STEM program is just the start of it. In other conversations, issues included funding a salary increase to persuade a talented individual to stay with the school when he'd been approached by a competing institution with an offer of better pay; finding a couple of hundred dollars to fund a new junior history prize (something the teacher had offered to fund out of his own pocket); deciding which AP courses to offer (an important element in enhancing the school's marketplace appeal) when each could cost $350 per student to run even if provided on line; and how to cover the costs of travel to an important professional development conference when it became apparent that funding wouldn't be available from an external source. In each case, the sums of money involved would barely merit a discussion at a more financially stable institution.

In many ways, finding money for these kinds of matters is simply part of keeping the school on course. More challenging is the question of how to finance a change of course. One of the first things Rabbi Neuman had wanted to do after his appointment as principal was to make the physical environment in the school more welcoming. As he explains, "If a student comes to a school where the environment looks disgusting, he will feel unrespected. The outside affects how people feel inside." Having been a member of the faculty for more than ten years, he knew full well that the physical space was showing its age. The corridors and classrooms didn't look very different from when the fathers of the current student body, or perhaps even their grandfathers, attended the school. There wasn't money to bring in a contractor, so during the first summer following his appointment, Rabbi Neuman and the school's STEM teacher painted all of the ceiling grids, door frames, and radiators. They often worked late into the night. It was a small gesture that signaled the intent to create a different environment for both students and faculty.

While refreshing the paintwork could be accomplished through an application of elbow grease and an investment of time, addressing other needs requires more radical financial solutions. High on Rabbi Neuman's agenda is the challenge of creating a bes medresh space that would truly be designed for group learning. This isn't a cosmetic question of ensuring that after sixty years the mesivta will finally look more like a yeshiva than a repurposed public school, although that would certainly help the school's appeal to parents; it was about creating a setting that could advance the vision of students learning Torah independently or in small, self-sufficient groups. As we have seen, there is only so much that can be accomplished in an acoustically challenged breakfast room. The rabbi's first major fundraising goal is therefore to find a donor to underwrite an enhancement of this kind. By the end of his second year as principal, he is close to meeting this goal.[3]

It isn't just the physical space and the costs involved in improving it that undermine the effort to change course at the mesivta. Another impediment is the school's barebones leadership structure, a situation that also resulted from financial necessity. Repeatedly over the course of a normal day in school, Rabbis Neuman and Sauber are called on to address issues that would not be brought to them if the school could afford a deeper administrative bench. It surely complicates the task of taking the school in a new direction when the two rabbis are interrupted so frequently—for example, by a student coming to complain about his pop quiz score and its impact on his grade average, or by needing to defuse a situation created by a tenth grader filming himself squishing cake into the face of an elementary section student following a joint activity, recruiting a student to locate a teacher's missing chair, or tackling a situation where a student has refused to hand over his phone after using it inappropriately in class.

Being available to students in this way certainly helps build a culture of caring, or in yeshiva language, *shayachut* (connection). This is undoubtedly a feature of the school that students appreciate most—the fact that the rebbeyim are always available for them at all hours of the day. They feel that every student is known by faculty, something that comes across very strongly in student focus groups. But when the school's most senior staff find themselves required to function so much in reactive mode, it is hard to focus on taking proactive steps to improve the quality of teaching and learning, and ultimately to change the culture of the school.

4:07 p.m.: Math—More of the Same but Different

After the short time-out provided by mincha, the ninth graders head to math. Their teacher, like many of the general studies teachers, has already completed his responsibilities for the day at a different educational institution, in this case a local college. Thanks to the structure and length of the yeshiva day, he's available to teach a full set of classes at the mesivta. The long day has its advantages when it comes to the recruitment of general studies faculty.

A veteran educator, the math teacher methodically and animatedly takes the students through the algebraic steps required to derive an equation for a parabola. Most of the class is giving him its fullest attention, although a couple of students have their heads on the desk in classic "I-don't-want-to-be-here" pose. Although the students don't seem to have handed over their phones at the start of class, they don't seem to be distracted for at least the first part of the lesson.

Still, it's only a matter of time before one of them asks what undoubtedly is the most frequently posed question in general studies classes: "Is this on the test?" The teacher answers in the affirmative. This not unexpected news stimulates the students to perk up a little, although it's shocking how many students sit at their desks without taking any notes. How these students hold on to whatever is being proffered is hard to fathom.

Given how different the content and purpose of the class are from the Jewish studies part of the day, it is remarkable how similar is the prevailing pedagogic dynamic. As was the case in Gemara, Chumash, and Navi, the teacher dispenses the content from the front of the class. The students are the consumers. Their job is to develop the skills that aid digestion or simply to digest the content quickly and efficiently. The medium for doing so is a kind of Socratic dialogue between teacher and class, a high-octane verbal interaction in which the teacher prompts students to take a series of increasingly more advanced steps with him, or at least he makes sure they follow the steps he's outlined for them. It's a form of pedagogy that favors those who thrive on verbal reasoning, although its noticeable that some of the students who were quietest in the morning's Judaic classes have burst into life here. Evidently their passivity earlier in the day was less about aptitude than interest.

Here, in math, as was the case in an English language arts class observed after lunch, the teacher devotes less time to keeping students motivated, whether through inspirational stories or entertaining anecdotes. It seems that the prospect of a test later in the week does most of the motivational heavy lifting. Nevertheless, as this well-managed and well-paced class heads into its final minutes, more and more of the students fall by the wayside. They drift, with a couple even literally dozing off, or they start to play surreptitiously on their phones. When so much of the teaching is in the abstract, it would take exceptional verbal pyrotechnics to hold the attention of this group of fifteen-year-old boys for the full forty minutes after four in the afternoon.

Above All Else

Changing the ethos of teaching and learning at the mesivta is going to take time. It's not just that teachers are set in their ways or that the physical environment doesn't accommodate a more problem-based, learner-centric approach to either Jewish or general studies. Students, teachers, and parents carry with them expectations of what school should look like and of what should happen in the yeshiva day school classroom, for better or for worse.

Rav Teitz Mesivta Academy, Elizabeth, New Jersey | 169

This is the "grammar of schooling" that makes all educational change difficult to implement other than when tinkering around the edges. We have seen, moreover, that the transformation of the Mesivta Academy is further complicated by the school's financial challenges. These are just some of the factors that have disrupted the pace of change.

One other force is at play at this time of transition for the school. In some respects, this force drives change forward, making it all the more urgent. In other respects, this force acutely complicates all that the mesivta educators try to do, just as it complicates the work of Orthodox day school education in the most stable and secure institutions.

When you ask educators at the school what has changed most in their work during the past ten years, they do not first refer to the educational innovations being implemented in the school or to the turmoil created by turnover in the school's leadership. They point instead to the way in which the Internet and the mobile devices by which it can be accessed have invaded the lives of their students. This development has introduced ideas, images, and behaviors that are entirely at odds with the values of the school and the community it serves. The Internet has dramatically eroded students' capacity to concentrate. As some of the school's educators have noted, "It has created a society of ADHD kids," it has made pornography readily accessible to them, and it has resulted in socially corrosive addictions with "kids [who] don't know how to turn off their devices."

For Rabbi Neuman, these circumstances have made it all the more urgent to develop a more compelling educational experience for students and cultivate in the students the capacity to make the right choices. Every senior educator in the school highlights the burden these circumstances have placed on them as educators, in large part because parents have come to rely on the school to address issues they should be handling themselves. Parents are worried about pushing away their children, so they rely on the school to make the tough calls. They call the school to ask, "Can you take my son's phone away for the day?" and then, Rabbi Sauber notes, "they complain when their child hates school."[4]

The students' phones are never far away. In most classes, the protocol works reasonably well: students either put their phones away, or if they know they won't resist the temptation to reach for them, they deposit them on the teacher's desk for the duration of the class. At times, as we have seen, the students make use of their phones for constructive purposes: looking up the meaning of an Aramaic term in seder; accessing the translation to a passage of Chumash; seeking out a "battlebot" model in STEM, or gaining help with figuring out a quadratic equation. During our visits to the school, we observed an instance where a student was incapable of surrendering his phone. Playing on it during seder, he was asked to hand it over but refused. Rabbi Neuman was not able to address the issue at the time, but later in the day, he called the boy to his office. He wanted to take the student's phone away at least until the end of the day and more likely until the end of the week. The boy couldn't bring himself to hand the phone over.

At this point, the rabbi realized he was a confronting a serious issue. He told the boy he would have to call one of his parents and phoned the boy's father. In the course of the conversation, it became apparent that the boy's parents were painfully aware of the problem. The boy himself shared that over the course of his brother's bar mitzvah weekend, he spent most of the time playing the same game on his phone. He often stayed up most of the night to game. There was no question he was addicted. If it wasn't one game, it was another. He admitted that even if he were to give over his phone, which he did after the conversation with his father, there were plenty of other devices he could play on at home. In saying this, he was not being defiant; he was describing a reality where he had lost all self-control.

A short time after the first phone call, the father called Rabbi Neuman and asked him to confiscate his son's phone until the end of year. He made plain that the family needed the school's help. They were at a loss. "This is killing our son," the father said.

Thankfully, this episode was a rare, extreme incident. And yet it lays bare the urgency of the transformation playing out at the Rav Teitz Mesivta. The boys in this school, and their peers elsewhere, live in a world where mobile technology has invaded every moment of their waking lives. The technology has given them great power—power to do good and to do harm to others and themselves. In their quest to develop in their young charges the capacity to make the right decisions and in their efforts to inspire them, Rabbi Neuman and his colleagues ultimately want to enable their students to be *yirei shamayim* (God fearing) and to do positive things with the lives that Ribono shel Olam (the Almighty) has gifted them with. This educational goal is deeply traditional on the one hand; it is no different from that pursued by generations of yeshiva day school educators. On the other hand, in their approach to realizing this goal, the school's educators couldn't be more contemporary, not least in the potential they have to enable young people to survive and thrive in genuinely challenging and uncharted social and cultural circumstances.

The efforts of the leadership team at the Mesivta Academy constitute a work in progress. As all members of the team acknowledge, they face immense difficulties changing the teaching practices of all who work in the school and changing perceptions of the school in the wider community. And yet there is something both moving and inspiring about the dedication invested in this work by a small group of deeply committed individuals in a corner of the world that does not typically attract attention. The practices they are developing at the mesivta model something important for day school educators more widely.

CONNECTIONS AND EXCEPTIONS

As in the other high schools in our sample—TanenbaumCHAT (chapter 7), the Hebrew Academy in Miami Beach (chapter 8), and Yeshiva Darchei Torah (chapter 9)—much of the work of school leadership at the *mesivta* is tied up with addressing students' social and emotional needs. At times, the academic, social, and personal pressures on high school students seem almost unbearable, especially in schools that operate exceptionally long days.

These needs take on a special complexion in a strictly Orthodox, all-male setting where religious norms, from dress codes to how boys spend their leisure time outside school, diverge so much from American society in general. Under these circumstances, school leadership is heavily concerned with both managing and monitoring the borderline between the school's culture and the culture beyond its walls and protecting students from themselves, as Ami Neuman so poignantly puts it in this chapter. This is consistent with what we found at Darchei Torah, an even more strictly Orthodox institution.

To be a leader, actually to be a Jewish educator, in an Orthodox school carries additional responsibilities as a religious role model for students; that's a large part of what it means to serve as a rebbe. This is certainly not an expectation in more liberal schools where both faculty and students are more diverse; in those schools, how teachers spend their time outside school is their own business. At the mesivta, as at Darchei Torah and to some extent Hillel Torah, the expectation and aspiration is that students will learn from how their teachers conduct their lives 24/7, and not just from what they teach in class.

The mesivta was such a fascinating case at the time of this study because of how much the school was in a process of transition. The pedagogy depicted in this chapter—in both Judaic studies and general studies classes—is quite different from that observed at most of the other nine schools. Again, that may have something to do with the high school setting, where there is a tendency for most teachers to employ a lecture-style format for their classes (something noticeable at TanenbaumCHAT and Hebrew Academy too), but it is also indicative of a traditional teacher-centered culture (similar to that at Darchei Torah) that the mesivta's leadership is gradually seeking to shift. We have subsequently learned that these shifts have continued to take root as a consequence of staff turnover, a major expansion in the school's STEAM (science, technology, engineering, the arts, and mathematics) offerings, and, unexpectedly, the disruption caused by COVID-19.

If these features underline the ways in which the mesivta differs from other schools in our sample, in other respects it strongly resembles what was observed in other places. We provide two examples. First, as was the case at the other high schools, the mesivta did not devote many resources to work with parents. The only time parents intensely engaged with educators or were observed on the school premises was when their children were dealing with acute challenges. At those times, they turned to the school for special, even emergency, help. Otherwise they faded into the background. This seems to be a commonplace of high school life.

Second, the mesivta's difficulties in finding funds for resources to meet the needs of students (to ensure the school does not fall behind its competitors) without passing on the costs to parents are a widespread feature of the day school field more generally. This is a challenge shared by the great majority of day schools. Without special benefactors (as was the case at Hillel Detroit) or access to public funds (as at Hebrew Academy), the mesivta was especially hard-pressed to make ends meet, sometimes painfully so.

7

It's All in a Name

The Anne & Max Tanenbaum Community Hebrew Academy of Toronto, Canada

TanenbaumCHAT, The Anne & Max Tanenbaum Community Hebrew Academy of Toronto, presents an opportunity to examine some of the sharpest dilemmas confronting Jewish day high schools: How can they build community by welcoming students of all scholastic abilities in an educational environment that enables students to achieve the highest academic standards? How can they help students succeed in the intense race for admission to selective colleges while protecting their mental health and supporting them emotionally? How can they welcome students regardless of their Jewish religious orientation and their prior Jewish education while requiring that, throughout their high school careers, all of them take a significant number of serious Jewish studies and Hebrew courses? Finally, how can they offer day school education at a price significantly lower than that at most other private schools while remaining financially sustainable? The answers TanenbaumCHAT has found to these questions might not be readily implemented everywhere, but the means by which the school has wrestled these issues to the ground have wide applicability.

Do schools mirror communities? Can they change communities, or at least defy the circumstances in which they find themselves? These questions are part of a long-running debate in education about whether communities get the schools they deserve or whether schools have the capacity to transcend or transform those communities.

This longstanding conundrum comes to mind after spending time at TanenbaumCHAT, The Anne & Max Tanenbaum Community Hebrew Academy of Toronto. A high school with almost one thousand students, CHAT is perhaps the quintessential Toronto Jewish institution. Founded in 1960, as the outgrowth of one of Toronto's oldest Jewish elementary schools, some of its current students are the third generation in their families to call themselves CHATnicks. A disproportionate number of senior Jewish community professionals in the city are alumni of the school, as are many of the community's most prominent lay leaders. In a community that invests more than $13 million in subsidies for Jewish day school education each year, the school does not run a deficit on its $22 million budget, thanks, in large part, to an annual subsidy of $1.5 million from the UJA Federation of Toronto. (All dollar amounts in this chapter are in Canadian dollars.) In a community where rates of interfaith marriage are lower than in most other major North American cities, the school advertises that 96 percent of married graduates have Jewish partners. In this reality, with almost eight thousand graduates over the course of more than fifty-five years, it is hard to tell how much the school has helped forge this state of affairs and how much it is the fortunate beneficiary of a context that has been good for the Jews, Judaism, and Jewish education.

At first glance, the school seems to benefit from a virtuous circle in a milieu that would be the envy of other Jewish educational institutions. This, however, would be a serious misreading of the reality. Today, the context for day school education in Toronto is more challenging than it has been for decades. The Jewish community is reeling from the dramatic downsizing of previously robust elementary schools, among which are two of the largest feeder schools to CHAT. Just ten years ago, CHAT itself was reported to be the largest private school in Canada, with an enrollment of fifteen hundred students on two campuses. At the time of this study, there were 30 percent fewer students on its rolls. The school's northern campus, whose doors opened to much fanfare seventeen years earlier, had closed.

Enrollment issues aside, these are challenging times for high schools everywhere, not just for Jewish ones. Ever-intensifying competition for college admission has placed high school students under great stress. Schools have been under acute pressure to inflate grades. Students, made anxious by the race to college, have suffered from an epidemic of mental health challenges, exacerbated by some of the more destructive aspects of social media. Among Jewish high schools, there has been a scaling back of Jewish studies and Hebrew requirements to create space for more college-competitive courses and because, it is said, parents are more interested in the cultivation of Jewish identity in their children than in the development of high levels of Jewish literacy.

In large part, CHAT has withstood these pressures. Enrollment is rising again at a quick pace; the new ninth-grade class is 50 percent larger than it was two years ago. The school does not run an annual deficit even though tuition, set at $18,500, is at its lowest in ten years. With forty-seven grade 12 electives and more than fifty extracurricular clubs, student life is richer than ever before. All students take four Judaic studies courses out of an annual eleven-course load, and a Hebrew requirement for the first three years. More than a third of students take Hebrew Bible (Tanakh) and Talmud in Hebrew (ivrit b'ivrit style) in so-called "academic" offerings.

The school has had its share of good fortune no doubt, but its leadership operates within a variety of constraints, some shared by other schools and some peculiar to Toronto. The story of how the school has been able to thrive despite these constraints can be instructive even, and perhaps especially, to those who may consider their own circumstances less fortunate.

Truly an Academy

Unlike many elite private schools, TanenbaumCHAT is not surrounded by playing fields or extensive sports facilities. It does not even own its building. Since 1974, the school has rented the same drab two-story building, a former public elementary school, from the Toronto District School Board. Squeezed onto a corner in a lower-middle-class neighborhood where once there were more Jews than today, the school's immediate neighbor is an Orthodox synagogue that has certainly seen better days. Across the road is a Conservative synagogue, also showing its age.

Walk through the school's entrance, and you quickly sense what parents and teens might find appealing. Take a sharp left and you head toward a recently constructed science and engineering wing. (Apparently, more than 10 percent of the students are taking engineering, probably the hottest program today on Canadian campuses.) As you head to this new wing, you walk past a sizable gym festooned with pennants from the past decade, including those from the school's now-defunct northern campus. The corridor is plastered with artifacts from extensive extracurricular activity: MVP awards, posters from theater productions and musicals (some in Hebrew), photos and memorabilia from community initiatives and Israel-related events. Turn right, and you're in a building that dates back more than fifty years where the signage throughout is in both English and Hebrew, including the storerooms. Along one corridor you'll find long lists of donors and of landmark events in the school's history. Along another corridor are graduation photos from decades ago, when the graduation classes were smaller and hair was worn much longer. About a quarter of the current study body can find their own parents in one of those photos. The building conveys, then, a powerful story of tradition and innovation, community and individual achievement, Jewish cultural riches, and engagement with the world.

As for the students, in their appearance there's generally an absence of show or obvious material privilege. For the girls, some variation on gym wear seems de rigueur. Among the boys, there's more variety—a fair number of college sweatshirts, perhaps indicating something of the wearers' aspirations, and memorabilia from Israel trips or Jewish summer camps. More than a handful have *tzitzit* out (fringed garments traditionally worn by Jewish males). Before class starts and during their breaks, students sit with their backs to the lockers, computers open, talking quietly about work. Few have their phones out. If some Jewish high schools feel more like summer camps, this feels more like college. The atmosphere is calm, and people seem genuinely content to be here.

Those who have been associated with the school the longest will tell you that its story is about the interplay between the elements in the school's name: Community . . . Hebrew . . . Academy. During its first decades, the school's identity as an academy loomed large. It functioned as an academically selective institution and was run on religiously Orthodox lines for members of the broader Jewish community. Today it is a more inclusive institution, both educationally and religiously, although there are different views about how far that spirit of inclusion goes.

There are dozens of day schools in North America that call themselves academies. The term is supposed to indicate academic excellence and exclusiveness, mimicking some of the continent's best-known independent schools. Often this is just a matter of cosmetics. Here, one senses, the academy identity runs deep. It isn't only about marketing, although it helps in that respect too. Both students and teachers will tell you that at CHAT, it's cool to work hard and do well. Over the course of generations of students, a culture has evolved of "work hard, play hard," says one of the senior administrators who has been at the school for some fifteen years. The students proudly report that this is a place where they have to work hard. "It's like university," they say. A senior staff member says, "The kids push each other to reach the bar."

Certainly the atmosphere in class is intense. Whether in Jewish studies or general studies, teachers have to devote very little time to discipline. If a student is repeatedly late or absent or acts out in some way, classroom teachers hand the case over to the deans, who can be trusted to take care of these matters sensitively and efficiently. The students generally come to class in order to work. This is not, for example, a school where there is a continually revolving door of students heading back and forth to the washroom during class time, a sure sign of indifference or boredom.

Sitting in a math class during the last period of the day from 3:30 to 4:30 p.m., with more than twenty eleventh-grade students, an observer is struck by the close alignment of student interest and teacher energy. It's not that everyone understands the material—the class is solving progressively more complex exercises for graphing algebraic functions—but the students do seem interested in mastering the material. There are audible sighs of satisfaction when students figure out a problem. "Oh! I see now!" "Got it! Got it!" It is remarkable that at this time of the day, after eight hours in school, there isn't a less focused atmosphere. The teacher has to remind students that they can work together. "You don't have to do it alone!" she calls out with a laugh.

Confronting the Dark Side of Academic Intensity: Both Offense and Defense

The school's leaders take pride in the seriousness of CHAT's academic culture. They celebrate how successful their alumni are and how more than 90 percent of them are admitted to their college programs of choice. And yet they're also concerned about some of the less healthy dimensions of such success. They're mindful of how students have little room to make mistakes, when learning from one's mistakes was once a privilege and still is a developmentally necessary dimension of childhood. In the Canadian precollegiate education system where there are no standardized tests and the most popular and competitive university programs are looking for a 95 to 97 average, they know that an average of less than 90 is a "CHAT-fail," in student-speech. Twenty years ago, an 80 was quite fine.

They know that students complain when teachers grade quizzes on a scale of 5 because a 4.5, the first notch down from a perfect piece of work, will harm their grade average; it's only worth 90 percent. They're also aware that students gravitate to courses where teachers are known to be easier graders —those who'll give you a grade in the low 90s if they see you put in the effort. And they know that student grade grubbing—incessant haggling with teachers to increase their test scores by one or two points—threatens to create a culture where the final score is more important than the learning that those scores are supposed to reflect. Finally, with all classes linked to EDSBY, a learning management system for real-time student-teacher communication, assignment submission, and grade reporting, the school's leadership has learned that teachers should not post new grades during class hours because of the commotion created at such times, so obsessively do students monitor their standing. "They watch EDSBY like tickertape," says the head of guidance.

The school's response to these concerns is twofold: playing both defense and offense. On the one hand, its educational leaders work to limit the impact of forces that lie outside the school and are beyond their control by developing robust support systems that can help students thrive. On the other hand, and more subtly, they take steps to ensure that the school's culture goes deeper than college preparation. The strategy is to create an environment where values, in addition to academic success, are honored and celebrated and where students nevertheless are given every possible opportunity to achieve the highest levels of academic success and will be celebrated for doing so.

These two strategies, reactive and proactive, go hand in hand. Perhaps the most powerful proactive move the school has made in this respect is through its admissions policy. Very few students are turned away for being academically unsuitable. The director of admissions explains, "If parents are committed to their child being educated in a Jewish day school and the child does not have exceptional learning challenges, the school will try to help them succeed. This might involve suggesting, for example, that the student get tutoring support before the start of the year. It will certainly involve developing a student learning profile for that student." Of course, it's not clear, and hard to judge, whether because the school has such a strong reputation for academic achievement that some families don't even consider applying. What is clear is that the school's inclusive admissions policy makes a powerful statement: the school takes its identity as an academy seriously, and at the same time it is deeply committed to its role as a community institution that serves all students, regardless of ability. This is a stance that current faculty and administrators who had attended the school themselves identify as reflecting the greatest change in school culture since they were students.

Being as inclusive as possible is not a hollow promise. Fewer than twenty students drop out each year, a number that translates into a retention rate of 97 percent, higher than at most of Toronto's Jewish elementary schools. Maintaining such high rates of retention is possible because of the considerable ideological alignment of parents with the school's Jewish ethos and because of the extensive infrastructure that exists to support students behaviorally, academically, and emotionally. That infrastructure is the strongest form of defense.

The school's principal, an alumna of the school, sketches out the different components of this system. She frames her comments with something of a mantra: "It's about accommodation, not modification. We're not going to expect less of you. We'll help you." The basic concept is that all students engage in the same program; they access different kinds of supports according to their needs. As she sees it, the school has not lowered its standards to attract a broader cross-section from the community. CHAT has not lowered the bar, but helps students reach the bar: "If a child wants to be here, we'll help him or her succeed."

The support system has many tiers. First, a team of guidance counselors provides students with emotional support. All students are assigned a counselor who serves as their primary advocate over the years and is the first point of contact in addressing personal or mental health issues. Second, a team at the Centre for Differentiated Learning (CDL) focuses on addressing students' learning needs, making sure that teachers are aware of what these are and what accommodations might be needed. Finally, the deans are responsible for social and behavioral matters, conflict resolution, and chronic attendance challenges. All of these efforts are overseen by a single person, the director of student services, to ensure there is no duplication of activity.

There are specific variations to this overall framework. For example, CHAT offers three levels in Jewish studies in grades 9 and 10 (academic and intermediate intended for those who graduate from day schools and "new stream" for those who have never attended day school or at least not during the previous three years). The school also offers a track providing remedial Hebrew. Students have access to three levels of math in grades 9 and 10, and there are multiple options in grades 11 and 12, ranging from AP and college-level courses to more applied math and science offerings.

Other interventions are also in place, such as a weekly project support period that students can go to for academic help. A peer tutoring program is run out of the CDL and also a learning space run by teachers three times a week. Students who have an academic assessment can take an accredited learning strategies course where they receive guidance on organization and time management. A Jewish studies support class is also an option.

Reflecting on these extensive systems and their effectiveness, the head of guidance, another alumna in a senior administrative position, shares that "very many students will have some trouble at some point. . . . Things can become overwhelming for two days or two weeks for the vast majority." For a small minority, those challenges might last longer. As a perennial example, she cites what students call "hell weeks," when grade 9 students confront eleven midterms for the first time; suddenly traffic to her door surges. Her team helps students learn how to anticipate and manage such stresses. In fact, she derives great satisfaction when students come back after having started college to share how well developed their time management skills are, especially now they have to manage only four or five courses rather than eleven.

Broadening the Concept of Success: Playing Offense

If the focus was solely on remediation or on accommodating students' needs, no matter how effectively, it is doubtful whether the school could fulfill its mission as either an academy or a community school, and certainly not as one with a Jewish mission at its core. Its stance would be entirely reactive, and its horizons would be set toward addressing the most self-interested needs that draw parents to a school: the desire to help their child get ahead. No one communicates this message more thoughtfully than Jonathan Levy, the head of school, someone who, not coincidentally, started his own career in schools as a guidance counselor and is acutely sensitive to the social and emotional needs of students. As he puts it, it is not automatic that many of the students will come to a Jewish school, but in offering programs of a quality that would appeal to those who might have otherwise gone elsewhere, the school must do more than prepare students for academic success. It must prepare these young people for life as individuals in their families and their communities.

Surely it's no coincidence, Levy argues, that what students remember of their high school experience is not one class or another, no matter how stellar; it is the sports team they played on, the musical or talent show they performed in, or the Shabbaton (a residential Shabbat retreat) they attended. These experiences provide moments of personal significance, and of belonging to something larger than themselves. These moments place the intense investment in academic success within a larger framework of meaning. Such experiences, he argues, are as much an antidote to the ever-intensifying academic pressure students experience as are the elaborate support systems that help students address their learning challenges.

Admittedly, some students probably view their participation in extracurricular or volunteer work as another opportunity to build their college application. That possibility certainly exists. Yet such a cynical reading of student extracurricular participation seems out of place when walking around the school after four-thirty in the afternoon when classes are over for the day. On a Thursday evening in December, many hours after the school day has ended and when it's dark outside, between three hundred and four hundred students, at least a third of the student body, are still on the premises. A large crowd of chorus and musicians are in the music room preparing for a show. Set builders are huddled off to the side doing their thing. Around the corner, a smaller but more raucous group are in the gym for a competitive interleague basketball game against a rival independent school. On the other side of the building, another smaller group is wrapping up a *mishmar* session —a voluntary, teacher-led after-hours Jewish learning program. Coming to the end of their session, they transition from Talmud to pungent-smelling pizza. Upstairs, in a suite of classrooms furnished to look like a business center, another three groups are participating in a student-led business club. The school is still humming with life. It gives one pause to consider that there are more students on the premises at this time than in many Jewish day schools during the course of the day. Surely more is going on here than just the accumulation of additional experiences to put on one's résumé.

On a different evening earlier the same week, cynicism seems even more out of place. On a bone-chilling evening typical of Toronto in the winter, a crowd of about three hundred students, family members, and friends assemble in the theater of a local public school for the student-led annual talent show. (Ironically the theater belongs to CHAT's main public school competitor.) The event consists of some twenty acts in which soloists, small groups, and large bands take turns performing, interspersed with witty commentary and videos provided by a couple of seniors. Over the course of the evening, more than one hundred students take to the stage, a number equivalent to about 15 percent of the student body. The acts provide an intimation of the school's diversity. Some of the boys wear *kippot*, but most do not. Some of the students seem somewhat, almost painfully, introverted but seem to find their voices when their turn comes. Others relish their few minutes in the spotlight, enjoying the attention. For many, it is evident that taking part is the important thing; they don't seem especially musical or comfortable, but a handful of performers really do dazzle the audience with their talents.

At the end of the evening, the audience is invited to submit votes by text for their favorite act. This feels a little jarring after a couple of hours in which these young people had a chance simply to have fun being themselves. For the assembled crowd, the voting is innocuous, mimicking any number of television shows. But perhaps the vote at the end of the evening does tap into the school's ethos of accommodation, not modification, of growing by facing up to challenges. By coping with the experience of winning and losing, people grow whatever the outcome. It's not quite a school of hard knocks, but certainly a form of tough love.

Putting such quibbles to the side, these after-school activities help substantiate the constructive role played by extracurricular experiences in broadening an appreciation of what the school values. Undoubtedly, enabling students to achieve academic success is of primary importance at CHAT, but it is far from being the whole story. Providing young people with an opportunity to excel or simply to express themselves outside the classroom is also an important principle here, as well as for the healthy balance such experiences provide to a focus on academic success. Both are important elements in the school's story.

That story cannot be fully told without close consideration of the Jewish dimensions of life at the school.

Coming for Community

At the time of its founding, CHAT was conceived not only as an academy but as a community day school, even if the community it served was a fairly narrow one. When it opened its doors, Toronto's only available Jewish high school options were affiliated with the ultra-Orthodox community. The families originally attracted to CHAT were members of Modern Orthodox congregations or were situated at the traditionalist end of the Conservative movement. Like the associated Hebrew schools from which the school was birthed and from which most of the students originally transitioned, CHAT's religious ethos was essentially traditionalist. The school's Jewish studies program was designed and delivered by religiously Orthodox Jewish educators for a population of students who were assumed, but not required, to be observant. The Jewish studies program established at that time was constructed on four pillars: four required courses each year of high school in Tanakh, Talmud/rabbinics, Jewish history, and Hebrew. For the first couple of decades, all of the Judaic studies courses were taught in Hebrew, reflecting the strong Hebraist leanings of the school's original sponsors and founding leadership.

Since the 1960s, the denominational variety of Toronto day schools has expanded. At the elementary level, this first saw the founding of Conservative, Reform, and secular options, and then in later decades pluralistic ones.

At an early stage of this expansion, in the 1970s, a Modern Orthodox yeshiva high school (the Bnei Akiva Schools of Toronto) also opened. Although the Bnei Akiva Schools never enrolled more than three hundred students in total, the confluence of its opening with denominational diversification at the elementary level, and higher levels of retention of those more diverse elementary students into high school, has meant that the proportion of students enrolling at CHAT who are not religiously Orthodox has increased steadily. Today, about 80 percent of families are estimated to identify with a liberal denomination or no denomination at all. Although the profile of the student body has changed, the structure of the curriculum is more or less the same as it always has been. The requirement that all Jewish studies classes be conducted in Hebrew was dropped, but the requirement to take four Jewish studies/Hebrew courses all the way through high school has remained. The extent to which the content of the curriculum has evolved to reflect the changed composition of the student body and how much its delivery by current faculty has also changed is a matter of debate.

What makes the situation at CHAT so fascinating is that those who enroll at the school have no lack of other choices. In neighborhoods where public schools are weak, Jewish day schools can exist as proxy selective schools. Parents pay school fees upward of $15,000, and students endure Jewish studies requirements as the price of gaining access to a good education in a safe environment. That is not the case here. Toronto's public schools have greatly improved in recent decades. The competition for places in public high schools with special programs in the arts, sciences, or languages is especially intense. Some public schools even close on Rosh Hashanah and Yom Kippur because more than half of their student population is Jewish. At one of these schools, Westmount Collegiate, there are probably more Jewish students than at any other school in Toronto. If young people come to CHAT, it is not because they lack alternatives or because it provides a quality of general education they couldn't get somewhere else and for a lot less money.

It is reasonable to conclude that a decisive consideration for families in choosing the school is CHAT's Jewish offerings. A recent study of the transition from Jewish middle schools to CHAT and to other high schools—funded by UJA Federation at a time when CHAT's enrollment was rapidly declining —revealed not only the extent of sensitivity to the high price of tuition; it also indicated that those who left the day school system at grade 8 and did not continue onto CHAT were turned off by two things. First, they balked at the number of hours devoted to Jewish studies and the concomitant impact on students' course load. Second, they communicated the notion that CHAT was too insular. As a student in one focus group who did not continue on to CHAT from his day school put it, "It is time to get out of the Jewish bubble. We live in a multicultural society. I would like to have a chance to be exposed to the real world."

Students who have chosen to come to CHAT view these same phenomena from a different perspective. In a focus group with current ninth and tenth graders, a number of them highlighted what they call the curriculum's "balance": the chance to experience a rich school experience, to "learn about Judaism" and "become knowledgeable about its traditions." These students, and especially those who have transferred to CHAT from public schools, appreciate the opportunity available at CHAT to explore their Jewish identity and to embrace it, something they perceived as not possible in public school. Above all, they highlighted the experience of "jelling with Jewish friends"— others with whom they feel especially comfortable because of shared backgrounds and a shared culture. What those outside the school see as a Jewish bubble, these young people experience as a powerful and palpable sense of Jewish community, a sizable part of the school's appeal.

Flash Points

The enthusiasm of these students for the Jewish dimensions of CHAT's culture does not mean that they don't have complaints about aspects of their Jewish experience in school. They do, as do other students and certain Jewish communal professionals outside the school who interact with it or with its families.

Few people who have enrolled at the school (whether parents or students) openly question the number of hours devoted to Jewish studies. They seem to have accepted the heavy Jewish course load as a given, perhaps because the school's leadership has refused to budge on this issue over many generations. It is nonnegotiable, reflected, for example, in the fact that in grade 12, when students are entitled to include two "spares" in their schedule—that is, to take nine courses instead of the standard eleven—they are not allowed to drop any Jewish studies courses. In the same way, if students in the lower grades are having challenges in general studies, they cannot free up time for additional support by dropping Jewish studies. By holding the line so firmly, the message has stuck: a complete Jewish education, at least as purveyed at CHAT, requires a significant and continuous investment of time.

The flash points are instead around two different issues: the extent to which students can select which level of Jewish studies they take and the extent to which the content of the curriculum truly reflects the diversity of the school.

More Than Just Holding the Line

For decades, the school has offered different levels of the same Jewish studies programs: academic, intermediate, and new stream. Historically, academic courses were the default for all those coming from day schools. New stream, offered only in grades 9 and 10, was established to help students not coming from day school to make up lost ground and become fully integrated by grade 11. Intermediate courses were developed for students transitioning from day school who struggled with Hebrew. These courses were offered in English, not Hebrew. The rabbinics course itself was also an evolution of the Talmud course, involving less wrestling with text and more exploration of the conceptual issues raised by the text. With academic, intermediate, and new stream courses all being worth the same number of credits, there has been growing pressure from parents and students to be streamed into the intermediate offerings; it's universally agreed that they're less demanding. The school has tried to resist such pressures by various means: by rejecting the notion that if students are in an intermediate course for one subject, they should be for all Judaic subjects; by limiting the number of years over which intermediate options are available; and by severely limiting the number of students granted this accommodation. One of the senior administrators said, "We know there are cases where it's the right thing for the student, but it's problematic for the system." A strategy being considered is to put superstar teachers in the academic classes to make them more attractive. And yet it has become ever more difficult to hold the line, especially when the intensity of Jewish studies in the day schools feeding into CHAT has progressively eroded. In fact, with Hebrew now optional in the middle school grades of one of those feeder schools, some have started to make the case that students from these schools should go into some version of new stream. Their Hebrew is not much more advanced than those coming out of public schools.

If the nuances of this issue seem convoluted, they reveal patterns indicative of a broader set of challenges faced by the school and its response to such challenges. CHAT does not exist in a vacuum. Just as the general studies program is battered by trends of intensifying competition for college admission and pressure for grade inflation, so the Jewish studies program is being squeezed by trends toward less intense Hebrew programming in feeder schools. These are unavoidable circumstances over which the school has no control. The school's resistance to these challenges is not just a matter of holding the line because of some abstract commitment to high standards. The school's response derives from something deeper: a view that taking things off students' plates doesn't necessarily make life easier for them, that young people grow through exposure to challenges and not by being coddled. In some quarters, these are unfashionable values, but they seem to be rooted deep in the DNA of the school.

A second value is also at work here. The school's leadership has for decades been invested in merging students from often quite distinct feeder school communities and cultures into a single integrated culture. Tracking them into different classes can result in more traditional students being in one class and less traditional students in another. Out of this concern, new stream classes have only been offered in grades 9 and 10. By grade 11, it should not matter which elementary school a student came from. That argument has become harder to sustain when the differences between feeder schools are ever wider. The school's resistance is not only about maintaining academic standards; it is about the formation of community and how that occurs. In this respect, the academic and community dimensions of the school's identity don't compete; they align.

"There's No Conspiracy Here"

A second flash point, perhaps less visible but probably more venerable in that it has been a focus of controversy over decades, concerns the extent to which the school affirms the identities of the great majority of students who do not identify as Orthodox. Students complain that the Jewish studies curriculum reflects narrowly Orthodox Jewish concerns. In the words of one student focus group participant, "They limit us in the examples of what it means to be Jewish. They don't offer examples of what it means to be an observant Conservative Jew." Another student grumbles that "everything we learn here is so outdated and has absolutely no significance for our lives. The discussions from Hillel and Shamai are from thousands of years ago." These complaints about the content of the Jewish studies curriculum are echoed in criticism of the lack of diversity among those who teach Jewish studies, especially among those who teach rabbinics and Tanakh. A student complains, "It communicates an implicit message that to be knowledgeable, you have to be Orthodox." In particularly controversial cases, although rare, students have experienced disparaging remarks from teachers. For example, when asked about the position of Reform or Conservative Judaism on some issue, a teacher is said to have responded, "Don't worry about it; we don't teach that here."

The response of the school's leadership is clear and consistent: "Those kinds of comments are not acceptable. . . . There is no tolerance for teachers who disparage students in this way." This seems to be the case. The problem is that while those who teach Hebrew are typically secular Israelis and those who teach Jewish history are more diverse in their profiles, most of the Tanakh, rabbinics, and Talmud teachers are Orthodox. That doesn't mean they're intolerant. On the contrary, during the hiring process, the administration makes every effort to identify open-minded candidates who will not only tolerate but embrace difference. In fact, one of the Tanakh teachers most often identified by students as a role model for her leadership, humor, and open-mindedness is a strictly Orthodox woman. Her lifestyle is about as different from that of her students as one could imagine. And yet there is no avoiding the fact that just in terms of physical appearance, it is somewhat incongruous to see such a high proportion of Orthodox individuals teaching in a context where the great majority of students aren't Orthodox.

The administration is aware that occasionally teachers say something inappropriate. It acts quickly to address these cases when they come to light and has made clear it will not tolerate *kiruv*, Orthodox outreach, with its implicit devaluing of non-Orthodox practice. Says one of the assistant principals, "The problem is that we simply can't find enough individuals from the non-Orthodox community who are able to teach the curriculum to the high standards we want." During the years when the school hired great numbers of *shlichim*, a practice curtailed due to the tightening of Canadian regulations for hiring foreign workers and the overall downsizing of the institution, it faced the same problem. Very few non-Orthodox couples were willing to spend three years abroad teaching Judaic studies. Today, at least, there are some exceptions—a secular Israeli with a PhD in Jewish studies teaches Tanakh; a woman rabbi who also leads a Reform congregation teaches rabbinics—but these individuals are very much in a minority, and students notice.

These issues are evidently sensitive. Critics outside the school complain that the school does not offer an egalitarian or non-Orthodox minyan in the morning. Veterans in the school respond that there have been efforts over the years to get one off the ground but that insufficient numbers of students come since minyan is not compulsory. Indeed, it is ironic, given criticism of the school's Orthodox tendencies, that this is one of the few Jewish community day schools in North America that does not require students to participate in some form of prayer, whether once a week or once a month. That position reflects a distinctive ideological orientation: one that is nondenominational rather than pluralistic. "Hands-off" is another way of putting it. The approach is studiously to resist any effort to compel students to engage in religious practices in which they would not otherwise choose to engage. In a sense, the school's style is to focus on cultivating Jewish ideas, not so much Jewish behaviors. Jewish practice is left to the individual. As the head of school explains, "We want them to be serious about their Judaism. How they act on it is their own choice."

Aware of the school's image in relation to these matters, the head is especially proud of two programs that demonstrate, in his words, "who we really are." In 2018, for the first time, the school held a community *yom iyun*, a day of Jewish study in which rabbis from all of the congregations with which students' families are associated were invited to come teach in relation to the topic of *ben adam l'chavairo*, interpersonal relations. Invitations were sent to fifty rabbis. Thirty-five came from across the spectrum of the community. The day was a roaring success, generating a spirit of Jewish learning for its own sake in multiple forms. It is set to become an annual event. In a similar vein, for the last few years on Purim, the school has offered five different *megillah* readings with the goal of reflecting the denominational diversity of the student body. For the school's leadership, these moments help to affirm the diverse identities of community members.

Perspective is everything. The director of student activities, another alumna, observes that she perceives the staff and the range of Jewish experiences being offered today to be much more diverse than when she was a student twenty years ago. The kinds of conversations students have with staff are much more honest and authentic. It used to be a case of "don't ask, don't tell." Addressing a complaint that school Shabbatonim, a key part of her portfolio, are run as Orthodox experiences, she points out that they run three minyanim at every Shabbaton—Orthodox, egalitarian, and alternative/explanatory. It's true that public spaces at these programs are Shabbat observant, but that's because a sizable minority of the students are observant themselves. She contrasts the situation to the previous school where she worked, also a Jewish community high school, where for all its pluralism (and perhaps precisely because of its pluralism), there were barely any Orthodox students. Despite its location in straitlaced Toronto rather than on the West Coast, "CHAT's community is way more diverse."

Seriously Stimulating

What's striking about these controversies, no matter how intently felt, is how few in number they actually are. With such a diverse student body whose prior experiences of Jewish education differ so much from one another before they came to CHAT, it is remarkable how satisfied the students are overall with the Jewish dimensions of school life. There are those, for example, who especially appreciate the hands-off approach when it comes to observance. In student focus groups, a number of participants acknowledged that they would not have enrolled in the school if there had been compulsory prayer. Coming from elementary schools where they had resented being required to participate in religious practices, they were grateful that this was not the case at CHAT. Other students single out student-led Shabbatonim as a highlight. They're not troubled by the policy of Orthodox norms in public spaces. It seems that students truly enjoy losing themselves in these moments of Jewish intensity.

Remarkably, students generally report high levels of satisfaction with the Jewish studies curriculum. There is no question that it has a traditional bent: the texts studied and the issues raised come from the traditional canon rather than from more liberal or secular sources. The grade 9 curriculum, for example, is concerned with personal injury and damages—issues from Seder Nezikim (the Talmudic tractates concerned with damages)—rather than more exciting topics. And yet even with the students' complaints previously noted about the curriculum's lack of relevance, most seem to enjoy and appreciate their time in Jewish studies classes.

The secret, it seems, is that Jewish studies classes typically are conducted at a very high level. The work is serious and intellectually demanding, on a par with the best of general studies. The tone may be a little more informal and slightly less intense than classes from which the students report their grades to colleges, but students' work is graded just as frequently and as carefully and those grades are monitored just as closely by students. Some day schools take a view that Jewish studies is a form of edutainment, where students should be left with a positive feeling about themselves as Jews or, in a different but similar argument, where students work should not be graded. The idea is that students should enjoy the experience for its own sake and see that Jewish learning is driven by intrinsic rather than extrinsic values. The long-standing view at CHAT, as expressed, for example, by Paul Shaviv, a former head of the school, is different: "To be successful, the Jewish studies program has to be structured in a way that fits a school, and that students recognize as a school model. The JS lessons have to be taught according to a planned curriculum and have to have assignments, homework, tests, exams and marks." Shaviv continues with the following example: "Experience shows that students cannot cope with moving from first lesson Eng Lit to second lesson Civics to third lesson Hassidic *farbreng* [happening] and then back to fourth lesson Chemistry."[1]

This continues to be the operating principle at CHAT, as the following two examples demonstrate. The first is from a Jewish history class.

Passionately Dispassionate

Organized around a large U-shape table in the business studies center, an eleventh-grade Jewish history class resembles a college seminar. The teacher, a youthful PhD with an intense style, introduces the topic of Polish violence toward Jews during the Holocaust, as seen through the case of the pogrom at Jedwabne. She sets the scene by reminding the class about recent Polish legislation outlawing talk about Poland and Poles during the Holocaust in ways that imply Polish culpability. She adds a personal dimension by telling a story about her time in Poland when doing her doctoral work and her fascination with which events from the Holocaust have been publicly memorialized and what language was used to talk about those events.

The pace then moves up a number of gears, with data and information coming at the students from all sides. The teacher has a presentation on a screen, while students have a text in their hands and are taking notes on their laptops. Their work is focused around a big question: How does one account for local violence against Jews—of Poles against their Jewish neighbors? "Neighbors" is the title of the historical text the students are analyzing. The teacher makes clear that the goal is to approach this question with as much objectivity as possible. "You have to understand all sides," she reminds the class.

Some of the students broaden the discussion by reflecting on their experiences while on the March of Living (an educational travel program to Holocaust sites in Europe), talking about their interactions with Polish locals. The teacher takes what might have been a diversion in her stride, responding to their reflections with intensity and seriousness. She moves the discussion beyond what might have remained an exchange of anecdotes by asking students to imagine how Poles perceive heritage travel to Poland and how Poland is presented to such visitors. Her point is clear: we must try to understand the Polish perspective.

The students are then given about twenty minutes to read through the text, which she warns them is "kind of graphic." Either working in pairs or working by themselves, the students must answer the following questions:

> What factors went into local anger against the Jews?
> To what extent did the understanding of Judaism and Communism impact Polish action?
> Who was really responsible? (Poles? Germans?)
> Why has this event created such a furor in Polish society?

With about fifteen minutes of the class remaining, the teacher solicits responses to the first question, recording the contributions on the board while students take notes on their laptops or on the handout. Not everyone is keeping up, and a few seem to have drifted off. The board is soon full of student responses organized to reflect a nested set of explanations from the macro to the micro. The teacher introduces the concept of redemptive nationalism as an idea that captures some of the students' suggestions. She then surprises the class by jumping to the third question, "Who was really responsible?" It's a move that pulls in those who had previously drifted off. In fact, the class catches fire. It quickly turns into one of those moments when the teacher can take a step back and let the students run with the topic as they take turns to debate the issue, all with great seriousness. For about five minutes, she does not need to offer her own comments while the students go back and forth.

With the clock ticking down, the teacher jumps back in. She comments on how meaningful it is to hear students express so many different viewpoints. She then reminds the class of their homework. Finally, before the classes finishes, she hands back a set of test papers. It's noticeable that the papers are all face-down. That way, the grade remains confidential if the student so wishes.

A few features stand out in this class. At no point did the teacher have to call students to attention or discipline the proceedings in any way. One might suggest that students were self-regulating because of the compelling nature of the content. At the same time, the teacher paced the lesson with great skill. She enabled students to share their own personal experiences and offered some of her own, while at the same time she worked hard to coach students to engage with the challenging material before them. There was room for personal responses and even passion, but ultimately she was urging the students to think and act dispassionately.

Of course, it's tempting to resist the conclusion that the class is indicative of students' experience in Judaic studies in general. The form and content of this lesson could just as easily have been classified as general studies. In some schools, study of the Holocaust might not even be the responsibility of the Jewish studies department. Jewish history, let alone Holocaust studies, might be an outlier in this respect. To address this argument, we'll need to look at a radically different example from the Jewish studies program.

Exceptional Circumstances

It's first period on Friday morning and also sports jersey day. The great majority of the twenty-one students in this ninth-grade Talmud class are wearing the uniform of one Toronto sports franchise or another. The teacher is not. A member of the school's senior administrative team, he cuts a more rabbinic figure and wears a large, crocheted kippa.

The sports jerseys are just one indicator that this scene is far removed from the conventional yeshiva day school Talmud class, the school setting where Talmud is most often taught in North America. There are many more indicators: The class is coed, a reality hardly requiring comment at CHAT that already distinguishes this setting from most other day school Talmud classes. At the start of the class, a number of boys are not wearing kippot, a circumstance suggesting that a good proportion of those present don't identify themselves as religiously Orthodox. The class is being conducted almost entirely in Hebrew by the teacher, an Israeli, and all of the students. Finally, no one has a volume of Talmud in front of them. The students are working from sheets in their folders or from their laptops. All of the material is saved on EDSBY.

The content comes from the second chapter of Tractate Bava Kama, concerned specifically with questions about the scale of compensation people have to pay if their animal does damage to someone else's property. The teacher starts by leading the students through a review of some of the concepts they've employed so far, concepts he reminds them they'll need to explain on their next test: *tashlumei nezek* (fines for damage), *tashlumei hanaah* (fines when the animal derived some benefit), *and achila al yedei hadechak* (eating out of necessity).

It's clear very quickly that the teacher's approach is less about covering the text line by line and much more about getting the students to be comfortable with and to work with Talmudic legal concepts. With the review complete, he introduces a new concept, *okimta*, an approach to dismissing part of a case because it rests on exceptional circumstances. He introduces a series of cases, in one instance smiling while pulling a furry animal from his desk to demonstrate what he means. He asks the class to explain in conceptual terms what makes these cases exceptional.

Although this interaction requires constant back and forth between teacher and students, it's striking that most students take part in the intellectual jousting, stretching to make sense of what are essentially bizarre cases: a deer that eats meat, a person who takes a wild animal for a walk. (The last scenario prompts an interlude in which a student checks on Google how many tigers are left in the world. After all, how often might people be walking about with tigers?) The students seem to enjoy the surrealism of it all.

One of the students who had been quiet until that point then probes the teacher: "What if an ox goes down a path that it had never been down before? Does that count as exceptional?" The teacher asks the student to repeat the question while inserting the term *okimta*. He then bounces the question back to the class, prompting one of the students to ask the teacher to define the concept again before they take turns responding to the teacher's question.

When it seems that the students have grasped the concept, the teacher asks them what they think of the following true-life scenario from the news, not from the Talmud itself. He tells them—in Hebrew still—about a cyclist who was determined to check the breaking capacity of a driverless car and in doing so harmed himself badly. He continues: "You're all intelligent people in this class. Are the makers of the car culpable? What are the concepts that help us here? Remember, you're bound by legal language."

The students have about five minutes to discuss with one another what they think. They start to report back their ideas, but they run out of time before going too far. (In the winter, Friday classes are about ten minutes shorter than regular classes.) Amid the noise of packing up, the teacher urges everyone to make sure to bring back their notes at the start of the next week. He wishes them Shabbat shalom as they pack up and head out in good spirits. He chats with one or two of them in Hebrew as they head out the door.

It's difficult to explain what happened here and how a class focused on such esoteric material and conducted almost entirely in Hebrew could have elicited so much student engagement. No doubt as one of the school's senior administrators, the teacher carries a certain amount of authority, which helps in holding the students' attention. The students also seem to appreciate his wry sense of humor and genuine interest in their ideas; they enjoy the spirit in which the class is conducted. It's possible, too, by gathering together some of the most capable students, academic-level Talmud stimulates a kind of self-affirming elitism among the students: they sense that not everyone can do this. The teacher's approach helps fuel this notion. And perhaps most profound, it is probable that these students respond positively to being stimulated by having to think hard and creatively. The way to their hearts, to their feeling good about Jewish learning and Jewish experience, is through their heads. They get a kick from the intellectual experience, and experience the class as a feel-good Jewish happening.

These two classes help both convey and uncover the heart of the CHAT experience. It's serious, it's often tough, and in being so, it can be deeply rewarding, interesting, often fun, and Jewishly meaningful. This type of class, of course, doesn't work for everyone, especially if they don't feel fully acknowledged for who they are. But it's remarkable how many are willing to buy in, figuratively and literally.

The Tuition Revolution

The concept of buy-in provides an opportunity to recount one of the most dramatic episodes in recent history at CHAT: how the school and the local Jewish Federation responded to what many were calling an affordability crisis at the school: a diminishing number of families were buying in to what CHAT was offering.

For a period of about ten years, the school was trapped in a problematic spiral, exacerbated by a steady shrinking in the size of the classes graduating from feeder schools in Toronto's northern suburbs. Each year, to ensure that costs were covered, tuition was raised. Between 1999 and 2016, tuition rose from $10,900 to $27,300. Over the second half of this period, with each increase, enrollment declined further, especially at the school's northern campus. Though that campus was built to accommodate some seven hundred students, there were fewer than half that number by 2017. In this situation, it was no longer possible to offer the same program to students at the school's two sites; the small numbers in the north limited the range of choices CHAT could offer. At Federation, there was a further concern: with each hike in tuition, the school's identity as a community school was being jeopardized. CHAT was fast becoming a selective institution for the shrinking minority who could pay. It was estimated that about only a quarter of the students were receiving some form of relief. The remainder were paying full tuition.

Federation took the initiative and engaged in a market research study to understand why people were staying away and at what price point they would come back. The study concluded that a 25 percent reduction in tuition would yield the most dramatic change in demand. Working quickly, benefiting from years of carefully cultivated relationships and now with the data to support what had long been a hunch, senior Federation leaders were able to recruit two major donors with a deep commitment to day school education. They made a joint gift of some $14 million, a gift that would make it possible to reduce tuition from more than $27,000 to $18,500 beginning in the 2017–18 school year and then keep it below $19,000 for each of the next five years.

For the school, this proposal presented a dilemma. Of course, the opportunity to slash tuition and potentially increase enrollment was compelling. But how was a school to function with an almost complete freeze on what it could charge? Any projected budget shortfall would need to be covered either by cuts to expenditure or more aggressive fundraising, something that had not been part of the school's culture over the years. There was also the question of what would happen after five years when the gift ran out. Wouldn't the school then have to increase tuition dramatically?

Not everyone in the school community wanted to be bound by such a straitjacket no matter how gilt-edged. Others saw the gift as an opportunity to soften a difficult decision to close the northern campus, which had been looking increasingly inevitable. The only way to make the revenue model work was to consolidate both campuses on one site, which would enable significant cuts to administrative overhead, a key step in maximizing the benefits of the gift.

For Federation, closing the northern branch would be a blow. It would be perceived as abandoning the tens of thousands of young families who lived nearby and send the message that opening the branch up north was an act of overreach. In more prosaic terms, CHAT, as the Federation's lessee on the campus, would now need to find a sublet for the space.

Although there were painful dimensions to this scenario for both school and Federation, all parties were prepared to follow through. The campus closure and the dramatic cut in tuition were announced at the same time. Made public in March 2017 and designed to take effect in September, the cuts came too late in the year to make a significant dent in enrollment numbers that fall; the numbers continued to decline. The following year, however, the change in enrollment was dramatic. Entry into grade 9 in September 2018 rose 50 percent. In addition, there were unusually high levels of lateral transfers into the higher grades. The school enrollment grew for the first time in ten years and was projected to rise again the next year, bringing the numbers back above one thousand students for the first time in four years. There is also a real possibility that any tuition rise when the gift expires will be significantly moderated thanks to the income generated by the better-than-expected increase in student numbers.

The mood at the school changed for the better. There even was talk of creating a waiting list for admission to grade 9. Fundraising for the school also seemed to be receiving a boost. Its focus was on program and facility improvement and not on subsidizing tuition.

In financial terms, these events do not mean that the school is fully out of the woods. Enrollment is related to more than affordability; it is also dependent on the overall demographic situation in Toronto and especially on how many students are rising through the Jewish elementary schools that feed into CHAT. It's already evident that enrollment in these schools is substantially down in grades 1 through 3, a trend that will start to hit CHAT just when the tuition reduction initiative is scheduled to end. The school's leadership must spend the coming years planning for that time, along with upheavals in day school demographics. Increasing retention from grade 8 to grade 9 also is on the agenda. Since the introduction of the tuition incentive, retention has climbed and is set to exceed 78 percent, a high point since the year 2000. The school must explore too whether it can increase the flow of new stream students coming from outside day schools. This too may compensate for the decline in numbers coming out of the Jewish middle school system.

Leading from Within

At this moment, when CHAT has emerged from an unusually stressful period and is looking toward a challenging future but from a position of relative strength, the current head of school is especially well suited to addressing the school's most pressing needs. Jonathan Levy was appointed in December 2016 when the most painful elements of the previous period were climaxing. His predecessor, who stayed in position until August 2017 (when he fulfilled a long-time plan to emigrate to Israel), had the misfortune over his four-year tenure to preside over one of the most traumatic periods in the school's history. Through no fault of his own, he was associated with that trauma. He had to lead a process that involved letting go of many staff whose services were no longer needed. Levy, by contrast, had the good fortune to take up his position when the most painful decisions had been implemented.

Levy's appointment wasn't only about good fortune. He took up his position at a moment when school morale was in need of healing and it was critically important to merge what had become two distinct cultures on the two campuses. He was the right person in the right place at the right time. Prior to taking up the position as head, he had served for two years as principal at the southern campus and before that for six years as principal of the northern campus. He was intimately familiar with the culture at both campuses and had worked closely with staff from both. He had been a member of both communities.

Levy's prior experience also proved useful. Initially, he worked for nine years as a guidance counselor in Montreal day schools, with a graduate degree in social work. Having specialized in youth protection, he knew well how to engage people in the most difficult conversations. At a moment when the first task was to help people adapt to change, in a context complicated by being a unionized workplace (as are all Toronto day schools), his interpersonal skills and professional expertise have been at a premium. Bringing the faculty together as one united team has required extensive facilitation and support. Ensuring consistency across classroom practice among a newly integrated faculty is still a work in progress, especially since teachers are sensitive when they perceive that their department heads are overstepping their supervisory responsibilities. At the best of times, these are delicate matters. In the context of reintegrating and realigning faculty who may not have previously worked with one another, the task is all the more challenging and urgent.

If one can talk about leading from behind or leading from the front, then Levy exhibits the capacity of leading from within. In interactions with members of his senior team, he does not dominate the conversation. Not long ago, he was their peer rather than supervisor. In team conversations, he acts as an equal participant while ensuring that all keep their eyes on the horizon —on where they want to go and what, if any, sacrifices will be necessary to achieve goals. He is especially skilled at framing and focusing the discussion, ensuring that actionable decisions are reached. Reflecting his background, he frequently advocates for the students. He does not believe in coddling them, but he's also aware of the limits on what it's possible to ask of them. "The suitcase is full," he likes to say. "If you're going to add anything to it, something has to come out."

There's more to Levy's headship than his ability to deploy his skills as a social worker. A day school graduate himself, proficient in Hebrew, he is the child of two highly regarded Jewish educators. With a PhD in social welfare, he models the best of Canadian Jewish day school education: Jewish literacy, communal responsibility, and educational achievement. Having a passion for Canadian sports helps too. He feels a deep responsibility to maintaining the school's serious commitment to Jewish studies, appreciating the ways in which such an education made him who he is. In his own words, education provides the school's raison d'être. He deeply appreciates the needs of individual students even while that appreciation is leavened by a commitment to ensuring that students receive the most serious possible Jewish education in a community day school context.

In a school of CHAT's size, Levy has limited direct contact with students, something that seems a bit painful for someone who started out in youth work and used to coach teen sports. It's a situation he tries to address by heading out into the corridors to mix with students at the start of the day and during recess. That's his way of staying in touch and engaging in day-to-day concerns with individual students.

Levy brings a more low-key style of leadership to the school than did his predecessors. The parents sense that he is one of them, something that is literally true: his own children are in the school. At a time when the school has recommitted to its community mission and continues to focus on maintaining the highest standards in Jewish and general studies, Levy personifies the integration of these different strands in the school's identity.

Community. Hebrew. Academy.

The best way to complete a picture of what distinguishes the CHAT experience is to turn again to the voices of students. In a focus group with eleventh and twelfth graders, the students were asked what stands out for them as a most memorable experience during their time at CHAT. The responses to this question help reaffirm the prominent themes of this study.

"Grandparents Day—Standing in the gym with 1,000 grandparents, joining for the Hatikvah, and seeing what it meant to them."

"Grade 12's last day of school, involving a carnival with blow-up castles. The feeling of being stress free. Realizing that this is a school where we work hard and play hard."

"Serving as a guide for public school students coming to a traveling exhibit from Anne Frank's House, hosted here at CHAT. Seeing that I had the knowledge to represent the Jewish community to non-Jewish people."

"The school's annual club fair for the last three years and being bombarded every time by the school spirit."

"Havdalah at a school Shabbaton, with everyone linking arms and feeling that we're one big family."

This range of responses well captures the aspects of school life we have highlighted. First, students note the significance of extracurricular experiences such as the carnival and the club fair in the context of an intensive academic environment, for their mental health benefits and their cultivation of values that extend beyond academic success. Second, they find satisfaction in learning and in becoming expert in particular areas of learning, especially—as in the Anne Frank's House example—when that learning results in being empowered to lead others. Third, they note how powerful school experiences are when embedded within a community larger than the individual student and her or his immediate social group, whether within a multigenerational community as at Grandparents Day or as part of a multifaceted community as highlighted by the Havdalah experience.

These memories come from the melding of an academy and community experience in a rich, highly literate Jewish milieu. What these young people reflect is that at TanenbaumCHAT, they have found meaning as members of a values-based community, discovering their passions and the pleasure in serious study, and then graduating from high school with an understanding of how significant their Jewishness is in their lives.

CONNECTIONS AND EXCEPTIONS

TanenbaumCHAT is an unusual school; some would say it's unique. For a community day school with a denominationally diverse student body, the intensity of the school's Judaics program is certainly rare. Its inclusion of students with diverse learning abilities while maintaining high academic standards squares a circle that has long challenged other schools with similar commitments to a community ethos alongside academic excellence. These features highlight the degree to which schools are shaped by local community culture and their institutional histories. Powerful norms created over the years are hard to shift. They create an environment that supports this endeavor.

The contrast with the Hebrew Academy in Miami (chapter 8) is instructive.

The academy attracts less diverse families than CHAT in religious terms and finds it hard to balance its commitment to inclusion with maintaining elite academic standards. Its leadership is working hard to shift these things, but in many respects, their efforts go against the grain of a local Jewish culture with different priorities. TanenbaumCHAT is a significant player in the local communal ecosystem; its alumni take up leadership positions across the community, and from these places of influence—at the Federation, in synagogues, and in local elementary schools—they help maintain a broad commitment to the school's values and norms. CHAT is also fortunate in being able to recruit from a deep pool of mission-aligned faculty who are readily attracted to Toronto, a city with a high quality of Jewish life. These circumstances have enabled the school to deliver on its commitments. The closest analog amid our sample of schools is Hillel Day School of Detroit (chapter 2), which has similarly served as a strong link in the chain of Jewish communal continuity, but because Hillel runs only to eighth grade, its contribution to community life has been less readily appreciated compared to CHAT. That said, the two schools have been recipients of sizable philanthropic gifts from benefactors who have sought to ensure that these two communal institutions can continue to admit students regardless of financial need.

CHAT's embeddedness in a broader societal context is also evident in relation to some of the most acute challenges the school faces. In this respect, the school is no different from other high schools, and especially those that are not part of a kindergarten to twelfth-grade institution. On the one hand, these schools find themselves at the end of the day school food chain; what they can accomplish with their ninth-grade students is heavily dependent on what skills students bring with them from feeder schools. And in this respect, it's rare to find a high school whose educators don't complain of a decline in standards in middle schools. On the other hand, they must respond to the intensifying social and academic pressures that plague all high schools. Every high school faces its own form of these pressures; in some, it might be drugs, alcohol, or technology abuse, and in others it might be pressure to go "of the derech," that is, defy Jewish religious norms. As we have seen, a particular expression of these pressures at CHAT is the challenge to manage the intense stress that comes from competition to gain entry to elite colleges. It is much harder, it seems, to protect high school students from these kinds of pressures than it is to shield elementary-age students.

III

K–12 Schools

8

How a Day School Transforms Itself

Hebrew Academy (RASG), Miami Beach, Florida

The Hebrew Academy in Miami Beach is a K–12 school in transition. Situated in a changing geographic environment where the cost of housing for student families and teachers has become prohibitive and the Jewish population has become highly diverse in both religious outlook and Jewish subethnic origin, the Hebrew Academy balances its long-standing commitment to Modern Orthodoxy with steps to attract a more religiously diverse student body. The school has also been transitioning in its pedagogic style. Once regarded as academically lax, the academy has tightened requirements and upgraded its curricula. It has invested in a chief innovation officer who has brought new general and Jewish studies curricula to the school, promoted project-based learning, and enrolled the school as a pilot for several Israel-based online learning programs in Jewish studies. Precisely because this process of upgrading has evolved over more than a decade and under different school heads, its path has zigzagged, even as it has continued to move each of its divisions successively toward curricular and pedagogic improvements. Not every school can reform itself on straight line. The Hebrew Academy may well reflect the experience of many other day schools moving gradually but surely as they up their game.

A fifth-grade, coed class at the Hebrew Academy (RASG)[1] in Miami Beach is being initiated into studying Mishna, the codification of rabbinic religious debates and rulings constituting the foundation of the Talmud. Seated around tables accommodating four children each, the twenty students are learning about rules pertaining to the Passover Seder—in this case, the four cups of wine imbibed at that ritual meal. At first glance, there is nothing particularly unusual about the class. In a Modern Orthodox day school such as the Hebrew Academy, students generally begin to study this foundational rabbinic text in grade 5 or 6.

Upon closer inspection, novel features surface. First, students are not studying from a book; rather, each student holds a Chrome Book device because both the texts and accompanying exercises are online. The focus of the class, moreover, is not solely on the meaning of the text but also on its construction: students learn from the outset about the structure of a Mishna and key words tipping off the reader to the logic of the argument. From their first exposure to Mishna, students are taught about how they themselves can make sense of the flow of a Mishna by looking for signposts and information-packed language. The program takes the Mishna apart in order to explain its components. This is a level of sophistication about learning how to learn Mishna not usually present in beginners' classes.

Equally noteworthy, the entire class is conducted as an exercise in blended learning. The teacher leads students actively through the online program, which is also projected onto an interactive whiteboard at the front of the classroom. He prods them to answer questions orally, including the connections of the current material to what they studied previously; explains the concepts and why learning about the structure of the text is so important; and asks about the implications of the text for what they will be doing at their home Seder.

The program he uses is a digital platform with color-coded charts breaking down the text into its components. To keep students engaged, the platform includes videos requiring students to rearrange the text, respond to questions, and take sides in rabbinic debates. It also tests students on the material and thereby provides the teacher with immediate feedback on how well his charges have grasped the material. He has the opportunity to revisit material when the program indicates what students haven't quite mastered.

All the while, the teacher actively paces around the room, and an assistant responds to queries from students. This is a class demanding a great deal of interactivity—with the teachers, the online program, and fellow students seated at the same table. Students are engaged. No one is tuned out. For homework, students will have to use Google Voice to read the text, a further way for the teacher to ensure that everyone has mastered the Hebrew text of the Mishna.

The class provides a graphic example of how blended learning is making its way into Jewish studies in day schools. That it has been adopted in general studies classes is nothing novel: many good programs already exist in the broader American marketplace. But Jewish studies have lagged, not least because the market for them is relatively small and production costs for digital learning platforms are high. In this case, the program, Mishnayot Behirot (roughly translated as Mishna Study Made Clear), is one of several new programs developed in Israel for day schools abroad. Not only is the Hebrew

Academy an avid consumer of such programs, in the case of the Mishna program, it is the first North American day school piloting the new online curriculum. The teacher has undergone advanced training in how to use the program and provides feedback to the producer of Mishnayot Behirot about shortcoming or unclear aspects of the program.

That the Hebrew Academy in Miami Beach is ahead of the curve with this program—and more generally has adopted several different types of innovative educational approaches in both its general and Jewish studies classes—speaks to the dramatic transformation of this school over the past dozen or so years. The Mishna class, however, represents something more dramatic: it is part of a radical reorientation, somewhat akin to an ocean liner reversing and altering course in mid-sea.

Facing Up to Challenges

That the Hebrew Academy has undergone significant changes in recent years should hardly come as a surprise. As documented in the previous chapters of this book, Jewish day schools have reformed how they approach pedagogy, understand learner needs, and address the social and emotional lives of their students. The Hebrew Academy is no different in its adaptation to the new educational environment. But in the case of this school, change has been driven not only by new ways of thinking about schooling but also by the need to address the poor reputation it had earned as an unserious place of study. The school contended with eroding enrollments, particularly in the transition from the middle to the upper school. Demographic changes added still another variable to the mix.

By the 1990s, the Hebrew Academy was regarded in the wider Jewish community as lacking in academic standards and poorly run. A long-time teacher described the prior reputation of the Hebrew Academy as very "homey" and also "Mickey Mouse." "Nothing was professional; it was about warm feelings: we just want you to get a Jewish education. Colloquially, it was called Camp Hebrew Academy. Classes were canceled at the drop of a hat. Academics were not valued. Giving kids a hug was the priority."

That judgment may be a bit harsh, but it was repeated in different ways by other long-serving teachers and administrators. Several spoke about the late twentieth century as a time when many families showed little respect for school guidelines. Parents scheduled family vacations as they pleased and pulled their children out of school as they saw fit. Student attendance was treated as a highly flexible matter. This also was a time when parents would demand to see teachers during lunchtime to complain about some issue affecting their children. From all accounts, it was a chaotic time in the school.

Not surprisingly, the Hebrew Academy has found it difficult to persuade some alumni to enroll their children in the school. Some retained memories of how weak and disorganized the school had been when they were students and, not surprisingly, have opted to send their children elsewhere. As parents, these alumni were looking for a well-run, academically serious place for their children.[2]

To make matters even more difficult, demographic realities complicated the school's recruitment efforts. The costs of living in Miami Beach had skyrocketed and Modern Orthodox families were moving to northern Dade County—to Aventura and North Miami—and even farther to Broward County, especially Hollywood, because housing prices there were more reasonable. Orthodox day schools in those areas had the advantage of being located close to where students live, thereby obviating the need for students to make the long commute to Miami Beach, a trip that could take anywhere from a half-hour to an hour depending on traffic conditions.

As for those Jews who did live in Miami Beach, immigrants from Latin America, Israel, and the former Soviet Union were settling in the area. Their levels of Jewish observance were more flexible, if not lax. At the same time, parents of all backgrounds were looking for a school offering a rigorous academic program and sophisticated pedagogy.

These circumstances have pushed the school over the past dozen or so years to clarify how it intends to compete in this challenging environment. It has forced the Hebrew Academy to define its identity explicitly, address its former inadequacies forthrightly, and rebuild its reputation. Gradually it has taken important steps to address its challenges. Its educational leaders forthrightly acknowledge they still have a way to go, but much has improved in the school. This chapter is about the steps taken by a school to remake itself, a work in progress, to be sure, but one that shows signs of major achievement already.

Addressing a Diverse Population

To appreciate how extensively the school has remade itself, a bit of history is in order. Founded in 1947, the Alexander S. Gross Hebrew Academy is the oldest Jewish day school in Florida. Since its establishment, the Hebrew

Academy has defined itself as an Orthodox day school. But what kind of Orthodox school does it aim to be?

For much of its history, the school had staffed its Jewish studies program with teachers more in line with a so-called Yeshivish perspective: the men tended to be graduates of leading Haredi (ultra-Orthodox) yeshivas and the women were products of seminaries connected to the leading yeshivas of higher learning. The school also worked to recruit students into its high school program who had attended Bais Yaakov day schools for girls, as an example, thereby displaying its preference for a student body that tilted to the "right" end of Orthodoxy. As part of this package, the school followed the non-Zionist orientation of the Yeshivish world, and, according to more than one alumnus, placed no emphasis on building students' connections to the state of Israel.

With the arrival in 2007 of a new school head, Hebrew Academy shifted significantly.[3] It signaled its identification with Zionism and the state of Israel unequivocally though its curricular emphases and student trips to the Jewish state. The academy also enrolled students in its middle and high school divisions who previously had attended public school or non-Orthodox day schools. To bring these students up to speed, it intensified a *mechina* (preparatory) program in Jewish studies. Moreover, as time went on, the Hebrew Academy in practice, though not in official ideology, functioned more as a community school by admitting students whose background was not "mission appropriate" for an Orthodox school—they came from families that were non-observant Orthodox or secular. In the words of a board member, "We want the diversity. We're open. We're a big melting pot. Some families are very religious, some are Modern Orthodox, and some are not religious."

This approach, in fact, is common in many Modern Orthodox day schools situated in communities lacking a critical mass of similar-minded families committed to supporting the school. In contrast to the major centers of Modern Orthodoxy, such as the Five Towns on Long Island; parts of Manhattan; Teaneck, New Jersey; sections of Los Angeles; and Toronto, among other tightly knit communities, Modern Orthodox day schools in other places don't have the luxury of enrolling only students from a homogeneously Modern Orthodox pool of families. As one observer put it, the Hebrew Academy in this sense is "a typical modern Orthodox school out of town."

By casting a wider net, schools like the Hebrew Academy admit students whose home practices and religious commitments vary widely. According to the estimate of one administrator, 15 percent of families sending their children to the school are not observant of most Jewish religious rituals; in high school, which admits a particularly diverse student body, one-third of the students come from homes where the stricter rules of Kashrut (dietary laws) are not observed. Whether these estimates are precisely accurate is less important than the awareness shared by numerous interviewees that synagogue attendance, daily prayer, and the observance of dietary and Jewish ritual laws vary greatly among the families of students. As a consequence, the school is able to attract families on the less observant end of the spectrum because they know their children will not be the only outliers, while simultaneously some parents on the more observant end have opted to remove their children from the school in order to place them in a day school with a more homogeneous, observant population.

Why did the Hebrew Academy choose to broaden its appeal to a wider range of families? As noted, the Jewish population living in the vicinity of the school had undergone a significant transformation. Numerous personnel in the school note how the Orthodox Judaism of most parents takes a "relaxed approach." Modern Orthodoxy, noted one interviewee in the school, "is about *not* being Haredi; not about being ritually observant. Few could define a Modern Orthodox ideology. The Latin Americans are not familiar with that lexicon."

This outlook translated into behavior too. Levels of religious observance and sensibility range considerably. Even among the Modern Orthodox, text study is not valued across the board. Accordingly, as one administrator put it, "when the school started teaching Talmud to girls . . . it caused no controversy [among parents, only among the then ultra-Orthodox faculty]. When the Mishna program was changed, there was minimal reaction. And when there were substantial changes to the Navi [the books of the Prophets] program, including eliminating it for a period of time, [it caused no ripples]. . . . The pushback [from parents] is not around the content (the substance or details of the program), it's around the quality of the experience." In short, the kind of Orthodoxy practiced by most local families differs from what is more common in the larger Modern Orthodox enclaves where ideological debates rage over the roles of women in the Jewish religious space or over the advisability of adopting some of the cultural sensibilities of the wider society. These are nonissues in the school community of the Hebrew Academy.

At the same time, the school's immediate neighborhood is home to a large population of Orthodox Jews who adhere to a Yeshivish outlook. They have their own constellation of yeshivas and would not send their children to the

Hebrew Academy.[4] The ideal students favored by the school during the twentieth century are now few and far between—or not interested in the Hebrew Academy.

The school also has been reaching diverse subethnic Jewish communities scattered throughout Dade and Broward counties. According to one count, the school's roughly six hundred students include children of immigrant families from eighteen separate countries. many more families today are from Latin America, the former Soviet Union, Israel, Morocco, and France. This diversity has enriched the school but also has burdened it with the task of socializing students into the ethos of the Hebrew Academy. Each of these populations has a somewhat different understanding of what it means to be an Orthodox Jew or is more interested in how well the school can develop the Hebrew-language skills of students and inspire them to identify with the Jewish people, and especially Israel.

It therefore made sense for the school to prioritize its Modern Orthodox approach and Zionist allegiance. This has enabled it to carve out a distinctive identity among other schools in the area. More important, these commitments comport with the outlook and values of families the school attracts. They help the school distinguish itself from Haredi ones and signal an openness to families that maintain strong bonds to Israel and Jewish peoplehood though not necessarily ritual observance.

In line with its ideal of creating what one board member described as "a kind of melting pot," the school refuses to cluster students by levels of family observance, as some parents have demanded. Despite the requests of some mothers, for example, who asked that their children to be placed in the same class with other students whose mothers only wear skirts and not pants in accordance with more Centrist Orthodox practices, the school is committed to ensuring that religiosity is never an issue in class composition. In this sense too, the Hebrew Academy functions more like a community school rather than as an institution solely for a specific type of Orthodox family. In short, the school has adapted to altered demographic realities.

The Enhanced Academic Emphasis

In addition to the Hebrew Academy's ideological reorientation, the educational administration, with the strong support of the board, has issued a clear message that the school takes academics seriously and is committed to offering a Jewish and general studies education superior to that of its competitor schools. A board member identified what is at stake succinctly: "We have to offer the best education to survive in a competitive market."

This is seen as the key to the future vitality of the Hebrew Academy and a response to one of its pressing challenges: enrollment. For a period of time, the student body shed 15 percent of its student body annually. Over a decade ago, the school hired a full-time admissions director to bolster enrollment. She brought in a consultant who determined the primary problem was not recruitment of new students but retention of those already in the school. The biggest losses occurred in the transition from middle school to high school. To address attrition, the school invested in a stronger STEM program and introduced robotics in order to upgrade its scientific and technological offerings. Other steps the school took included training teachers and staff in what they called "school-family care"—better communication with parents and generally spreading news about positive developments. A second initiative has focused on building stronger ties with synagogues, including collaboration on some programming; the school also has hired a marketing director to publicize its value to the broader Jewish community, as well as the parent body, and as part of that effort, it has created a robust Web platform to communicate with families considering the school. In addition, a board committee is working on plans to help families facing affordability challenges.

Most important, the school has worked to substitute a rigorous academic approach in place of the widely perceived loose style of the past. Symptomatic of the concerted effort to remake its programs and image, the school hired a full-time dean of academics and innovation. equivalent to an associate head of school. Rabbi Avi Bossewitch sees himself as "being the leader of research and development." He has been the catalyst for leading the adoption of over thirty programs from nursery to twelfth grade and developing a culture of innovation among the staff. Such a position is not usually funded in day schools, which therefore says quite a bit about the outlook of the board that it has budgeted for such a full-time position.

Working with principals and assistant principals in each of the four divisions of the Hebrew Academy, Rabbi Bossewitch has played a major role in moving the school toward greater cohesion, the adoption of new educational technologies and progressive educational models, and a more rigorous approach to student learning outcomes. In the first area, he has worked to build continuity for students as they progress from the early childhood center to lower, then middle, and finally upper school. He also has pressed the staff to evaluate student outcomes rigorously, made more feasible by some of the online platforms.

Working with the faculty, Rabbi Bossewitch has advanced five key academic areas across the entire school: Light of Torah and Israel; Character and Middot (proper Jewish character traits); Blended and Personalized Learning; Innovators, Leaders & Entrepreneurs; and STEAM (science, technology, engineering, the arts, and mathematics). Bossewitch educates himself about new curricula in the general studies and Jewish studies markets by attending educational seminars and workshops for school administrators. He has brought at least a half dozen new curricula into the Jewish studies program, such as the Mishna digital platform. Other new curricula focus on STEM, social and emotional learning, and Israel education. All are part of an effort to steer the school in a new direction and tighten what had previously been a loose educational enterprise.

Upgrading General Studies

This direction is evident in both general and Jewish studies. Administrators and teachers speak about the shift in approach to learning. In line with progressive education today, the sage on the stage model of teaching is being phased out. Beginning in the lower school and then progressing upward, classes are far more interactive than in the past. Teachers have been urged by their supervisors to "to let the reins loosen a bit." This means allowing classes to evolve and not structure lessons tightly. General studies teachers have become far more adept at being facilitators of learning. The goal is to create an environment attentive to student learning needs and styles.

Personalized and blended learning have been introduced throughout the school. This effort and others have been facilitated by the local Central Agency for the Advancement of Jewish Education (CAJE), which runs workshops for Jewish day school teachers in Dade County. The Hebrew Academy sent its teachers to learn methods of introducing personalized and blended learning. (While we visited the school, a large group of teachers were attending a three-day workshop on blended learning sponsored by the CAJE in partnership with the AVI CHAI Foundation.) In addition to personalized and blended learning, the school has also expanded the integration of PBL: project-based learning. For example, in the lower school, PBL was implemented initially through a new unit devoted to sustainability and urbanization. Middle school faculty won local and national recognition for some of the interdisciplinary units.

Hebrew Academy, Miami Beach | 213

To provide a Jewish perspective on some of the issues raised, one of the Jewish studies teachers brought Jewish texts to bear on the subject matter. The purpose, of course, was to integrate Judaic perspectives into the general studies work of students.

A further innovation came with the introduction of a "mini-mester" the week after the winter vacation, which at the Hebrew Academy, as at many Orthodox day schools, falls in the second half of January. Teachers are encouraged to develop subject matter they normally never get to teach by creating their own courses around topics they find particularly compelling, and students are free to choose from these courses. One mini-mester option was a course on medicine in which students visited hospitals and doctors' offices. Another was a class on ethical issues, particularly in the area of medical ethics. And in yet another course, a Hebrew teacher taught about human biology with the goal of having students learn the Hebrew names of body parts. Another focused on ritual laws regarding which animals are permissible according to Jewish law and which are not. Others were about health and fitness, art in Miami, photographing architecture, or the design of buildings students could then display for their parents. All of these efforts were based at least in part on PBL. Some took students out of the school to expose them to professional offices or corporate headquarters. Teachers have been impressed with the maturity that students who went on those trips displayed.

The middle school of the Hebrew Academy has been the quickest to adopt blended learning and PBL. Much depends on the receptivity of teachers to embracing new teaching modes, and for the most part, personnel in the middle school responded with great openness. The embrace of technology was on display in a middle school literature class. Eighteen students were seated around tables of between three and six students. Posters in the classroom explained how different genres of writing are composed most effectively.

In this class session, the teacher prepared students to write a public service announcement. The teacher used an interactive whiteboard to project powerful, clever images that make public service announcements. She then showed a three-minute public service announcement alerting students to a potential shooter in their midst. It included images of students who seem to be bored in school and then urged their classmates to reach out to individual students who may seem alienated or bored. After screening the video, the teacher asked students to reflect on what made this public service announcement powerful. The class discussed imagery employed in the video and the compelling story it told. Students then were assigned a project to be completed by small groups to prepare their own video of a public service announcement. The rest of the class hour was spent with small groups sketching out a planned video and the teacher circulated as a guide to these small groups.

Symptomatic of the Hebrew Academy's drive to compete academically with other schools, its middle school students have participated in science competitions sponsored by the Cadena Initiative, an international program to spur social entrepreneurship. For three years running, students at the Hebrew Academy won first prize in a competition involving South Florida Jewish day schools. The winners went on to an international competition held in Mexico City.

For a variety of reasons, the high school has lagged in adopting some of the new pedagogical methods but is being pressed by the administration to catch up. Evidence of change was on display in a number of settings. A tenth-grade class in history, for example, was assigned to deliver three- to five-minute TED Talks. The exercise was meant to teach students how to engage in public speaking. Though some parents complained about the assignment and asked for their children to be exempted on the grounds that they can't give such a talk, only a single student was exempted by the school psychologist. Every tenth grader gave a TED Talk, not the usual assignment for high school classes at the Hebrew Academy of yesteryear.

Science classes in the high school have been especially challenging because of the outdated facilities, which the school intends to remedy with the pending construction of a new building. In the meantime, the school improvises. The assistant principal for general studies in the high school reported about her experience at a Prizmah conference where she saw demonstrations of how to do a lab virtually. After the conference, she successfully lobbied the board to approve the acquisition of virtual lab apps or programs.

Cutting across the various divisions of the Hebrew Academy are new initiatives to prepare students at all levels for the challenging job market they probably will encounter as adults. One striking example of such an initiative is the school's adoption of an Israeli curriculum to train future entrepreneurs. Entrepreneurship for Kids (EFK) seeks to encourage children from grades 6 to 12 to acquire the skills and qualities deemed necessary to succeed as entrepreneurs. Though it neither expects nor encourages all students to become entrepreneurs, the program assumes that the skills it teaches will help students do well when they enter the labor force. It particularly seeks to encourage girls to develop those skills. The Hebrew Academy was the first North American Jewish day school to adopt this program.

Shifts in Jewish Studies

As is the case in most Modern Orthodox day schools, the Hebrew Academy divides every school day equally between general and Jewish studies. In the middle school, for example, students take separate classes daily in Chumash (Pentateuch), Navi (the Prophets), Halacha (Jewish law), Mishna, and Hebrew language. In the high school, Navi is replaced by classes in Jewish history, philosophy, and law. Morning and afternoon prayer services are also part of the daily routine.

As also is true in many Orthodox day schools, resistance to change is greater when it comes to Jewish studies than general studies. Some teachers are insistent that the way they were taught is best suited for current students too, and many parents who attended Jewish day schools agree with them. Learning from books, rather than online platforms or workbooks, is deemed superior because that's the way it has been done for hundreds of years. Methodically going chapter by chapter through a particular book of the Chumash (Pentateuch) was good enough for our ancestors, so why not continue that way now? Similarly, working one's way through a tractate of the Talmud, rather than studying texts thematically drawn from multiple tractates, also is the tried-and-true way. Gradually, though, these approaches have given way to new approaches at the school (as they have in other Orthodox day schools included in this book).

Change in Jewish studies also came with the decision to teach girls and boys the same material. The school has long separated the sexes in grades 6 to 12 and devised different Jewish studies curricula for each. In recent years, though, that policy was changed so that girls and boys now study the same material, albeit in separate Jewish studies classes. Initially, when the change came, it took a while for girls to catch up because they hadn't been exposed to Talmud study. Those kinks have been worked out. One of the rabbis who teaches Talmud to both male and female middle schoolers speaks of the high level of interest his female students exhibit. According to several teachers and administrators, the decision to teach Talmud to girls proved uncontroversial to parents but did rile some in the rabbinic teaching corps, prompting a few to quit as part of the broader shift away from Yeshivish Jewish studies teachers.

The equal investment of female and male students in Talmud study was dramatically evident in two high school Talmud classes, both taught by the same teacher. Both classes were conducted using a Socratic method. In the boys' class, virtually all of the dozen students responded to the unending stream of questions the instructor threw at the class. The questions were about the content and structure of the text, its relationship to other material they had studied that year and in previous ones, and the implications for ritual practice.

The parallel girls' class included both eleventh and twelfth graders, presumably because it was for advanced students with a high level of proficiency and engagement. They used a workbook developed at the Shalhevet High School in Los Angeles (the Lahav curriculum), which contains three- to four-page excerpts from a dozen different tractates of the Talmud, including commentaries in Hebrew and English. Students were asked to develop their own theory of underlying principles to explain when custom trumps laws and when it does not. In this class, the emphasis was on students first working out answers with a partner (Hevruta) and then explaining their positions to the rest of the class.

In both classes, the approach was conceptual. Students were asked to discern patterns of thinking on the part of the rabbis. What is the purpose of the rabbis, and what underlying principles are at work? In short, these classes built on the texts to analyze the rabbinic mind.

Both the upper and middle schools have adopted an Israeli-produced curriculum about Jewish law. In the high school, the focus is on ritual laws regarding the observance of the Sabbath, dietary laws, and prayer; in the middle school, the topic is Jewish perspectives regarding interpersonal relationships (ben adam l'chavairo). Workbooks featuring eye-catching graphics, case studies, and color-coded sources aim to stimulate active learning environments. The consensus of the school leadership is that the workbooks have ratcheted up the level of student engagement. Classes feature far more discussion than in the past about how the rabbis went about developing Jewish law and exploration about questions of religious authority. The workbooks also help students think through a theme that they then trace from the Bible to the Talmud and, ultimately, codes of Jewish law. The approach empowers students in new ways because it helps them understand how Jewish rituals and laws evolved and the rabbinic thinking about them.

Hebrew-language study in the school occurs in designated Ivrit classes. In the lower school, Hebrew language is taught four days a week for one period, and then on Fridays, the focus shifts to learning about Israel employing the Hebrew language. By middle school, students are placed in classes in accordance with their levels of proficiency, and all Hebrew classes therefore meet at the same time. Somewhat ironically, though, for all its commitment to Israel and its very name, the school did not offer other Jewish studies classes conducted in the Hebrew language (*ivrit b'ivrit*) except in the designated language slots. That changed recently with the introduction of a pilot program for teaching of Chumash in Hebrew.

The primary reason for this is the difficulty of finding Hebrew-language teachers who live as observant Orthodox Jews, a challenge that many Modern Orthodox and Centrist Orthodox day schools face. As a result, there is a sharp division and relatively little contact between the Hebrew language staff and the Jewish studies teaching corps. The latter are all Orthodox and observant; few Hebrew teachers live their lives that way. The school brought one Israeli couple teaching in the high school to serve as *shlichim* (Israeli teachers who are placed in a school for two to three years) but has found the costs of bringing schlichim is prohibitive, beginning with the cost of the recruitment process, moving a family, offering scholarships to children in such a family, and finding suitable housing for shlichim—and that doesn't begin to cover the time necessary to educate shlichim about the many differences in school cultures in the United States as compared with Israel. Still, there are some Israeli teachers in the school, including in the Jewish studies division, who have emigrated to the United States, and the school seems to be hiring them in increasing numbers. Perhaps their arrival will close the wide gap between the Hebrew and Jewish studies teachers. At present, the Hebrew-language instructors are not seen as part of the Jewish studies department.

Tefila, prayer, is both a twice-daily occurrence in the school and also the subject of some Jewish studies classes. As in so many other Jewish day schools, the time devoted to Tefila is fraught with tension. Teachers work to involve students but often are required to spend most of their time during prayer monitoring and disciplining students. As a middle school teacher put it, echoing what so many of his counterparts at other day schools have said: "*Davening* [the prayer service] is the most difficult part of the day for me. As a teacher, I feel like a policeman. It's a contentious way to start the day." The reason, he explained, is that students tune out. He contrasts how "classes in other subject matters have a clear function and kids understand why they have to take those classes. When it comes to prayer, students just feel that they are compelled to do this and don't necessarily find it meaningful." The biggest problem is that some boys are disengaged and some then go on to talk with each other rather than participate in the prayer. There's a large correlation, he claims, based on what he calls "family reinforcement"—parents who take their children to synagogue versus those who do not; the former children are much more likely to participate in prayer in the school than are the latter.

As this teacher struggles with what is a near-universal problem in those day schools requiring daily prayer attendance by students, he has decided to experiment with new approaches. His plan for the second half of the school year is to use different prayer books and to spend some time during his Jewish law classes talking about what individual prayers mean. He's doing this in the hope that this approach will resonate with students and help them relate more positively to the prayers. On two days of the week, he plans discussions about the meaning of prayers during the time devoted to prayer. Significantly, when it comes to girls' prayer, he intends to frame the discussion around what God means to them, their understanding of God, and how they relate then to God.

Commitment to Israel

Perhaps more than anything else, Israel serves as a glue holding together the increasingly diverse families enrolling their children in the Hebrew Academy. Love and passion for Israel is a common denominator, especially when levels of religious observance differ. Every morning, students sing Israel's national anthem, "Hatikvah," and recite a prayer for Israel's soldiers, the (*mishabeirach* for *chayalim*) to the tune of *eretz shel shoshanim*. Israel, moreover, is ubiquitous in the halls and classrooms of the Hebrew Academy. Even classrooms devoted to general studies are festooned with the Israeli flag and maps of the country. Hanging on the walls are pictures of Israeli leaders, past and present.

Classes on Israel are taught in every division of the school. In the upper school, students learn about the country's history. On a day one of us visited classes, a student reported on the Nakba, the Arab view of what 1948 represented: a catastrophe. The school is well aware of the need to prepare students for anti-Zionist critiques they will encounter eventually at college.

The school educates its staff by connecting faculty via Skype with teachers in Israel and brings some master teachers from Israel to serve as mentors to its staff. And as noted, the Hebrew Academy is an adopter of curricula developed in Israel. These points of contact are identified with pride by the school's administration, often with references to the good company the Hebrew Academy keeps: its connection to Israel is in sync with the most prominent and well-resourced modern Orthodox schools in North America.

The Hebrew Academy also offers class trips to Israel. One is for tenth graders who take a course on the history and culture of Israel during their sophomore year as preparation for their school trip and as a means to debrief after the trip. They then embark on a trip lasting two weeks. High school seniors also may go on a Senior Heritage Trip, first visiting Jewish sites in Europe related to the Holocaust and culminating in Israel. Because the March of the Living involves students from a range of observant and nonobservant backgrounds, some parents are reluctant to send their children on this trip.

The lower school offers a unique Israel experience, Yom Tzahal, a day during the Hebrew month of Heshvan when students learn about the importance of the Israel Defense Forces in Israeli society. In the month after the High Holidays, a day is set aside to learn about the Israel Defense Forces. Students are invited to wear an article of clothing that connects them to the forces. Some wear khaki shirts or pants with the IDF insignia. Time is devoted that day to teaching about the IDF, and an invited speaker from the called Friends of IDF organization addresses students at a large assembly.

As in most other Jewish day schools, Israel Independence Day is a major event on the school calendar. On the eve of the celebration, the school sponsors a commemoration for those who died during Israel's wars and attacks by terrorists. Parents and members of the wider community also attend. That evening, as Israel Independence Day begins, the school organizes a fireworks display over the nearby beach for the entire community.

In the past few years, the celebration continues the next afternoon at Marlins Park, the home of the local major league baseball team. Attended by students from area Jewish day schools and their parents, some four to five thousand people gather to participate in a parade, entertainment, and choir competitions. The event concludes with a barbeque for the assembled celebrants. Israel is a feel-good, uncontested focal point for the Hebrew Academy.

These combined efforts highlight the extent to which building students' connection to Israel is a high priority. It is an area of consensus among parents. Though the Hebrew Academy elevates Zionist identification far more than many other schools, its sincere commitment to nurturing a love of Israel in its students also serves to bind the school together as a community.

Meeting Students' Needs

The Hebrew Academy has instituted an unusual program to address student needs. To begin with what is common to many other schools, the Hebrew Academy has become far more learner-focused in recent years. It helps that class size is limited to between twenty and twenty-four students; high school classes are considerably smaller. Through blended learning and on-line platforms, it has become far more feasible to keep track of each student's progress and address student needs as they arise.

More unusual is a major school undertaking, the Academic Enhancement Program (AEP). The program's coordinator is a speech therapist by training who had worked for a decade at Christian schools. She was recruited by the Hebrew Academy in 2013 to develop a strong support system for students re-quiring special attention. Initially the program functioned with a single per-son offering assistance in general studies and a half-time person for Jewish studies. By 2019, it fielded a team of ten people, including two psychologists, a speech therapist, and teachers.

Serving students from kindergarten through twelfth grade, the AEP sup-ports students requiring special attention in general studies and/or Jewish studies with the major emphasis on math, language arts, and Judaica. (The name Academic Enhancement Program was chosen to avoid attaching a stigma to its work or to the students who require special attention.) Elemen-tary school students may spend up to two hours of the day, up to four days weekly, in this AEP. Middle school and high school students can spend be-tween forty-five and sixty minutes in such a program daily. There's also an English as a Secondary Language enhancement program and, as noted pre-viously, a preparatory (Mechina) program for students entering the Hebrew Academy with insufficient Judaica knowledge and Hebrew-language skills. (An outside firm provides math at a high level for advanced students.)

What sets this program apart from many others in Jewish day schools are the costs parents must bear. Many states provide financial aid to cover the costs of remedial support, but Florida does not. Above and beyond the regular tuition fees, then, parents pay $700 a year for support in one subject, $1,300 for two, and $1,800 for three. English as a Second Language costs $575 per year for special tutoring, and the Mechina preparatory program costs an extra $1,875.

Between 15 and 18 percent of students at the Hebrew Academy are en-rolled in the AEP, a number the school tries to limit because it does not want to be seen as a school primarily for students with learning difficulties. The school counsels some families to remove their children if it cannot remediate their problems, especially when a child interferes with the learning experi-ence of classmates. But the board also is committed to helping students and ensuring that no one falls between the cracks.

The AEP team also does standardized testing and curricular testing to provide the school with feedback about the learning that has taken place. One of the psychologists on staff and invited guest speakers spend time teaching students. The purpose of these interventions is to discuss kindness and character. "The focus is on the whole child," notes the head of the AEP. "We want to have a happy and healthy child too." These efforts are consistent with a broader initiative in Jewish day schools to include social and emotional learning (SEL) as part of a school's offerings.

What sets this program apart from initiatives in SEL in other day schools are the additional costs levied on families. Essentially, the AEP has privatized its services so that families availing themselves of its programs support the effort through fees beyond tuition. That is at once a novel approach to the extra burdens SEL imposes on the budgets of day schools but also drives up costs to parents.

Ongoing Challenges

Even as the Hebrew Academy has worked systematically to remake itself, it has contended with a number of challenges that impede its efforts or place pressure on its finances. One is the difficulty of hiring and retaining teaching staff. Good general studies teachers are in great demand in Florida, so much so that schools offer hiring bonuses and other perks, such as generous pension plans. The Hebrew Academy finds it hard to compete with the packages that local independent schools and public schools offer.

Staffing Jewish studies classes also is a challenge. With the migration of Modern Orthodox Jews to northern Dade County and into Broward, Jewish studies teachers have also settled in those areas, where they may find jobs at three Modern Orthodox day schools closer to home than the Hebrew Academy. Adding to the challenges are the shift of the school away from hiring rabbis with a Haredi outlook. Where formerly the school had staffed its classes with products of the Lakewood yeshiva, its reorientation toward a more Modern Orthodox and committed Zionist perspective meant that these teachers were no longer mission appropriate. But how might the school replace them?

In some cases, the school has hired Yeshivish teachers who are amenable to working in an environment that does not reflect their own Jewish outlook. The school works with these teachers to help them navigate teaching students whose families do not conform to levels of observance preferred by the yeshiva world. Chabad personnel also have been hired increasingly because they are trained to show respect for a range of Jewish viewpoints. None of this is simple, though. When these personnel choose to send their own children to Haredi schools, they deliver an implicit message about the legitimacy of the Hebrew Academy. Here, too, the school is beset with a challenge that many Modern Orthodox day schools face.

The process of bringing these teachers in sync with the evolving outlook of the school is ongoing. Like their general studies counterparts, the Jewish studies staff are given professional education opportunities. Though many of the teachers of Judaica have made their peace with the school's Zionism and its celebration of Yom Ha'atzmaut, and also are open to working with students whose families are not as observant as the teachers might like, resistance persists among some when it comes to employing new approaches to pedagogy, such as blended learning or learner-centered pedagogy. Staffing issues thus impede the administration's plans to reorient the school.

Some parents also present challenges as the school refashions itself. Blended learning, for example, has left some parents worried about whether their children are receiving a proper education. One teacher with advanced training in blended learning, for example, realized she had to introduce this approach to pedagogy more slowly, not because her students objected but because parents were not ready for it. For this reason, the school continues to use textbooks in history and the sciences, supplemented by online resources. Gradually most parents are realizing that online learning provides instant assessment of what students understand or still are struggling to grasp. As the math programs have used such assessment to identify areas of weakness, student learning has risen to higher levels. Similarly, in language arts, student writing and fluency are measured to reveal areas of weakness and then used to quickly address deficiencies. PBL also had to prove itself to parents because it is foreign to their own educational experiences. As parents have come to understand the advantages of new teaching methods, they gradually come onboard.

One further challenge of a different sort also has stretched the school: bolstering security. Like so many other Jewish and other types of schools, the Hebrew Academy has invested significant sums to provide for the safety of its students and faculty.[5] Increasing antisemitism adds to the sense of vulnerability so many school leaders must address. In the case of the Hebrew Academy, not only are all its buildings walled off behind high metal gates, it has spent over $1 million in recent years to install more than one hundred cameras and secure its complex with locked doors. It has a staff of four armed guards checking every person seeking to enter its compounds. The sums spent on security, though necessary, are dollars the school might otherwise have invested in additional new curricula or professional development for its teachers.

The Roles of the Board

The school's board is aware of these various challenges and takes responsibility for the budgetary implications of addressing them. To help reshape perceptions about the school, the board approved the hiring of a marketing person, arranged for the huge outlay on security, and is involved with the financial ramifications of competing for the services of teaching personnel.

Beyond that, the board sets policies for financial aid. The greater diversity of students at the school also has brought a far more diversified population of parents to the school. Families range across the socioeconomic spectrum. The Hebrew Academy attracts students from very wealthy homes and from homes with very limited resources—and every kind of home in between. With its commitments to the wider community and its conviction that every Jewish child deserves a day school education, the board must find the means to offer scholarship assistance to aid a wide swathe of families. As one administrator put it, "It's set into the DNA of the school that you don't turn people away for financial reasons." Roughly 60 percent of students receive some support, which places huge pressures on the school to raise philanthropic dollars.

This means the board must ensure that significant sums are raised to aid those who cannot afford paying full tuition: only 65 percent of the school's budget comes from tuition. And although the Greater Miami Jewish Federation contributes some money to the school and parents can apply for aid from state tax incentive programs available in Florida even to Jewish day school students,[6] the burden of ensuring the availability of scholarship funds rests on the board. Not surprisingly, among the board's major preoccupations are enrollment trends, especially retention.

In the past, board members were not always prepared to limit their involvement to acting on their fiduciary responsibilities but also intervened in some areas of educational policy. This blurring of lines was unhealthy and was cited by educational personnel as unhelpful meddling. Though the board did not call for the firing of specific teachers, it directed school heads to scrutinize the performance of some educators. Some board members also voiced complaints about curricula employed in the classes of their own children. Matters were further complicated because over a period of three years, the school was without a head; searches had not turned up candidates with the proper Modern Orthodox credentials. During that period, board members took on an outsized role. Not surprisingly, this caused internal friction.

Once a new school head was chosen, those issues were actively addressed. Outside consultants were brought to the school to run workshops on responsible board management. And the current school head devoted his first months to working individually with every board member, clarifying what is and is not under their purview. The lines of responsibility between the board and the educational administration are becoming clearer.

Whatever problems existed in the past, the board's tight oversight resulted in a balanced budget every year. That is remarkable given the huge sums allocated for scholarship assistance and large outlays for academic upgrading. Raising money has been the province of the board, though that is changing under the school's new head, who is assuming a larger role in the area of development. To keep the budget in the black, board members also monitor expenditures to eliminate wasteful spending. The budgeting process is carefully managed to plan ahead as realistically as possible.

No less important, the board has supported major academic initiatives, the introduction of new curricula, and extensive professional training for the teaching staff. It has not stinted on support for the academic enhancement of the school or on the introduction of new technology. These efforts all come at a significant financial cost. The board has supported the school's transformation, a point of pride for its members.

The Student Perspective

It's natural to wonder what students have to say about the school. To answer that question, we interviewed high school seniors in small groups. The graduating class was chosen because it has lived through so many of the transitions within the Hebrew Academy.

The students interviewed confirmed the general outline of change traced in this chapter. They complained about excessive homework assignments, especially in AP classes, and the amount of homework that piles up because there is insufficient coordination among teachers. Others recalled how hard the eleventh grade was due to the pressure of preparing for SAT exams and working to boost their grades to improve their transcripts. Students felt they put a great deal of pressure on themselves, and their parents added to those pressures. Of course, these laments echo what might be heard in any high school. They underscore just how much the Hebrew Academy has successfully socialized students to aspire to high levels of academic performance, a primary goal during the school's transformation.

Students of course mentioned uses of new technologies. They acknowledged how much more often middle school classes employed blended learning than did their high school classes. The high school's lag in adopting new pedagogical methods was not lost on students. But they also noted that in high school, they worked on projects in small groups, made videos explaining what they learned in Talmud classes, and wrote blogs on what they learned in science classes. In addition, Hebrew-language classes assigned homework online.

High school seniors also spoke about their Jewish studies classes. Homework assignments in Judaica classes were deemed far less onerous than those in general studies. Few devoted more than an hour or two weekly to homework assignments in Judaica, and they were not troubled by the different expectations for these courses. Girls noted that they were exposed to Talmud study only in their final three years at the school. They spoke freely about how much they enjoy the highly interactive nature of Talmud study and also how they can apply what they learn in Talmud classes more so than in other classes. Highlights of the school year include a school-wide Shabbaton and also class or grade Shabbatonim when the entire class stays with families in a particular community.

What students stressed about the religious outlook of the school was the gap between the school's official Orthodoxy and the reality of many students' lives outside the school. In the building, boys wear a kippa and all students keep kosher. A segment of the students are not as observant in other situations. Students lauded the fact that they are not being judged by their behavior outside the school building. They accept the more relaxed approach, even if they personally are observant. They spoke warmly about the efforts of rabbis to explain the reasons for the observances and to speak personally about their own beliefs.

In most ways, students spoke very much like their peers at many other schools. They wished for a later start to the school day because as adolescents, they need to sleep longer, and they also wanted a shorter school day. They noted the school does random drug testing, although they hadn't heard of cases of actual drug use. Smartphones get confiscated, and that happens a lot in school, students claim. These are standard student preoccupations. So too was the response of students when asked what they liked most about the school: the predominant answer was the camaraderie with classmates. Small class sizes meant that students can ask questions and engage in conversations with teachers and fellow students. The school's rich array of sports and other extracurricular offerings also creates a closely knit connection with other students, they noted. Summing it up, one student stated, "We lean on each other. Period."

Epilogue: The Continuing Story

During the 2019-20 school year, we revisited the school to gauge the initial impact of a new head of school. Rabbi Shaye Guttenberg previously headed a Jewish day school on the West Coast, where he developed a record as an innovative educator. He spoke about the educational philosophy he intended to impart. Central to his outlook is a shift from regarding education as a commodity that teachers transmit to a role teachers must play helping students figure out on their own how they will acquire knowledge and what to do with that knowledge—that is, how to share their knowledge with others. Central to his thinking is that learning today is best done by students in groups who work on projects. He is working on infusing this approach throughout the school's divisions.

Along with intensifying the school's adoption of progressive educational methods in both general and Jewish studies, he also will press teachers to bridge the gap between the Jewish and the general studies. All teachers will work together and attend each other's classes on occasion in order to break down artificial disciplinary barriers and the walls between the school's Jewish and general studies offerings. Integrating far more technology into the high school is another agenda item.

The new head envisioned big changes in character education to help enrich students' emotional and social learning. Rabbi Guttenberg embraced the vision of the leadership team and school psychologists to strengthen positive education across the school. He has affirmed his strong commitment to nurturing a "Torah environment that will develop the character of students as practicing Jews." Bible and Talmud classes will involve students in project-based learning.

Rabbi Guttenberg sees his role as primarily outer directed: he defines himself as the communal voice for the school. He is its public face and will deliver its message to the wider community, parent body, and other stakeholders. The dean of academics and innovation, Rabbi Bossewitch, is assuming a far more directive role in the school's educational offerings. In the past, he offered options to teachers—new curricula, ways to teach, exposure to new methods. Now he is empowered to be far more directive so as to craft and implement a joint vision with the new school head. He says he is now the "principal's principal." Working with administrators and teachers, he will implement further educational changes.

To be sure, the vision that Rabbis Guttenberg and Bossewitch articulated early in the school year were aspirational. Time will tell how successful their efforts to transform the Hebrew Academy will be. Educational institutions are notoriously slow when it comes to making changes, and the school faces challenges that may impede the process. But then, almost all schools face obstacles. The Hebrew Academy has already come a long way over the past dozen or so years. In so many ways, it is a very different school today than it was in the 1990s. This track record of successful change augurs well for implementing the current educational leadership's determined agenda to press forward with more educational innovation. Indeed, the school's health, in their view, depends on delivering a different educational product. "When you show value," Rabbi Guttenberg states, "people will come."

CONNECTIONS AND EXCEPTIONS

Of all the schools in our sample, Hebrew Academy (RASG) may be the most representative of the broader day school field. Founded in 1947, the school's continuity is testament to the deep appeal of the day school dual curriculum to a Modern Orthodox community that wants the best of all worlds for the next generation. Today, the school faces a much more congested marketplace than when it was founded, with competition from the right and the left. Because of rising property prices, it must also attract families from beyond the neighborhoods from which its families historically came. Hillel Torah (chapter 1), the other Modern Orthodox school in our sample, has experienced some of these same challenges but not to the same degree. Hebrew Academy is more typical of the broader field, and especially of those Modern Orthodox day schools located in cities outside the Tri State Area (New York, New Jersey, and Connecticut), where it is that much harder to recruit both mission-aligned families and mission-aligned Judaica faculty.

The school's transformation over the past two decades is indicative of how the broader day school field has steadily professionalized against the backdrop of rising parental expectations about what children should gain from a day school experience. These changes—in particular, the intensifying integration of learning technologies across the curriculum and the expanded provision of student support services—have not been as dramatic as those at, for example, Hillel Day School (chapter 2) and the Pressman Academy (chapter 4). The steady if uneven implementation of these changes at Hebrew Academy is probably more representative of how things have played out at great many longer-established day schools. In this respect, the journey taken by the academy looks more like that taking shape at the Rav Teitz Mesivta (chapter 6). These two long-established schools, the first day schools in their communities, seek to recruit the children and even grandchildren of alumni and must work doubly hard to overturn assumptions about what classroom life is like in the school today. In both schools, that's a work in progress.

While working through such challenges, the single asset that is probably most decisive in attracting and keeping students at the school is its community and family-like spirit. Immigrant families especially are drawn to the academy by these embracing qualities, even if the families are not fully aligned with the school's *hashkafa* (religious ideology). In this respect, the Hebrew Academy highlights a core feature of the broader day school story. Ultimately, day schools are self-chosen communities, a theme we have seen repeatedly in these chapters. Even the larger ones promise an opportunity to belong and to connect, an experience that can't be guaranteed at public school.

Having highlighted the extent to which Hebrew Academy is representative of many other institutions on the broader day school landscape, one exceptional feature of the school's situation is worth noting since it is a matter of widespread interest in the day school field: a significant minority of families obtains tuition support through the Florida tax incentive program. Similar programs exist in only a few states, and they make a decisive difference in the affordability of day school education. In this respect, Florida is ahead of the rest of the nation.

9

The Yeshiva as Teiva (Ark)

Yeshiva Darchei Torah, Far Rockaway, New York

Yeshiva Darchei Torah is a phenomenon. Over almost fifty years, during virtually all of which it has been led by the same Rosh HaYeshiva (head of school), the school has grown from a fragile start-up in an inhospitable New York suburb to a thriving community of twenty-five hundred boys and men between the ages of three and twenty-three, embedded in the heart of a strictly Orthodox neighborhood enclave. This chapter recounts how members of the yeshiva community draw inspiration from the yeshiva's growth, and it highlights some features of life in this institution that have made it such a magnet: the yeshiva's unusual investment in serving students with a wide range of learning needs; its role of taking care of young people who have encountered difficult circumstances in their home lives; and its inclusion of opportunities to pursue general studies within the limitations of a traditionalist yeshiva setting. The chapter introduces readers to both the intense educational demands and the distinctive spiritual rewards associated with the yeshiva experience in its most traditionalist form.

Monday morning. The clock hits 7:35. The Mesivta Beis Medrash (the high school study hall), with space for more than two hundred chairs set up alongside long tables, is more than half full.[1] From a large lectern near the back and with a deep and powerful voice, one of the mesivta principals begins to recite the *birkos ha-shachar* (morning blessings) at a slow but steady pace. Teenage boys continue to hurry in, kicking traces of light snow from their shoes. By the time they finish putting on *tefillin*, all are wearing jackets and black hats, some of which seem to have been left on the tables over the weekend. When a student takes over as *shaliach tzibur* (prayer leader) from the front of the hall, he can barely be heard over a full room of adolescent voices raised in prayer. *Rebbeim* (rabbinic mentors) are dispersed around the room to keep a discrete eye on things and offer words of encouragement to those who are finding it hard to stay focused. In large part, they're able to concentrate on their own prayer; very few students are either involved in conversation with their neighbors or have adopted classic disengaged head-on-table mode. The yeshiva week is well and truly under way

Prayer demarcates the day for students in Yeshiva Darchei Torah's Mesivta Chaim Shlomo (its high school section). They gather for *shacharis* (the morning service) at its start, for *mincha* (the afternoon service) before they transition from *Limmudei Kodesh* (sacred studies) to secular studies in the middle of the afternoon, and at 8:30 p.m. for *maariv* (the evening service) at the end of a seventy-five-minute postdinner "night-seder" (an evening study session) before most head home.

These few details indicate that Yeshiva Darchei Torah is not a conventional day school. Indeed, members of this community don't think of it as a day school at all. In many ways, it isn't. Paradoxically, this most traditional of institutions embodies one of the great axioms of progressive education, as expressed by philosopher John Dewey: "Education is not preparation for life; it is life itself."[2] By the time they reach high school, the students who choose to remain at Darchei (about a third of those who started out in the early grades of elementary school) are praying together, eating together, and living and learning together, not just five days a week but also for a large part of Sunday and often on Shabbos (the Sabbath) too. The yeshiva, inhabited by almost 2,500 boys and young men and a staff of more than 450, is not for a great many of its inhabitants simply a provider of educational and social services. It can comfortably be described as "home" at least as defined by the *Merriam-Webster's Dictionary*. It is a place of residence, the social unit formed by living together, a familiar or usual setting, and a place of origin.

Taking a close look at Darchei Torah is an opportunity to test assumptions about what schools look like and what they're for. Much of what Darchei Torah accomplishes derives from experiences and elements in the yeshiva environment beyond the classroom, in the *Beis Medrash*, in special programs and in the interactions between rebbeim and students during the hours when they're not in class. This case therefore raises questions about the most powerful means by which schools come to have an impact on the lives of children and families. Furthermore, the breathtaking growth of Darchei from inauspicious beginnings in 1972 to its currently extensive kindergarten-to-post-high-school facilities, which take up most of a city block in Far Rockaway, New York, leaves one wondering to what extent this yeshiva is an anomaly, model, or harbinger: an anomaly in the sense that it might be the peculiar product of the special circumstances and people who have come together to make it what it is; a model, in terms of its deep fusion of *chesed* (acts of kindness) into the heart of the educational enterprise and not just as a supplementary or extracurricular activity; and harbinger with respect to the future of day school education in North America. So many students here are the offspring of parents and grandparents who attended day schools of a very different variety themselves and have now sought something quite distinct for the next generation in their families. What do these choices promise for the day school enterprise more generally?

How a Kindergarten Became a Kingdom

To unravel these questions, the first step is to reconstruct the history of how the yeshiva came to be the institution it is today. Spend a short time at Darchei Torah, and you'll soon hear or read about critical moments in its history. It's easy to understand why people enjoy recounting these episodes. They perceive the yeshiva's story to be touched by *siyyata dishmaya* (divine providence), evidence that a larger purpose has guided the fortunes of this place, one in which "the Almighty rewards those who help His children."

At the start of the 1970s, a small group of parents in Far Rockaway came together with the goal of founding a "community yeshiva." The neighborhood, home to few religiously observant Jews, was one of New York's less desirable. Far Rockaway is where the outer boroughs of New York meet the edge of the Atlantic Ocean, almost within earshot of Kennedy Airport. These families were not attracted to the Modern Orthodox, coed day schools in the adjacent Long Island neighborhoods. They wanted a traditional yeshiva for their sons. The yeshiva they imagined would provide in its early grades "an outstanding foundation in *chumash, Tefila, mitzvos, midos* and *yiras shamayim* [a mix of text study, prayer, values and religious inspiration] . . . and excellence in our general studies program." It hardly needs mentioning that, like all other yeshivas in the ultra-Orthodox community, it would not be coeducational.

In 1972, after a few years of organizing, the group accumulated sufficient resources to open a kindergarten and first grade, operating over the following years out of a series of rented spaces. Each year they added a grade. In 1977, needing a rebbe for the soon-to-open seventh grade, they recruited Rabbi Yaakov Bender, who would commute from Brooklyn. He made such an impression that after just one year and despite not having formal classroom experience previously, he was asked to become the *menahel* (principal). One of the yeshiva's testimonial publications reports: "Rav Bender accepted, and laid out his philosophy of *chinuch* [education]: He believed that excellent learning and excellent *middos* [dispositions] must always go hand in hand, and that a yeshiva has an obligation to educate every single *talmid* [student], whatever his strengths or challenges."

These principles have become the hallmark of the yeshiva, which, more than forty years later, continues to be led by Rabbi Bender as Rosh HaYeshiva, possessing, it seems, as much energy as he did in his thirties. The yeshiva grew steadily and for about a decade rented space on the campus of the local YMHA, ironically occupying a building once used by a Modern Orthodox day school that had fallen on hard times and relocated to merge with another day school. Rabbi Bender and his family moved to Far Rockaway within a few years of his becoming menahel.

Another significant milestone was reached in 1991, one often described in school lore as another "Darchei Torah miracle." The New York Jewish Federation, facing significant financial challenges at the time, resolved to sell the Y's eight-and-a-half-acre campus, part of which the yeshiva was renting. Although the yeshiva was more than a year behind on its $72,000 a year rent, its leadership saw a special opportunity in the purchase of the $2.2 million campus. They managed to raise $1.6 million, but with one more payment deadline to make, they were still $600,000 short. Another yeshiva publication reports on what happened next:

> An individual, approached for help, explained that he wasn't in a position to donate, but he did have connections in Jewish media and could arrange for an article about Darchei Torah to appear in *The Jewish Press*. Just as in Megillas Esther (The Book of Esther), *malachim* (angels) arranged for words in the *sefer zichronos* (Book of Chronicles) to come to the king one sleepless night, the *Ribbono Shel Olam* (the Almighty) arranged for one of the generation's great Torah philanthropists to lift up the newspaper and notice the piece. He was intrigued at the article's description of Darchei and the unique fusion of excellence in learning and excellence in *chesed* that had become their "brand."

Conversations ensued, and after seeking the advice of his rebbe, the philanthropist and his wife offered to underwrite a large share of the project. The campus continues to carry his family's name.

The next turning point in the Darchei story involves the addition of a *mesivta* (a high school section). For more than two decades, Darchei operated as an elementary school, and each year its students had to fight for admission to high schools and mesivtos around the country. As one narrator puts it, "Everyone wanted only aleph (A1). . . . That has never been the Darchei philosophy." Each year, it was a struggle to ensure that all of Darchei's students were appropriately placed. Again, this is a story taken up by one of the yeshiva's publications:

> All that changed when Rav Bender welcomed Mr. and Mrs. Ronald Lowinger's autistic son, Chaim Shlomo, into the fifth grade. The Lowingers had tried many schools and options for their son, and were thrilled when he seemed to finally find his place at Darchei. . . . But where could they send their son when he finished eighth grade?
>
> With Mr. Lowinger's encouragement and support, Rav Bender opened Mesivta Chaim Shlomo—the Maurice and Edith Lowinger Mesivta High School—in 1995, and it was comprised of two classrooms. . . . One year later, Chaim Shlomo Lowinger was welcomed as a *talmid* [student] of its second ninth grade. Shortly afterward, the Mesivta moved into its own, newly constructed building.

The opening of the mesivta and the cementing of Rabbi Bender's relationship with the Lowingers was a decisive turning point. The mesivta didn't so much serve as a capstone for the yeshiva as a building block in the yeshiva's growth and, in turn, to the gradual transformation of the neighborhood into what Rabbi Bender likes to call a "mini Lakewood" (a small-scale replica of the yeshiva community in New Jersey). With the opening of the mesivta, the yeshiva began to enroll boys from other communities around the United States to live and learn at Darchei, something made possible by the purchase of adjacent houses and their conversion into dormitories.

In 1999, when the first cohort of students was due to graduate from the mesivta, the yeshiva took another step. The young men of the mesivta were given the opportunity to continue learning at Darchei in a new *Yeshiva Gedola* (senior yeshiva), again created with the support of the Lowingers. Many boys planned to continue their studies in Israel, an almost universal practice in the Orthodox community. Now they had an opportunity—again, in the company of an influx of young men from farther afield—to spend three years closer to home before transferring to one of the major yeshivas in Israel. A beautiful Beis Medrash was opened soon after as the centerpiece for this new framework. The young men of the Yeshiva Gedola serve as role models and a resource for the younger students.

This story is not merely of academic interest. How Darchei Torah began life as a kindergarten and has become a kind of *mamlechet kohanim*—"a priestly kingdom"—makes a palpable difference to those who inhabit the yeshiva today. It informs their self-image and self-confidence. In the eyes of its members, the yeshiva's vigorous growth, and the gradual transformation of the adjacent Far Rockaway neighborhood into a religiously observant enclave stand as testament to the values that infuse this community. Its leadership didn't just get lucky at some of those key inflection points; the yeshiva attracted people whose lives were touched by its values and in turn helped sustain those values. Those values are all the more compelling for being associated with such vigorous growth. At a time when many Jewish educational institutions in North America are experiencing decline, the yeshiva's history inspires confidence among its faculty and families that the path taken by Darchei Torah is indeed the path of Torah.

Unpacking the Yeshiva's Appeal

What explains the appeal of Darchei Torah? First, this is a place that takes traditional Jewish literacy seriously, as evidenced by the increasing amount of time students devote to Torah study such that by twelfth grade, they're spending a minimum of thirty hours a week on *limmudei kodesh*. Furthermore, seriousness is not just reflected in the hours allocated but also in the expectations of students, starting with fluency in *aleph beis* (the alphabet) by the end of kindergarten and culminating with the aspiration that a sizable proportion of the boys will complete a tractate of Talmud each year of high school. In recent years, this final goal has been fulfilled by about a third of the students, culminating in an annual event, the yeshiva's *siyum hagadol*, a celebration of completed studies, part of which includes a torch-lit parade through the neighboring streets to celebrate this accomplishment.

Impressive as these milestones are, it is doubtful that Darchei would have flourished if this was the whole story. There is no shortage of schools in the New York area that make similar claims. A second element in the yeshiva's appeal are the stringent demands it makes of families with respect to the social and religious practices they observe in their own homes. Such expectations help the yeshiva ensure that families enrolling their sons are genuinely mission appropriate. Those expectations also serve an additional function: they enable parents to feel comfortable about the homes of their sons' school peers. Establishing public standards of this kind is part of what draws parents and is also a reason some families withdraw at the end of the elementary school or middle school grades.

Today, these expectations are par for the course in the yeshiva world. What distinguishes Darchei Torah are three additional dimensions: its investment in serving students with diverse learning needs, the all-pervading nature of its commitment to chesed, and what one interviewee called "the solidity of its secular studies program."

Serving all Students

The yeshiva's commitment and capacity to serve students with special learning needs is unusual, even as it has been a constant element in the story of its growth. The yeshiva world can be elitist, celebrating scholarly achievements and sidelining those who lack the intellectual wherewithal to hold their own. From an early period in its growth, Darchei Torah was a pioneer in providing special resources for children with learning needs. Not only did the school resist turning away weaker students, it invested in facilities to serve them: it established a multifaceted learning center for students in the elementary and middle schools and a vocational center for students in the mesivta. As the yeshiva grew in size, it also developed an elaborate organizational structure of grade-level teams to ensure that individual students would not fall through the cracks.

What is especially interesting is that the school's reputation for serving needy students has not turned off families that might be concerned that their own child would be held back by weaker classmates or might not see the yeshiva as sufficiently selective. On the contrary, those families seem to find the yeshiva's inclusiveness genuinely appealing, offering their own children an opportunity to grow. Why that is so requires some unpacking. A vignette brings to life the distinctiveness of Darchei Torah in serving students with a wide range of learning needs.

Occupying the southeastern corner of the campus is a facility that at first glance seems entirely incongruous in a yeshiva: the Weiss Vocational Center.

Since the yeshiva opened its mesivta, only about half the boys who graduated from eighth grade have started ninth grade, a high rate of attrition. The high school program is intense, running six days a week. Students must be willing to embrace a regimen that involves many hours of traditional Torah learning as well as approximately twelve hours a week of general studies, enough to complete sufficient credits for the state Regents exam and optional AP courses by the end of twelfth grade. It's easy to assume that the mesivta program appeals to an elite, self-selecting few.

And yet since the mesivta opened its doors in 1995, a significant minority (about 10 percent) of the seventy-five students who start ninth grade each year have not been able to handle the academic program, whether *limmudei kodesh* or general studies. These boys participate in a modified program of Gemara, Chumash, and Halacha and don't take the regular Regents curriculum. Instead, during general studies time, they spend between forty-five and ninety-five minutes a day in the vocational center.

Today the program mainly operates out of a specially constructed building subdivided according to the various trades taught. The building was itself a special project of the program's director, a long-serving rebbe who took time out from teaching to supervise its construction. Walk through the doors into this beautifully faced building, and you find yourself in a facility that rivals what's on offer at many technical colleges. Near the entrance, in a display case, are the business cards of yeshiva graduates who have set up their own businesses employing the trades they learned here: window installation, home construction, electrical services, photography, and various kinds of renovations. One part of the building is set up for teaching advanced electrical wiring under the guidance of another rebbe. In the next room, various full-size bathrooms are under construction. The boys have been doing all of the design, tiling, plumbing, and boiler installation. At the end of year, they'll take everything apart, leaving just one example for next year's students to use as a model. Across the corridor, a small group of students are learning about camera systems with a Darchei graduate who is in the home security business. Across the parking lot, still operating out of a trailer, is the woodwork shop. Less ornate but well equipped, it's a hive of activity with boys building bookcases and *shtenders* (lecterns), useful yeshiva furniture.

When the vocational program was launched, there was a concern that those who took part would be stigmatized for taking a less demanding option or, in a very different scenario, that the program would prove so appealing because of its uniqueness in a yeshiva setting that it would draw to Darchei ever larger numbers of academically weak students. In a marketplace where there's intense competition for the brightest students, that was a risky move because stronger students might stay clear. And yet this facility gets to the heart of what makes Darchei distinctive: an acute concern for the welfare of individual students with an unusually wide variety of personal, educational, and economic needs. In the words of Rabbi Bender, even in an institution with more than twenty-five hundred students, they are committed "to ensuring that no *neshama* [soul] is uncared for."

Ironically, the vocational program has become so appealing that some of the strongest students in the mesivta now opt to take one of its courses when they they've completed the credits required by the Regents. In the school's calculus of values, what started out as an act of chesed for a minority of students has become a special opportunity for the institution as a whole and is something that draws families to it.

Chinuch *with Chesed*

When you ask students, parents and the yeshiva's leadership what's special about Darchei Torah, they are most likely to point to the quality of chesed. In the words of an alum, "It's a chesed empire." Chesed is everywhere; it touches the lives of students, teachers, parents, and members of the local community. Sometimes it's expressed through individual acts and sometimes through specific programs. Certainly the phrase "random acts of kindness" is not appropriate here, as the following examples demonstrate:

The yeshiva is well known for admitting students from challenging home circumstances, single-parent families, and straitened economic circumstances. It also includes students with physical disabilities.

From the yeshiva's early days, it has kept a commitment never to miss payroll, something that is a widespread problem in the yeshiva world. As one of the administrators says, "You can't expect someone to go into the classroom and be owed money."

Quite recently, the yeshiva established a $1.7 million fund to help faculty defray the costs of paying for life-cycle events such as weddings and bar mitzvahs. As a board member expresses it, "What better way to show *hakoras hatov* [appreciation] to our *rebbeim* and staff than to run a campaign like this?"

The yeshiva is currently giving organizational and financial support to enable another high school to start in the community. This will help ensure that those students who leave Darchei at the end of eighth grade and are not suited to the demands of its own mesivta program will not be without a school option in a highly competitive market.

The staff redesigned a Motzei Shabbos (Saturday night) learning program so that it is no longer viewed as a father-and-son event, as is the case in many other yeshivas. It is now called *dor l'dor* (from generation to generation)—students learning together with an older person. The purpose is to include boys who do not have a father.

The yeshiva established a substantial fund for boys who come from single-parent homes. The money is designated to provide gift certificates to buy new clothes before Jewish holidays and pay for tuition at sleep-away camp, "where they can be the same as everyone else."

The yeshiva runs a once-a-month support group, staffed by a psychologist and one of the senior rabbis, for boys whose parents are divorced.

The executive director recounts how he responds when a parent becomes unemployed and can't pay tuition. "To people in this situation, I say, first, I want to *daven* [pray] for you; what's your name? . . . Send me your résumé; we're well connected. . . . Don't worry. . . . Then, when you can start to contribute again, you should, no matter how little. It's a *zechus* [privilege] to pay tuition."

When students want to give *tzedaka* (charity) and be sure that it goes to people in need, they stuff money into Rabbi Bender's jacket pocket— what he calls, "the rabbi's fund."

These acts—practices, really, in ethical terms—draw from the same reservoir of values that Rabbi Bender has championed since he came to Darchei Torah. His philosophy is helpfully articulated in two published collections of his responses to questions posed to a weekly education roundtable convened by the newspaper *Yated Ne'eman*. The first collection, *Chinuch with Chesed*, includes, for example, a passage in which the Rosh HaYeshiva bemoans how exclusive many yeshivos have become: "Just the line, 'we cannot service your child,' which parents hear constantly, is despicable. Children are not used cars that need servicing. They are *neshamos* [souls] who deserve every consideration."[3]

Thanks to Rabbi Bender's writings about these matters and in no small part thanks to word-of-mouth in the yeshiva community, Darchei Torah has become known as a place that cares. Rabbi Bender reports on cases of parents and grandparents from other neighborhoods who have waited on his porch to plead that the yeshiva take in their child. Others have lobbied some of the most prominent donors to the yeshiva for help in placing their son in the school. For the great majority of parents, the more fortunate, the point is not just that their own child will be treated with chesed but that their sons will see chesed modeled by the rebbeim and by fellow students. They know these values will be celebrated in *vortlach* (the stories students will hear during the course of the day) and *shmoozen* (inspirational talks that form a significant component of the yeshiva's pedagogy).

It's 8:30 a.m. A few boys linger, waiting to catch a word with Rabbi Bender. The Rosh HaYeshiva encourages them to introduce themselves to me while they wait. Whether by accident or design, their stories share a similar theme. One tells how he came to Darchei in tenth grade after being bullied for most of ninth grade in another local yeshiva. His complaints had been ignored until he fought back against a boy from a high-profile family. Finally, his parents (and his yeshiva) understood he needed to be elsewhere. They turned to Darchei as a lifeline. A second boy, also in ninth grade, said his family lives about an hour from Far Rockaway, in a community where there are no day schools or yeshivas. During elementary and middle school, his mother brought him to and from the yeshiva every day, something that involved her spending four hours a day in the car. Now he is relieved to be boarding on the campus. A third boy lives close by. His parents are both *baalei teshuvah* (newly religious) Russian-speaking émigrés. When quizzed, he reveals that he's the first person in his family to learn Gemara. These boys have a special reason to be grateful for the yeshiva's intervention. The affection they display toward Rabbi Bender, who gives them each a warm hug, seems more like that of grandchildren with their *zeide* (grandfather). The yeshiva has changed the course of their lives.

Taking Secular Studies Seriously

Another way the yeshiva sets itself apart from competitors is in its relative openness to general education. In recent years, some alumni of yeshivas in the New York City area have leveled a strong critique of those schools for offering a substandard education. Organizations such as YAFFED (Young Advocates for Fair Education) have agitated against the yeshivas by mobilizing in relation to a state law that requires private schools to offer an education "substantially equivalent" to that offered by public schools. Much of the criticism has been directed at Hassidic schools, where the language of instruction often is Yiddish and the time allocated for general studies is very limited.

Against this backdrop, Darchei Torah has gained a reputation as a yeshiva that takes secular studies seriously, albeit within a set of self-imposed constraints. The most obvious indicator of this seriousness is the number of hours set aside for the general studies program: in kindergarten and pre-1a, half the day; in the lower school, a little more than three and a half hours a day; and from fifth grade to twelfth grades, three hours a day, four days of the week. (Although in the high school grades this works out to less than a third of the boys' time, it is much more intensive than at most equivalent yeshivas.) Darchei Torah ensures that all boys who complete twelfth grade fulfill their New York State Regents requirements by the time they graduate, and each year it offers seven or eight AP classes, with the subjects varying based on demand.

Beyond these courses, the yeshiva conveys a message about general studies in less tangible ways. For example, if a child is suspended for *limmudei chol* (general studies), he may not attend *limmudei kodesh* (Judaic studies) classes either. Discipline expectations are consistent across the curriculum, even if —in the yeshiva's scale of values—one form of learning is more valuable than another. Finally, the yeshiva's leaders do not convey that secular studies is *bittul Torah* (wasting time that could be devoted to Torah study), a position others in the yeshiva world certainly take. At Darchei, general studies are not regarded as merely instrumental—to provide students with the tools to earn a living. One of the rabbis said, "If you're going to do something, you do it seriously."

General studies nevertheless operates within boundaries that preserve a hierarchy of values and norms. Although in kindergarten and the elementary grades there are women teaching general studies, from sixth grade, only men do so. From the earliest grades, general studies classes are scheduled during the last part of the day. As the students pass through the grades, the general studies program is ever more focused on the core of the curriculum. By middle school, students no longer have library time or gym; instead, once a month the boys go out for sports. Science is also integrated into other subjects rather than taught independently. The students do not engage in assignments at school or at home requiring the use of the Internet or a library outside of school. Teaching in the highest grades requires a good deal of creativity with so much resource material now online that is off-limits. With so little time available, the pedagogy tends to be designed to cram students for their next test. As a general studies administrator admits, students don't develop strong research skills. Students do get exposure to computers throughout the grades, but the focus is on mastering applications—the suite of Microsoft Office tools, for example—that are needed to run an office or home. The students do not go on the Internet.

These limits are attractive to those parents who want a more intensive Jewish education than what is offered at Modern Orthodox day schools.[4] They appreciate the yeshiva for protecting their sons from online distractions, while it ensures their children will graduate with the credentials needed to participate in some appropriate form of higher education.

Typically the parents whose sons continue to the mesivta do not wish for their sons to go on to undergraduate studies at a college or university. Those who are interested in a university education almost certainly switch out by the end of middle school. It is a pattern the yeshiva does not discourage, knowing full well that a majority of students who enroll in the elementary grades will leave before the start of high school for day schools offering a more robust precollege experience. Those who do remain or enter the yeshiva at this stage expect that if their sons do go on to secular higher education, they will attend a community college under Jewish auspices, such as Touro College or Lander College (one of Touro's divisions), or a New York area city college such as Queens or Brooklyn, where they will find a sizable population of yeshiva alumni. Alternatively, if boys stay in yeshiva for more than five years after twelfth grade, increasingly the norm for strong students, they might obtain a BTL (a bachelor's of Talmudic law), a degree enabling them to avoid going to college altogether.

Holding It All Together

Though it may not seem so from the outside, the student body drawn to Darchei Torah is quite diverse. Approximately 10 percent of students have some form of identified learning disability; a higher proportion are academically gifted. Only about a third come from families able to pay full tuition, while about 5 percent come from homes experiencing some form of family dislocation, whether due to the loss of a parent or divorce. In the kindergarten and elementary divisions, where there are about 180 students in a grade, all live within a walk or drive of the yeshiva but come from religiously diverse communities, at least within the Orthodox community. In the mesivta, where there are about 75 students in a grade, about a third of the boys (a large proportion of whom come from other parts of the United States) are boarding for between three days a week and all of the time. Otherwise, most of the students live within commuting distance of the yeshiva.

How does Darchei Torah integrate these populations? In the early childhood program, the only consideration is age: students are grouped within a three-month birth span. As the director of ECE says, "I don't care how Yeshivish you are; we're all together." In the elementary and middle schools, the organizing principle is the neighborhood from which students come. This ensures that students live within walking distance of one another for Sabbath get-togethers, and families know that their son is in a class with others like him in terms of their families' religious orientation. Finally, at the lower elementary levels, there is one smaller class for students with specific learning issues. Still, throughout the grades, the school assumes that both weaker and stronger students benefit from being in class together as often as possible.

By contrast, in the mesivta, there is less religious diversity. Those who stay at Darchei or enter the yeshiva tend to come from homes eager to place their sons in a yeshiva with religious intensity and stringencies. In the upper grades, there no longer is a need to group students by neighborhood, so they are grouped by ability. Like yeshivas everywhere, and especially the so-called out-of-town yeshivas, competing to woo the strongest students, Darchei needs to ensure that its star pupils are challenged. The stronger students therefore have numerous options to participate in a variety of learning opportunities: a seder before morning prayers, one at night after evening services, an extra class on Friday afternoons after the official end of the week, and then all kinds of special shiurim with the yeshiva's leading personalities.

Rabbi Bender explains how he sees these things:

> I sincerely believe that the correct way is by having three tracks in the yeshiva and accommodating all who want to learn. The weaker student feels great to be part of a yeshiva that has *chashuveh* [important] and top *bachurim* [boys], and has someone to look up to and model himself after. . . .
>
> A yeshiva itself is an organic entity. Growth and *aliyah* [self-improvement] come as much from its atmosphere and aura as from the *shiurim* [classes] themselves. Ensuring that every *bachur* [student] is welcomed within it and is part of the *davening* [prayer], and the *ruach* [religious spirit], and the Shabbosos and Yamim Tovim, guarantees them life, despite the fact that, come *shiur* time, they may be divided by level.[5]

This sounds ideal, and often it is, but the reality can be more challenging. The pressure on even the strongest students is immense. When navigating the turbulent years of adolescence, no boy is immune to distractions beyond the yeshiva walls, and even more so if living in dorms, away from the support of home. The first in line to help with these challenges is a *mashpia*, an experienced and approachable individual who in addition to his responsibilities as a tenth-grade rebbe functions as a student counselor. Every day he has open-door hours when boys can come to him with issues that require confidential advice or input from someone other than their own rebbe. Most commonly, those who seek guidance are "finding yeshiva hard" or are "finding it hard at home." On other occasions, the challenges can be more acute. Boys might get involved with smoking or with girls, for example, and the mashpia helps them find ways to stay "on the derech," yeshiva parlance for the straight and narrow, before things get out of hand.

Study and Stories

A twenty-four-hour period with the mesivta students opens a window on the nature of the yeshiva experience for students of different aptitudes.

As has been the custom in yeshivas for the past two centuries, the bulk of the student's day is occupied with Gemara, within two frameworks: *b'iyun* (in depth with a wide array of commentaries) and *bekius* (at speed so as to cover ground —that is, going through many pages of Talmud). As is standard yeshiva practice, everyone in the mesivta and the Yeshiva Gedola is learning the same *masechta* (tractate). While this is the same for all boys in the mesivta, the challenges come in different forms for students of different abilities.

Besides devoting a considerable portion of every morning to shiur with the rebbe with whom they learn b'iyun six days a week, the more able students also have shiur with some of the senior rabbonim in the yeshiva. Every evening, a group of advanced eleventh-grade students join the *mesivta menahel* (principal), Rav Trenk, for night seder in a small Beis Medrash. In the shiur room, Rav Trenk's style is austere and intense. In the yeshiva's lingo, there is no *bittel* (fluff or padding) here. At 7:15 promptly, without any small talk and before all of the boys settle down, the Rav picks up from where they left off at the end of the last shiur. They're learning the seventh chapter of Bava Metzia. He does not question boys about what they remember from last time. It's assumed they have reviewed the material, in many cases with the help of the recording devices they position near the front in order to catch his every word.

Over the next hour—pausing only to ask a few clarifying questions to check that the boys are following—the Rav makes his way through the text. The style is remarkably focused. They are no tangents, no interruptions, no schmooze. Remarkably, the great majority of the students seem to be following—a minority annotating the text, the majority simply trying to keep pace. One student in the front row has fallen asleep and a couple have spaced out; it is 8:00 p.m., after all. It seems that the challenge here is to keep up and then digest later what's being covered. This is truly survival of the fittest. With most of the page complete, the Rav comes to an abrupt stop. It will soon be time for *Maariv* (the evening service). No grand finale, more a case of to be continued tomorrow.

The next morning, after breakfast, the same boys are back in the same location, joined now by the strongest students from the tenth grade. Some of their rebbeim are there too. They're here for a once-a-week shiur with Rabbi Bender, the Rosh HaYeshiva. They're learning the eighth chapter of Bava Metzia.

If the pace of the shiur is just as demanding for the students as it was the previous evening, the style is radically different. Rabbi Bender is warmly greeted by a number of students when he arrives, including one young man with evident special needs who takes a seat next to the Rav at the front. The rabbi also playfully salutes the "sleepers' corner" at one end of the room. In a marked contrast to the previous evening, as he proceeds through the Gemara at a rapid pace, he connects the text to reflections on life. One insight is especially powerful. The Rabbi contrasts the halacha's approach to the *Eved Ivri* (essentially an individual with severe financial debts) and that of contemporary society. He notes that in Judaism, we don't send this person to jail—"jail is a terrible place," he reflects. Instead, we send him to live with a family. It's in a family home where we can get him back on track. This, in turn, leads the Rosh HaYeshiva to tell what he calls a *gvaldike* (wonderful) story about the Bryner Rebbe. One of his students had been an orphan for ten years and was about to get married. For the week before his wedding, the rebbe cleared everything out of his own study and had the *bochor* (young man) come live with him, saying, "I want you to observe how I interact with my wife." After a pause to let the story sink, the rabbi is back inside the text until he has to leave at 10:05.

The intensity and pace of these two shiurim are breathtaking for an adult, let alone a teen. It is noticeable that in neither shiur did the boys "interrupt" to ask clarifying or challenging questions. For these strong students, the primary goals are to keep up while their rabbonim set a fast pace and then stay on top of the multiple *sugyos* (sections of the Gemara) they're learning at any one time.

For weaker students the challenge is of a different order. For these boys, the goal is to stay focused for a great many hours each day and to make sense of complex, intellectually challenging material.

It's 9:15 a.m., and Rabbi Feder is about to spend most of the next six hours with the fifteen students in his shiur group. There will be breaks for recess, lunch, and mincha, but in total he is settling in for about four hours of contact time with the same group of students as he does every day.

Like his fellow rebbeim in the mesivta, once trusted with the responsibility of leading a shiur group, he is given a great deal of independence to determine how he uses his time. He is responsible for covering three topics: Gemara, Chumash, and Halacha. In reality, he has one responsibility: to ignite his students' enthusiasm and capacity to serve Hakadosh Baruch Hu (the Almighty) through limmud torah. The specific difficulty he faces is that his students are not academically strong enough, and probably not motivated enough, that he can leave them to learn b'chevrusah (in independent pairs) for too long or too far away—say, in the Beis Medrash downstairs. For most of the time, he needs to keep them tethered to him or at least working independently in his classroom.

It's a daunting task with a group of students who, as Rabbi Feder generously puts it, have an incredible amount of energy. It is as if he is managing a complex pressure cooker while continually monitoring any number of temperature and pressure gauges.

He begins the day with Chumash, which he uses as a chance to engage in a Musar (moral discipline) schmooze with the students. He knows that if he formally included Musar in the schedule, the boys would switch off. This way he can catch them by surprise. And so it is that for the first three-quarters of hour of shiur, he more or less holds the students' attention, jumping off from the weekly Torah portion about the clothing of the kohen gadol (high priest) to explore the concept that "clothing makes a person."

After a half-hour break, Chumash is followed by Gemara. Now the job of keeping the students' attention is of herculean proportions, especially when the content is so complex. Rabbi Feder does not back away from tackling some of the toughest problems inspired by the text. Before turning to the text itself, he leads the students, orally, through the issues, drawing examples from across the centuries in one continuous flow.

Weaving these examples, Rabbi Feder needs to call on any number of methods to hold the boys' attention and to intercept the smallest possible distractions. He prefers not to write much on the board; instead he verbally provokes and prods the boys to respond and confirm the ideas he's raising. When he doesn't get a response with respect to a textual issue, he switches gears and recounts a story that sheds light on the matter at hand. (It's hard to know whether these stories are extemporized or whether he's banked them ahead of time.) At other moments, he'll raise or lower his voice to dramatic effect. Whether he chooses to stand or to sit conveys a signal to students as well. Watching the mood carefully, he sees which boys he can trust to move things forward, which boys to quiz until they get the point, and which boys not to push (today) even if they truly seem miles away. It's hard work for everyone. Some boys are so antsy they're literally struggling to stay in their seats. But without ever losing his cool, the rebbe somehow pulls the class forward. By the time he distributes a worksheet to review the material, it seems that most are in a position, in pairs or by themselves, to answer questions that span the Gemara text itself and various classical commentaries. When it's time to take a break for lunch, it feels like it has been well earned.

Yeshiva, especially in the older grades, can be a demanding experience. For weaker students, it is surely a challenge that the normative pedagogy in the yeshiva is so heavily teacher centered. That pedagogy embodies the-sage-on-the-stage approach. As forward thinking as Darchei Torah is in the social and emotional realm, it is a highly traditional institution when it comes to pedagogy and instruction. That places a burden on students and on the rebbeim too. Rabbi Feder's artistry in holding the attention of his class was probably exceptional. Students, however, seem to accept the goals of the Mesivta and its way of doing things. If a student did not want to be there, it would be very difficult to sustain his cooperation. Of course, there are those who act out and test the limits. They might refuse to get out of bed in the morning and look for ways to miss minyan (the morning service) at 7:30. They might seek to set themselves apart in subtle ways through the coat they wear, their hair style, or simply not tucking in their shirt. But it is noticeable that whatever acts of rebellion surface tend to revolve around marginal matters. It is rare that they extend, for example, to skipping class or socially disruptive acts. Rabbi Bender reports that in forty years, he's expelled three boys in total.

Even while boys may find themselves struggling to keep up or stay focused, they seem genuinely invested in the yeshiva's core values, and they're happy to be at Darchei Torah. The boys display evident affection and respect for their rebbeim, even the most austere ones. Rabbi Feder's shiur group may test his patience but they also articulate a sense of deep loyalty to him. He in turn conveys a great deal of respect for the challenges they have taken on and the trials that some of them must overcome emotionally and academically. The talmid-rebbe (student-teacher) relationship can be a powerful one, especially at this age. And here there is a powerful sense of mutuality, almost interdependence. As for the boys' relationship with one another, if high school is often the incubator of friendship for life, then in this context, where boys spend so many hours together and are engaged in a shared effort to master their learning or simply keep their heads above water, the outcome can be a deep sense of camaraderie lasting into adulthood. Educationally and socially, the yeshiva truly establishes lifelong patterns of behavior.

Keeping the Ark Afloat

There is no shortage of families who desire the Darchei Torah experience for their sons. Recruitment is not a problem for this yeshiva. There is intense competition for places in every grade. Indeed, the yeshiva's leadership is weighing whether to open a ninth class in each of the elementary grades.

The economic challenge for the yeshiva is not how to fill sufficient seats; rather, each student costs the school money since the great majority of families whose children are admitted cannot afford to pay full tuition. About two-thirds of families do not pay full tuition, which ranges from $14,000 in the elementary school to $17,000 in the mesivta. About two hundred families can barely afford to pay anything. Overall, tuition covers about $21 million of the yeshiva's $32 million budget. The remainder needs to come from other sources.

Fundamentally, Darchei's situation is similar to that of other educational institutions serving the Haredi community. In this sector, it is rare for families to have fewer than four children. Families with twelve children are not unusual. A significant minority of the parents in these families are working in education or in some form of Jewish communal work. If the take-home pay of the main breadwinner is even $75,000 (a rebbe's salary, for example) there is no way such a salary can cover school fees for every child.

Darchei Torah receives about $1.3 million from government agencies for mandated services, special education, and busing. The government is also starting to fund STEM education. Preschoolers who live in a New York borough, and not in Nassau County, which Far Rockaway abuts, get some government support too.

This leaves a $7 million hole in the school's budget every year. Some funds are generated by summer camp programs and from renting out facilities. Otherwise, almost all of the remaining money must be raised through fundraising, the bulk of which (maybe 85 to 90 percent) comes from parents and grandparents, the very people who are groaning under the tuition burden. Over the course of the year, families are asked to contribute to an annual raffle, a dinner, and a special breakfast devoted to the yeshiva's resource center. The yeshiva's ideological orientation—in particular its non-Zionist ideology, a commonplace feature of ultra-Orthodox yeshivas—means that although quite a number of grandparents might help with their grandchildren's tuition, they are less willing to make any additional donations, something that many schools can bank on.[6]

If the yeshiva has managed to remain financially solvent even while it has grown so dramatically, it is because Rabbi Bender and his colleagues have forged deep relationships with a small number of exceptionally generous families whose lives have been touched in profound ways by the yeshiva. Besides underwriting new construction projects, these families have helped make up the financial gap on a number of occasions. That they have done so, and that so many families have been willing to contribute in some way to the yeshiva is due in large part to these relationships. As Rabbi Bender's personal assistant reports, from Sukkos through the summer, the rabbi attends weddings, bar mitzvahs, or *shivas* (condolence visits) connected to a yeshiva family. These visits, and his participation in these events, reflect the weaving of the yeshiva into the lives of its families. At the same time, these visits build the relationships that underpin the yeshiva's fundraising. Other members of the administration have formed similar close ties with families, but ultimately the success of this effort comes down to what people call the personal dedication of Rabbi Bender for over forty years.

The Yeshivah as Ark

The story of an institution that's home to almost three thousand people is not the story of one person. Indeed, today, the educational arm of the yeshiva is led by a team of more than twenty individuals, division heads (*menahelim*) and principals. It is managed, too, by an extensive team of administrators and volunteer leaders, some of whom have been giving time and money to the yeshiva since its founding. The longevity of the school's staff and the multi-generational allegiance of families to the yeshiva's community are striking features of Darchei Torah.

And yet whatever the substantial and even decisive contributions of so many people, it is staggering how much of Darchei Torah's success and style can be traced to Rabbi Bender's personality, ethos, and example. After spending time at Darchei, it is hard to miss the distinctive contribution he has made and continues to make, whether to the kindergarten or the Kollel, the center for adult learning, or divisions in between. The most appropriate way to conclude an exploration of the yeshiva is with some accounting of Rabbi Bender's role within it.

Shadowing Rabbi Bender for the day, during his long work hours at least, we readily observed the values with which he has infused the yeshiva, the spirit with which he has animated it, and the principles on which it has been built. There is no day better suited for doing so than a Tuesday.

Every Tuesday for a great many years now, after giving a weekly shiur to the strongest students in tenth and eleventh grades, Rabbi Bender visits every class from middle school to the top grade of the mesivta (almost thirty classes) in order to hand back the weekly Limmudei Kodesh test papers of those who have done well this week or have shown improvement. These visits are a chance to give the boys a chance to show off what they've accomplished. It's an opportunity to check with individual students how a member of their family is doing (a parent who has come out of hospital, a sibling who had just gotten married) and to hear directly from the boys about what's happening in their lives (for example, those in eighth grade who have not yet confirmed which high school they will attend). Moving rapidly from classroom to classroom, Rabbi Bender also observes firsthand how boys and their rebbe are relating to one another. In some classes he doesn't linger long, and in others, prompted by a comment from a boy or a rebbe, he shares a *vort*, an inspirational story of some kind about, for example, an act of special chesed, an incident that demonstrates the greatness of a famous rabbi, or perhaps a special achievement in learning. Given that in schools the size of Darchei Torah, the head of school can go days without interacting directly with students, this is an unusually intense way to keep his finger on the pulse and ensure direct contact with the boys.

Tuesday is also the day when the yeshiva's senior rabbinic leadership meet for about an hour with Rabbi Brudny, Rosh Yeshiva of Brooklyn's Mirrer Yeshiva, one of America's leading ultraorthodox rabbis, in order to bring to him challenging questions with which they're wrestling—situations involving individual students or their families, for example, or questions relating to the ongoing development of the yeshiva. While Darchei's own leadership is populated by any number of learned individuals and experienced educators, members of the *hanhalla* (administration) want to make sure that their choices are informed by the highest levels of *Daas Torah* (rabbinic authority and wisdom). In a sense, they are modeling how they expect the yeshiva's families to conduct their own lives.

Tuesday, finally, is the day of the week when. during lunchtime recess, Rabbi Bender gets a special visit to his office from his many grandchildren. Briefly, with the assistance of copious quantities of candy, he enjoys the opportunity to be with at least a dozen of the youngest members of his family in the yeshiva.

Where Tuesday does not differ from other days of the week is that until 4:00 p.m., Rabbi Bender does not schedule meetings with parents or visitors. He uses part of the afternoon to get on top of email correspondence, a sizable part of which comes from parents seeking advice with educational and child-rearing questions. Otherwise his day is internally focused, in conversations and meetings with *menhalim* (principals), rebbeim, and talmidim. The internal needs of the yeshiva come first and take up the majority of his time.

After 4:00 p.m., invariably for three hours or more, his focus shifts outward, as he responds to yeshiva parents and other members of the community who seek to tap his wisdom on any number of issues. In the course of just one afternoon or evening, he is observed meeting with a graduate of the school seeking career and life advice; the parent of a boy who is no longer in the yeshiva and is concerned about the cult-like impact of a local rabbi on a cohort of boys, including his own son, most of whom are not Darchei students; the senior leadership team from a relatively new yeshiva in the New York area looking for advice about all kinds of educational questions; a videographer from a community group for single mothers that has requested a message of support for their fundraising efforts; and the parents and grandparent of a current student who are deeply concerned about their child acting out at home even while the boy is not exhibiting any issues at school.

Responding to this whirlwind of pleas for help, Rabbi Bender communicates a consistent philosophy to educators and parents, one that implicitly pervades Darchei Torah too: the most important thing is that children should be happy in school ("If your son isn't learning, that doesn't bother me, as long as he's happy"; "Homework is a sadistic invention to keep children off the streets"). In education, the carrot is usually more effective than the stick because being hard on kids often pushes them further away ("If you pressure them, you're asking for trouble"); whatever teachers' foibles are, the main thing is that they should love their talmidim and engage them ("If a rebbe's good and he cares, don't get rid of him"); keep kids as far away as possible from bad influences, whether people or technology ("If a kid brings in a phone, send him home . . . parents who allows Fortnite into their homes need psychiatric help").

Underpinning these nuggets of advice is a distinctive and consistent educational and societal vision, one that sees the yeshiva as a place where boys should want to spend time, where they're genuinely happy, where they're safe from corrosive influences, and where, as a consequence, they come to embrace a life of Torah and Mitzvos (learning and fulfilling the commandments) within a community of like-minded individuals. At the start of this chapter, we characterized Darchei Torah as a home. In some respects, Rabbi Bender's vision for the yeshiva, really every yeshiva, is more far-reaching than that. In his own words, "The Yeshiva is a *teiva* [an ark]." It is a protected space that enables the next generation to survive and grow spiritually in the healthiest ways possible. To describe this work as schooling is too limited. It advances a larger mission to which he's been committed more than forty years.

To return to the question with which we began, from the perspective of the members of this community, the yeshiva might be unusual, but it is far from being an anomaly. They see it as an example and inspiration to others. The question is whether it can truly serve as a model for other Haredi schools when so much of its success has been built on unique leaders and special principles.

CONNECTIONS AND EXCEPTIONS

Yeshiva Darchei Torah is a paradox. Its size, *hashkafa* (religious orientation), and the age range of its students make it quite unlike all of the other schools examined in this book. And yet in functional terms, the values and goals that animate this institution are consistent with the Jewish day school enterprise more generally, and certainly the other schools in our sample. Of course, through its intense focus on Talmud and the study of sacred texts more generally, the yeshiva gives distinctive expression to the goal of cultivating cultural virtuosos. But this goal is of a piece with other visions of cultural virtuosity elsewhere, whether in relation to Hebrew proficiency (say at Hillel Torah) or communal leadership (at TanenbaumCHAT). The yeshiva's much celebrated dedication to chesed provides a powerful example of how distinctive Jewish values can animate an entire institution, but we have also seen elsewhere how well-developed Jewish values can play a similar role in other places—for example, *ahavat yisrael* (Jewish peoplehood) at the Akiva School and *menschlichkeit* (decency) at the Pressman Academy. Finally, the yeshiva's unusual investment in programs and resources to help students with learning challenges might be exemplary in and of itself and exceptional in the ultra-Orthodox community, but it is fully consistent with the services we found at many other institutions, such as the Hebrew Academy of Miami Beach and Hillel Detroit.

In some respects, what makes the yeshiva so different from the other schools in our sample is, first, the extent to which it actively seeks to shape the lives of families. We have seen other schools, such as the Pressman Academy and Brandeis Marin, that aspire to make a difference in the lives of their students' parents. But these are pluralistic institutions; they don't make the same kinds of demands of parents and don't insert their values and commitments into how people's lives are conducted outside school. Such a role is central to the yeshiva's broader agenda for the cultivation of a Torah-centered way of Jewish life in America. That role starts with its own students and continues into a whole range of efforts to build up a local Jewish community governed by values consistent with the Yeshiva's priorities.

Second, consistent with such aspirations is the extent to which the yeshiva functions in classic sociological terms as a total institution, making behavioral demands of the students and occupying almost all of their waking hours. Again, making such demands conflicts with notions of autonomy to which most Jews in America outside the ultra-Orthodox community subscribe. Non-Haredi day schools (all of the other schools in our sample) want students to freely choose to act in certain ways; they wouldn't dream of compelling them to do so, and they are frequently challenged by discontinuities between their aspirations and those of their families. Such autonomy is out of place within yeshivot like Darchei Torah once families have opted in. Signing up one's son for the yeshiva means committing him, and also one's own family, to taking on a clearly articulated set of obligations.

These are some of the reasons why Darchei Torah's leaders are uncomfortable describing the yeshiva "simply" as a Jewish day school. The yeshiva is that and more. The Rosh HaYeshiva is an educational leader, but he also performs a number of spiritual and communal functions consistent with the Yeshiva's broader mission. The yeshiva provides schooling, but it also serves as a sanctuary for a particular kind of faith community.

Conclusion

Vital Jewish Day Schools

This book provides portraits of nine Jewish day schools, a small percentage of the nine hundred or so schools scattered throughout North America. Such a small sample can't properly replicate the organizational and educational diversity of the day school sector as a whole, especially when one includes the Hasidic institutions that make up about a quarter of the total. And yet, taken together, our sample of nine schools is sufficiently diverse organizationally and ideologically to support a series of conclusions about what Jewish day schools in North America today are able to offer students, families, and communities and what constrains them at times from doing so.

To be clear, there are two special respects in which these nine schools are unrepresentative: none, at the time we studied them, was experiencing such acute financial challenges that it was on the brink of closing, and none was gripped by internal turmoil with respect to the quality of its teaching or leadership that it was deemed by its constituents to be failing. In these terms, this is a sample of "good schools," a term Sara Lawrence Lightfoot employed to characterize the six public and independent schools she studied in a still influential book from the 1980s.[1]

We have purposely concentrated our attention on "good schools" not because we want to disguise the possibility that some Jewish day schools fall short of what they promise. We have been more interested in exploring what Jewish day schools in relatively good organizational health and in relatively stable circumstances are capable of offering. We aimed to document what these schools contribute and to make sense of how they have been able to do so. We could not have learned such things if we invested our time examining schools that are dysfunctional.

The schools in this book constitute models. By this we mean they serve as examples, even while they may not all be exemplars. They indicate what's possible but not, we believe, what's unusual. We have not disguised their names or the names of their senior leaders. We have wanted to make the point that these cases are real; they are neither fictions nor idealized composites that draw together the best parts from a number of settings. Curious readers will be able to find out more about each of them.

What Jewish Day Schools Offer Their Students

What, then, are the findings and implications of our study? We have offered indications at the end of each chapter. Here we weave together a series of general themes in terms of what schools contribute to the lives of children, families, and communities. Most visibly, there are five ways in which schools contribute to the lives of the young people who come through their doors each school day.

Nurturing Cultural Virtuosos

Day schools possess the special potential to nurture young people with the ability to contribute to Jewish culture; they cultivate Jewish cultural virtuosos. Compared with every other educational institution to which Jewish children have access, Jewish day schools are unusual in the amount of time they have at their disposal and, crucially, the extent to which that time forms part of a rhythmic cycle. At a minimum—in the case of the Akiva School, for example, which operates only until the end of sixth grade—students can be in school 190 days a year, for seven years.

Of course, there is a danger that this experience can involve boring repetition or rote learning; it can feel like drudgery returning to the same texts or concepts year after year. Undoubtedly there are times when that happens in all the schools we observed. We experienced some if it ourselves. Yet in the hands of skilled educators and school leaders, these recurring experiences can also be powerfully and positively formative, perhaps uniquely so.

This, for example, is what we saw on Yom Hashoah at Akiva when students in the highest grades shared with their younger peers self-researched stories of heroic individuals during the Holocaust as part of a Yom Hashoah ceremony in which, employing more or less the same format, they had participated in every year since they were in first grade. At Hillel Torah, it was a similar story; we observed eighth-grade students intensively rehearsing, in Hebrew, for a special Yom Haatzmaut performance that has always been the responsibility of their grade. Now the task of bringing the story of Israel alive in truly entertaining fashion had fallen on their shoulders. At the Pressman Academy, we joined the middle school students for Monday morning Tefila, and witnessed how, thanks to their experience of daily prayer in a whole range of formats over many previous years, they could now lead a congregation in prayer, chant Torah, and explain the meaning of what they were doing to their peers. At Brandeis Marin, we saw the seventh-grade students demonstrate to their families and younger peers how, over many months of work, they had translated Jewish values into a real-life effort to alleviate some of the gravest challenges that face the world today. At Hillel in Detroit, students fashioned artifacts by hand in the school's makerspace to reflect what they had learned about Jewish concepts, some with a great deal of originality. Sitting in on a ninth-grade Talmud class at TanenbaumCHAT, we saw how many prior years of study had enabled a select group of students to engage in intense debate with their teacher, in Hebrew, about subtle Talmud concepts. As at Darchei Torah, the Hebrew Academy of Miami Beach, and the Rav Teitz Mesivta, young people displayed a facility with challenging Jewish texts, something very few of their contemporaries in North America possess.

In these examples, students had gone beyond being culturally competent. They were displaying knowledge and skills that enabled them, at a high level, to tell stories about profound moments from the Jewish past, contribute to the well-being of society, engage in meaning-generating text study, pray fluently, and articulate Israel's significance. They were exhibiting virtuosity in some of the primary markers of Jewish cultural literacy and social responsibility.

Research about those who become virtuosos in music, art, and business highlights the benefits of doing the same tasks repeatedly. Psychologists attribute this process to neurological plasticity; they argue that our brains change through repeated exposure to experiences. Anthropologists attribute these same outcomes to the power of ritual: repeated performance that produces a bodily form of knowing. These are the kinds of formative experiences we observed: within a routinized structure (routine in the sense of regularized), young people had internalized important values; they were becoming expert in complex endeavors and were growing in responsibility.

Building Community and Lifelong Social Networks

In each school, we held focus group discussions with students and routinely asked about the highlight of their time in school. As was the case at the Hebrew Academy in Miami Beach, often their first response was how wonderful their fellow students are. Their reaction could be construed as a subtle critique of the educational offerings at school and the lack of anything exceptional that deserved comment. It's likely, though, that their response indicates something more profound. It highlights a feature of the day school experience that, for older students especially, constitutes the school's powerful community-building dimension.

This aspect of the day school experience is partly circumstantial. Students have chosen to be educated every day in the company of peers whose motivations likely overlap to a large degree with their own. This is something that can be assumed. It's a feature of all private schools, as schools of choice. Such schools exist as collections of individuals coming together in what sociologists call a functional community: a group of people with shared social, cultural, and economic needs.

Our observations of these schools and our conversations with students, especially the older ones, reveal something deeper: students express a deep emotional connection with one another. In part this comes from the length of time they've been in school together—in many cases, more than ten years —but there's more to it. These young people tend to see the world in similar ways, even in schools with more pluralistic orientations. They're bound together by strong, overlapping connections of kinship and shared values. Those values might be more particularistic in religiously Orthodox institutions and more inclusive in community day schools. In either case, they are felt to be countercultural and distinctively Jewish. This is not just a functional or circumstantial community. It is a community based on shared values where there is a powerful and palpable sense of being part of the Jewish collective.

The force of this experience explains why some students find the environment claustrophobic, a bubble from which they want to escape. It can all feel too insular. For the great majority, though, the environment is experienced as family-like. This quality is especially tangible in the smaller schools like Akiva and Brandeis Marin, where there are fewer than twenty students in a grade, and at Pressman, where students are brought together in cross-grade family groups once a month. In these cases, schoolmates are like cousins, loosely connected family members. For Darchei Torah students who spend more than twelve hours a day with their schoolmates, eat three meals a day together, and spend many Shabbatot in one another's company, these relationships seem at times to supplant those at home.

In most cases by design and sometimes as a collateral outcome of their efforts, day schools embrace their community-building roles. It's noticeable how at TanenbaumCHAT, for example, the school celebrates the number of alumni who have come back to teach at the school and the number of alumni who have married one another. At Hillel Day School and Hillel Torah, school leaders express pride in how many of their current parents are alumni. These schools are hubs for extensive social and interpersonal networks. One can understand why schools don't promote this dimension of their offerings more proactively; their core business is content, not cultivating contacts. And yet this thickening of social relationships is an important contribution to the Jewish lives of young people and their communities.

Caring for Souls: Tending to Students' Emotional and Academic Needs

Today's day schools demonstrate a widespread commitment to caring for the emotional and academic needs of students and to empowering students as agents in this work. (This may be the way in which contemporary day schools depart most radically from schools of even a generation ago.) We became acutely aware of this ethos at the Hebrew Academy when at the time of one of our visits, one of the students died in a domestic accident. The principals spent many hours at the student's home with his family, and a team swung into action at school to provide counseling and support for students. What was more unexpected, and also powerfully revealing, was the extent to which staff supported student efforts to work through their pain in a constructive fashion in the form of meetings and the creation of artifacts and Jewish ritual observances, such as studying sacred texts in memory of their deceased schoolmate.

This new emphasis goes to the heart of something distinctive about all nine schools in our sample and may well be indicative of the contemporary day school enterprise as a whole: their investment in meeting students' emotional and academic needs. Rabbi Bender at Darchei Torah applied traditional language to this enterprise, describing it as an effort to "ensure that no *neshama* [soul] is uncared for." In fact, the practices we learned about are often distinctly untraditional. The annual student focus groups and student-teacher meetings at the Rav Teitz Mesivta are part of a highly purposeful educational reorientation intended to give students a voice and enable them to shape their experiences. The same impulse lies behind council time at Pressman—weekly meetings intended to enable student voices to be heard and, crucially, to encourage students to listen carefully and empathetically to the voices of their peers. This too seems to be the goal of the restorative circles at Hillel Torah, an increasingly widespread practice at the school designed to enable conflict resolution and emotional expression. The diversity of schools engaged in this social-emotional work is as striking as are the various ways in which they're going about addressing these issues. Schools are grappling with mental health challenges among young people (a phenomenon some characterize as an epidemic), and they appear deeply committed to ensuring that students experience school as a safe space emotionally where they can exercise as much control over their lives as possible.

An analogue of this effort, and often an integral part of it too, as we saw at TanenbaumCHAT, with its multilayered student services department with guidance counselors, learning specialists, and deans, is the extensive investment schools are making in meeting the special academic needs of students. A generation ago, this was an area in which Jewish day schools lagged. It was common to hear of parents who were deeply committed to providing their children with a rich Jewish education nonetheless withdrawing them from schools that could not meet their learning needs. Such incidents still occur but it seems that much has changed. Schools have become much more adept at providing resources for students with special learning needs. Darchei Torah's state-of-the-art vocational center and its resource unit make it a field leader among ultra-Orthodox schools in this respect. The design of learning spaces at Hillel Detroit maximizes the possibility of meeting the learning needs of all students and has made the school a much-visited destination for those wanting to redesign their own schools to better serve students. At the Hebrew Academy of Miami—an institution that lacks access to the kinds of resources available at Hillel—a deep bench of learning specialists can be called on by parents in a fee-for-service arrangement. In all of the schools we studied, the budget line for "resources"—programs and interventions to serve students' special learning needs—has increased significantly since the turn of the century.

Listening to heads of school and board members talk about this transformation, it is evident that it is fueled in part by business considerations, a recognition that if schools don't respond to parents' demands for these kinds of support, they'll no longer be competitive in the marketplace. But it's not only parent demands that drive these initiatives: they stem from Jewish values central to school missions.

Modeling Particular (Jewish) Values
Plenty of public and private schools (maybe most) can claim to be values-driven institutions. And yet those values are often eclipsed by the respon-

sibility to ensure that by the time students graduate, they are on the way to being employable and law-abiding citizens. Surely, though, schooling is about more than the task of preparing young people for the functions they're expected to perform in society. Values-oriented schools strive for something larger. Schools can help young people become both the best possible versions of themselves and also producers of culture, not only consumers of it.

Educational leaders don't use this kind of language every day; some might not ever. School mission statements frequently don't do justice to articulating their larger purpose either; mission statements often have too much of a boilerplate or off-the-shelf quality. The best way to identify the extent to which schools seek to cultivate such outcomes in their students is to observe the choices educators make in the moment, to note the policies that schools formulate, and to deconstruct the kinds of interpersonal interactions they encourage. Ethnographic data reveal a set of animating values among the schools we studied that are widely shared and are especially prominent in some places. The values that stand out most conspicuously are *achrayut* (responsibility), *chesed* (kindness/caring for others), *Torah lishmah* (Torah study for its own sake), *menschlichkeit* (decency), and *ahavat Yisrael* (engagement with Jewish Peoplehood). Sometimes these values are formally celebrated in rituals, signage, or formally posted statements; sometimes they are simply enacted, embedded in everyday life. The following examples demonstrate what we mean:

> *Achrayut*—At the Rav Teitz Mesivta, we noted a number of examples of how the principal responds to students who act out, skip class, or engage in pranks. Rabbi Neuman's overriding goal is to protect students from themselves. He deliberately creates an environment in which students can learn from their mistakes without being ruined by them. That, he believes, is how they develop *achrayut*—becoming responsible for their own actions and those of others.
>
> *Chesed*—Darchei Torah provides any number of examples of how it inculcates *chesed* in students, from its inclusive admissions policy, the special attention given to students from disadvantaged homes, the extensive capital investment in facilities for students with special learning needs, the encouragement of stronger learners to form *chevrutot* (study partnerships) with weaker ones, and the endless stories (*vortlach*) students hear of special acts of chesed. As an alumnus noted, the yeshiva is well and truly a chesed machine.

Torah Lishmah—It may seem strange to single out TanenbaumCHAT as inculcating the value of Torah study for its own sake. This is a community day school where students are as frequently graded for their performance in the major disciplines of Jewish studies as they are in the subjects whose grades help them get into the top universities. But that's the point the school is making: Jewish literacy is serious, it is hard earned—especially in Hebrew—and as we observed in classes, it provides rich intellectual fulfillment, even joy, to those who achieve mastery. Ultimately Torah study won't make much of a difference to a student's college competitiveness. The school communicates that it should be studied conscientiously for its own sake.

Menschlichkeit—Eschewing the bells and whistles of some of its immediate Beverly Hills competitors, the Pressman Academy invests in programs designed to nurture *menschen*—well-rounded and grounded human beings who exhibit concern and respect for others. Launching a new life skills program for the whole school in order to cultivate ethical intelligence, it builds up the kinds of empathetic understanding students are already being asked to employ with classmates in weekly council meetings and in monthly family time with students from other grades. It's this ethos that draws parents to its doors.

Ahavat Yisrael—Akiva inculcates an appreciation of Jewish peoplehood as a value every day. The student body finely balances a mix of children from families who identify with every possible Jewish religious denomination or with none at all. Despite this ideological diversity, the entire school worships together every day, engages in meaningful Jewish text study, and marks the special events on the Jewish calendar in a spirit of mutual respect and inclusion. As the only Jewish day school for hundreds of miles, Akiva models for the broader Jewish community and its own students how the values of shared peoplehood trump those of ideological exclusiveness.

Observed in heightened form in these specific instances, it seems to us that these are the most widely shared values promoted by our sample of schools. There are others they promote, of course, but we have come to see these as the essential DNA of day school education today.

Educating for the Twenty-First Century

If schools promised only the outcomes we have just enumerated, no matter how admirable, we wonder if they would have any appeal beyond the Orthodox community and perhaps not even among some of that community's subsectors. Ultimately, without promising an education that comes close to matching or exceeding the academic quality of local independent and public schools, it is hard to see how day schools would attract interest beyond the youngest grades.

As will be apparent from the previous chapters, even schools with more traditionalist orientations are striving to be competitive with neighboring schools, despite the fact—as in the cases of Hillel Torah or the Rav Teitz Mesivta, for example—that there is little chance that parents would be interested in enrolling their children at those schools. It seems that the leaders of these two schools, like those in more liberal schools, appreciate that the goals of schooling have evolved, as have the most powerful means by which people learn. As a consequence, they are engaged in an ongoing (and often exhausting) effort to upgrade and update their offerings, as far their budgets will allow. Today, STEM and STEAM programs are ubiquitous. More than half of the schools in our sample boast makerspaces, which tend to be buzzing hives of activity at every hour of the day, including before and after school. One school has a greenhouse; a few have their own student-maintained gardens. Various distinctive forms of cutting-edge pedagogy are widely in evidence too. Our cases draw attention to the responsive classroom approach; flipped classrooms; social, emotional, and ethical learning; blended learning; design thinking; no-homework policies; and a no-grade/no-fail approach.

More generally, during our tens of hours spent in classrooms, we observed students and teachers engaged in the kinds of educational practices widely assumed to cultivate the skills and work habits needed to thrive in an economy that is changing so fast that most in this generation of young people may work in occupations we cannot even imagine. In some schools, it was rare to see children working by themselves; in almost every class, they were called on to collaborate with peers, including in one memorable instance connecting remotely to a student project-partner too sick to get to school that day. Often they were not sitting down or at desks while using their hands to manipulate construction equipment, work with design tools, or operate video and audio recording equipment. In the younger grades, reading and writing workshops were a strong feature of classroom life, and they too included working with groups of peers. Everywhere, teachers were employing problem-based learning, project-based learning, and technology-assisted learning. In all of these settings, the onus was on students to figure out things for themselves, not to swallow ready-made answers. One might say that "instruction" as a construct seems to be rapidly disappearing when so much learning depends on student-instigated discovery.

It's clear that many day schools are trying to ensure they don't get left behind in a time of rapid educational change. Yet these developments come with challenges. Parents want their children to develop the skills with which to thrive in an increasingly competitive economy, but they're also disoriented when schools look less and less like the ones they attended. Now, administrators are investing ever more time in running workshops for parents to keep them up to speed. If day schools once suffered from an image of being ready to initiate change only in response to parental pressure, the current dynamic goes in the opposite direction. It's no wonder that the head of Hillel Detroit defines his role as "communicator in chief": as school leader, he has to coax parents out of their comfort zones. A similar challenge faces the chief innovation officer at the Hebrew Academy, an Orthodox school.

Toughest of all in this environment, everyone—parents and teachers—is challenged by questions about how many hours it is healthy for young people to spend in front of screens or when they should access certain kinds of technology. This surely is one of the most challenging dimensions of learning today, and schools are feeling their way toward policies regarding student-owned, handheld devices. It was painful to witness, in one instance, educators wrestling with a case of technology addiction that was overwhelming both child and parents. Technology brings with it a dark side, not only advances in pedagogy.

Day schools were founded with a stated ambition of serving students, and their capacity to do so lies at the heart of their value proposition, certainly to those who pay their fees. But day schools also have taken on additional missions: to serve their parent bodies and the wider Jewish communities they inhabit. Our nine schools offer rich examples of how schools enact these additional functions.

What Day Schools Offer Parents

In a different context, one of us has closely examined the contribution of day schools to the lives of parents, in particular the parents of younger children.[2] That work pointed to the ways in which schools contribute to the

Jewish social networks of parents and in some cases to their Jewish cultural literacy while serving as sites of Jewish meaning for many of them. Our study confirms these findings while adding nuance to them. We see now how these Jewish community-building and culture-building functions assume greater significance the less intensive the Jewish lives of families were before they became connected to a school. For families at the more traditional end of the spectrum (and occasionally in more liberal communities) who typically live in close proximity to one another, attend the same synagogues with great regularity, and perform Jewish rituals at home with great intensity, whatever Jewish culture children bring back from school constitutes a nominal addition to their already rich Jewish lives. At one end of the spectrum, Darchei Torah may indeed have been the nucleus around which a community of highly observant families originally formed in Far Rockaway, but today the adults in those families do not depend on the yeshiva to enrich their Jewish lives socially or culturally. They have sufficient resources of their own. That's the case at the other Orthodox day schools in our sample with the interesting exception of the Hebrew Academy in Miami, where the school, because it enrolls a high proportion of migrants and immigrants, provides a site for families with thin social networks to connect with one another. The school's inclusive religious ethos also means that there is a proportion of less observant families who feel enriched by the educational programming offered there and brought home by their children.

Our investigation points to three ways in which schools contribute to the lives of parents.

Crucibles of Community

For families starting out with relatively underdeveloped Jewish social networks, their children's schools play a constructive role in their own lives as adults. The thickening of their relationships with other Jewish adults is an everyday consequence of what one might characterize as caring for one another's children, through car-pooling arrangements, sitting together on committees, or organizing playdates. By these means, the concern they share for their children helps parents make Jewish friends.

Some schools don't just rely on the serendipity of elementary school life to work its magic. They cultivate these relationships with intentionality. Hillel Detroit runs a family camp, family get-togethers around Sukkot, "movies and munchies" social events, mystery Shabbat dinners, adult-oriented programs on how to make a Seder table, and recipes for holiday meals, for example. As we observed, these efforts are designed to build community within the parent body and strengthen ties between parents and the school. Brandeis Marin employs a part-time head of community building, a portfolio that includes helping parents organize educational and social events for one another, integrating new families into the school community, and facilitating the admissions process. At Akiva, the school's small size means that any new family is immediately known and welcomed to a ready-made community—"the village," as one parent interviewee put it. As we explored previously, there are many reasons why more than a third of the students enrolled at Akiva come from families that are new to Nashville. In fact, the school is intentionally set up to provide these new arrivals with a social network they would otherwise lack.

Day school leaders invest effort in these activities both to build support networks for their schools or students, and also to aid families that might not otherwise know how to join a Jewish community. This outcome is especially helped by the integration of these efforts with special days in the Jewish calendar. When parents come into school to celebrate Chanukah, Purim, Sukkot, and Yom Haatzmaut (all mentioned by interviewees as memorable times at school), they join together not only with their own children but with the parents of other children who often make up a proximate and most attractive Jewish community.

Repair Shops

Previous studies of the relationships between families and Jewish schools have noted the extent to which in some contexts, parents build up their knowledge and understanding of Judaism through what their children bring home, through their children's inspiration, or through opportunities for adult education provided by the school. We came across examples of these phenomena among the liberal schools in our sample where, prompted by the desire to keep up with their children, parents devoted themselves to learning Hebrew (sometimes in classes provided by school), as well as in other ways, seeking to become more informed about Judaism. Their express goal was to contribute to their children's education and affirm what their children were learning in school. By attending a Jewish day school, their children have disturbed the equilibrium of their families' Jewish lives; school and home are not separate universes in that respect. And this moves some families onto a different, more engaged Jewish trajectory.

More profound still, we encountered in these schools parents who never had expected any of their children to attend a Jewish day school. (As one Akiva parent put it, "We didn't think of ourselves as those kinds of people.") Some parents explored the day school as an option for their child with deep skepticism. Dragged to the day school by a non-Jewish partner or a more engaged Jewish spouse, parents expected to encounter a traditional Jewish education of the kind that had embittered their formative years or one entirely alien to their lives. Some of the families we met admitted feeling deeply uncomfortable in public Jewish settings, especially in those with a religious orientation. Once they enrolled their child in day school and experienced its warmth and intelligence, they came to relate in altogether different ways to the organized Jewish community. Thanks to the prompting of their children, they arrived at a more positive appreciation of their own Jewishness and of how to express it in meaningful ways. As Peg Sandel, head of school at Brandeis Marin puts it, having come to the school "in defiance of themselves," they embark on a "journey of repair." In her words, "The school is repairing the harm done by previous generations." This has wider community implications but most immediately it contributes to the content of families' own lives.

Guides for the Perplexed

Day schools contribute to the lives of parents in still one more way. They are increasingly called on to help parents navigate the challenges of raising children today. Seasoned educators notice a discernable increase in levels of parental anxiety compared to previous generations, a change they attribute in large part to the invasion of social media and other forms of technology into the lives of young people. For this reason alone, it may be harder to raise children today. As veteran educators in our school sample reported, parents of school-aged children—members of what sociologist Jean Twenge calls Generation Me[3]—tend to be acutely anxious about their children's physical and mental well-being, as Greg Lukianoff and Jonathan Haidt have also argued.[4] Whatever the causes, schools cannot evade or ignore the needs of parents.

One administrator reported on the demands she receives from parents who want the school to do their parenting for them, even at the level of solving their children's social problems. At a different school, parents have asked administrators to confiscate smartphones rather than risk antagonizing their own children. And on top of these expectations, schools also help parents address other mental health issues, such as eating disorders and depression.

Schools address the anxieties of parents in a variety of ways. They run workshops and special programs, such as Pressman's Parenting Institute, which offers programs "designed to support parents, give them access to information, and help guide them in raising their children." In a very different milieu, Darchei Torah offers a series of classes on parenting each year in the homes of younger families. Hillel Torah runs a parent ambassador program in which volunteer couples help their younger peers with the "transition from early childhood to primary and then on to middle school." Schools are staffing up with all kinds of specialists whose task is to help parents help their children and teach children how to help themselves. They provide professional development for staff members to educate them so they can respond more effectively to whatever challenges students or parents pose. Overall, schools devote much more time now to engaging with the increasing number of parents who seek counsel about child-rearing challenges.

Jewish day schools are not alone in facing these challenges, and they're evidently reaching out to experts in other educational systems to learn how to be more responsive and effective in offering support. What's interesting is that in a context where schools are already tightly woven into the fabric of families' Jewish lives, they're also drawn even closer as they form a partnership in raising the next generation. Of course, their first order of business is to educate children, but they are becoming a one-stop shop for families in other related domains too.

What Day Schools Offer Communities

As noted in the Introduction, day schools at their inception in North America were seen as fortresses, defenders of tradition designed to keep at bay the worst aspects of the New World. They were criticized for being sectarian and separate, a charge their leadership often embraced with relish. Beyond the various ultra-Orthodox sectors, insularity is not a relevant criticism of day schools today. Advocates for most day schools have learned that it is not in their interest to maintain a separatist stance. It's not just that they would make themselves irrelevant to parents; they would jeopardize their own financial sustainability when it has become increasingly evident that their economic survival depends on communal support. The extended families of their students and alumni by themselves alone don't have the wherewithal to sustain day schools financially.

In a community where there is only one day school, Nashville's Akiva School offers the most compelling example of what the contemporary day school contributes beyond the services it provides to those who attend every day and to their parents: it models and cultivates nonpolarized community relationships, it is a physical anchor for the local Jewish community, and it is an incubator of leadership for that Jewish community. Akiva's case not only conveys the ways in which a day school makes these kinds of contributions to the community. It also demonstrates how those whose own children or grandchildren don't attend the school are ready to provide financial support. Akiva's special circumstances make all of these outcomes especially vivid, but we found evidence of these particular contributions across a great many of the schools in our sample, as we now endeavor to show.

Antidotes to Polarization

Our nine schools provide some evidence that day schools may temper some of the widescale polarization in the contemporary American Jewish community. Dozens of community day schools with a strong pluralistic orientation work to avoid privileging one understanding of Judaism over another. They nurture a culture of mutual appreciation and respect. In our sample, Hillel Detroit and Brandeis Marin offer strong instantiations of this ethos. They provide students with different experiences of prayer. Faculty hold a range of ideological commitments, and families affiliate with a variety of synagogues, or with none at all. These are common characteristics of a community day school.

Yet even some schools with strong denominational commitments provide a shared space for families with diverse Jewish lives. The Pressman Academy (a Conservative day school located on the premises of a Conservative synagogue) and the Hebrew Academy in Miami Beach (described in its philosophy statement as a "Modern Orthodox Dati Tziyoni [religious Zionist] school") fit this bill. Both schools draw a segment of families whose home observances differ from the practices observed at school and who affiliate—if they do at all—with congregations aligned with different movements from those with which each of the schools identifies. In both cases, parents periodically test whether the school is willing to give ground on certain principles, challenging school leadership from different directions. At Pressman, for example, some less traditional parents object to the school's insistence that food at birthday parties be certified kosher; more traditionally oriented parents complain about their daughters being required to learn how to chant Torah. Similarly, at the Hebrew Academy, controversies have arisen over the school's banning birthday parties starting before Shabbat ends and other parental complaints to end coed classes in high school general studies courses. These kinds of issues periodically surface, but they don't poison the climate. Parents generally understand and respect the schools' ideological orientations, and they appreciate the schools' commitments to inclusiveness and respect for all students, regardless of their own home practice. At the Hebrew Academy it is particularly striking that the director of admissions is happy sharing with prospective parents that "we're soup to nuts in terms of observance." In other communities, that's something an Orthodox day school would not advertise; in Miami, it is a distinguishing feature of the school that the administration is ready to celebrate.

TanenbaumCHAT offers a different model of how day schools contribute to a nonpolarized Jewish culture. The school is incorporated as a community day school—one might say, as a nondenominational rather than pluralistic one. As we saw, its Judaic studies curriculum and its faculty have been critiqued for being too traditional. The school's stance is that traditionalism is being confused with seriousness and that it is providing students with a rigorous grounding in the foundational components of Jewish culture and Jewish living—whatever their ideological orientation. If the school is proselytizing anything, it is the notion that all Jews who take their Jewishness seriously should be knowledgeable about their culture and should take responsibility for their community. It's a fiercely nonpartisan position, a characterization that comes close to sounding like an oxymoron. At the present historical moment, this stance feels profoundly countercultural, which makes it of special value to the broader Jewish community.

Anchors of Community

When middle-class parents choose to buy a house, the availability of good schools in the area is a significant factor in their decision. The presence of a good Jewish day school can have a similar impact on the life choices of some Jewish parents. The viability and intensity of the Jewish communities in which schools are situated is a second major consideration.

All of this was particularly evident in the Nashville Jewish community. Many of our interviewees, especially if they were traditional or observant, indicated that they would not have moved to Nashville to take up a job opportunity if there hadn't been a local day school. The same considerations influenced Jewish communal professionals such as rabbis in all four congregations and also some senior staff at the Federation.

Darchei Torah offers an equally dramatic case of how a day school helps build Jewish community. When the yeshiva was established, a few highly observant Jews were living in Far Rockaway; even the Rosh Yeshiva preferred to commute every day from Brooklyn. As the school has grown, a vibrant network of synagogues, kosher shops, and other facilities have sprouted nearby. In unusually entrepreneurial fashion, the school even purchased and redeveloped local homes, selling them to mission-aligned families, thereby further stabilizing the neighborhood. It's no wonder the school's leadership likes to think of itself as having created a mini-Lakewood in this part of Long Island. As they see it, an educational institution, the yeshiva, has been the nucleus around which an organic community has formed.

These two instances are extreme, but parallels exist in other places too. In Skokie, Illinois, the Modern Orthodox community is spread across four modest-sized synagogues. Because families don't travel by car on Shabbat, they must live near their place of worship, especially when Chicago winters limit people's readiness to walk far. These synagogue communities would have been fragmented and weak if it wasn't for the presence of Hillel Torah. The school does not so much provide the nucleus as the capillary system that enables these groups to function as a more substantial and stable community. If Hillel Torah did not exist, families would have had other options to the religious right and left. None would be a comfortable fit. One suspects that in time the Modern Orthodox community would have moved on to another part of town or another city where life would be less complicated.

Hillel Detroit plays a similar role for a more liberal population. Proximity to places of worship is not the issue here but the potential fragmentation of a web of community institutions is. Over generations, Hillel has enabled a network of families, many of whose members have played central roles as volunteers or professionals in the wider Jewish community to form relationships with one another. The school is part of a larger system that includes Camp Tamarack, the community's overnight camp, and half a dozen Conservative and Reform congregations. Parents talk about the school being part of a system. It might not function as the heart or even the capillary network, but it is a vital organ for maintaining the general health of Detroit's Jewish community.

The case of Brandeis Marin is noteworthy in a different way because it is situated in an unusual Jewish community. About 10 percent of the students are not Jewish, and as many as half of the families are not members of any other Jewish institution. For many families, the school is their Jewish community. Sharing facilities with a Reform congregation and with a Jewish Community Center, the school has become a portal to Jewish engagement and education for children and adults.

Seedbeds of Leadership

Where schools have been in existence for more than forty of fifty years, it is apparent that alumni play a critically important role in Jewish communal life. How much the current activism of alumni is a consequence of what they gained at school and how much was inculcated by the families in which they were raised is hard to determine. But there is certainly a relationship between a day school education and subsequent activism in Jewish life by alumni, a relationship one of us probed in a previous study of emerging Jewish leaders.[5]

This phenomenon was most observable at TanenbaumCHAT in Toronto, a community where the quality of life is such that there is a strong tendency among young people to settle down in town, usually close to where they were raised. We have already commented on the school's pride about the high proportion of current faculty who are alumni. The same is true for the alumni who serve as professional and volunteer leaders in the city's Federation, schools, and synagogues. There is a virtuous circle here in which this community high school, with its intense commitment to Jewish culture and Jewish life, is supported by alumni animated by the goal of enabling future generations to assume a leadership role in the city's Jewish life. A similar pattern exists at Hillel in Detroit, where local community leaders often began their conversations with us by stating, "You do know I'm an alum of the school." Hillel's alumni have been both beneficiaries of and contributors to the richness of local Jewish life, through thick and thin, since the 1950s.

There is a related and particularly intriguing pattern at the two Modern Orthodox schools in the sample, Hillel Torah and the Hebrew Academy, both of which have also been in existence for more than sixty years. In both instances, alumni of the schools are active in welfare, educational, and religious institutions in their region, within the Modern Orthodox community and beyond. What's different in their cases, uniquely so compared to other schools in our sample, is how many alumni have emigrated to Israel. In these explicitly religious Zionist institutions, this outcome is as much a source of pride as the number of alumni who today are making a contribution locally. These *olim* (emigrants to Israel) are enacting the schools' Zionist ethos in the fullest possible sense. No doubt, this phenomenon also means that a sizable proportion of graduates are sending their own children to school in Israel rather than to their alma mater. This is truly the price of success.

It's tempting to connect the active roles played by alumni in their local communities to the outcome noted at the outset of this discussion: day school alumni are likely to become Jewish cultural virtuosos. They continue to be closely connected with their Jewish peers and share a commitment to the values of *chesed, ahavat yirael,* and *torah lishma* (caring for others, love of the Jewish people, and Jewish study for its own sake). If indeed their schooling has provided a springboard to academic and personal success, then they are the kinds of people one might expect to play a leading role wherever they settle, whether in North America or Israel. By contributing in powerful ways to the lives of individual students, day schools are increasing the human capital of Jewish communities.

Overcoming Challenges

Taken together, these contributions to the lives of children, families, and the wider community present a formidable portrait of the contemporary Jewish day school and its special promise. And yet this picture would not be complete without drawing attention to the major challenges that at times impede these schools from delivering on what they promise.

All of these schools face distinct local challenges posed by the populations they serve, the geographic locations in which they're situated, and the institutional history their current leadership has inherited. For example, TanenbaumCHAT's maintenance of an intense Jewish studies program is being squeezed by shifting norms in its feeder schools and by ever-intensifying competition to get into good colleges that bring pressure to reduce the number of required Jewish studies courses. The Hebrew Academy struggles to stay ahead of the fallout created by skyrocketing property prices in neighborhoods near the school from which its families and its faculty have historically come and where they can no longer afford to live. The Rav Teitz Mesivta is fighting to turn around a reputation that the school has fallen behind competitor institutions, which makes it less attractive to its ideal constituencies. Each school faces a number of distinctive and occasionally idiosyncratic challenges of this kind. Wherever they're located, though, two related challenges stand out above all others as threatening their viability and vitality: ongoing struggles to ensure their financial sustainability and to recruit quality personnel—*kemach* and *koach adam,* as one might put it alliteratively in Hebrew.

School Affordability and Financial Sustainability
In both real and relative terms, the cost of day school education has been rising for the past thirty years, seemingly without limits. School leaders and community commentators started to sound the alarm about day school tu-

ition levels in the early 1990s during the great expansion of those schools. The issue, we believe, is not solely inflationary pressure on the costs of rising salaries and staff benefits. Almost every move schools make to raise quality comes with a price tag: up-to-date technology, appropriate resources for students with special emotional and learning needs, programming to connect students to Israel. All of these items place pressure on the bottom line, and these are only a few items on a long list of needs.

And so, while the vitality and richness of the day school product may well have improved, an increasing proportion of parents are not able to afford the full cost of this product. At the nine schools in our sample, the corollary is that the funds raised through tuition cover a diminishing proportion of their budgets, somewhere between just over 50 and 85 percent. At best, no more than 5 percent of a school's budget will come through a contribution by the local Federations. The balance therefore has to be raised from alternative income streams, from philanthropic gifts, or—in some cases—through specific forms of public funding. There is only so much that parents can contribute. Under pressure to satisfy the demands of the market and fulfill their responsibilities effectively, these schools, like other independent schools around North America, are in danger of pricing themselves out of the market they were created to serve.

In the blogosphere, at professional conferences, and at think tank convenings, all kinds of solutions to this financial conundrum are proposed. A recent review finds that about a third of day schools offer some type of alternative or creative tuition program—programs other than traditional scholarship or financial aid. The most common of these programs include capped or discounted tuition for middle-income families, indexed or flexible tuition, and tuition discounts for Jewish communal professionals.[6] For such programs to be realistic, though, funding must come from some exceptional source, and not from families that can pay full tuition.

Four schools in our sample have benefited from some exceptional sources of revenue. Thanks to time-limited multimillion-dollar gifts from benefactors in their local communities, Hillel Day School is able to discount tuition by about a third to all families, and TanenbaumCHAT has done so for four cohorts of incoming families. Akiva has been able to discount tuition thanks to the herculean efforts of one individual donor and fundraiser who has been remarkably successful in broadening the school's funding base, raising support from a great many people whose own children or grandchildren don't attend the school, and at the same time building up a great number of legacy pledges. Finally, the Hebrew Academy has been able to suppress tuition levels for its families by accessing a variety of special funds provided by the state of Florida for both public and parochial schools. These sources are of tremendous help now; however, most might evaporate in the medium-term future.

At the other five schools, financial pressures are vividly apparent. On the one hand, they're engaged in a relentless, exhausting struggle to generate additional income. Because Darchei Torah is so much associated with the personality and profile of its Rosh Yeshivah, a tremendous burden falls on him in an around-the-clock effort to form relationships with extended families at moments of significance in their lives; these, it is hoped, will translate into gifts to the yeshiva. In other schools, the burden is shared more equally between professionals and volunteers, in an exhausting and endless parade of fundraising programs: breakfasts, golf tournaments, grandparent days, fun nights, prize raffles, gala evenings, and targeted asks. On the other side of the balance sheet, there is an excruciating but also no less relentless scrutiny of potential cost-saving measures, such as tinkering with class sizes, teachers' benefits packages, pay structures, and back-office organization. This is not a case of trying to find ways of doing more with less, but essentially of doing more without having more with which to work.

The schools we have studied offer hope that the sky is not falling on the day school enterprise, but their experiences demonstrate how much creativity, hard work, self-sacrifice, and occasional good fortune are needed to keep disaster at bay and even to thrive.

The Hiring Challenge

The high price tag of day school tuition and the general cost of Jewish life have overshadowed a second though no less consequential challenge: finding sufficient numbers of quality Jewish educators and sometimes general educators too. It is surely no coincidence that the schools in our sample feeling the most pressure when recruiting teachers lie between the Centrist or ultra-Orthodox sectors, on the one hand, which draw on a large pool of individuals coming out of America's Haredi yeshivas, and, on the other hand, the community day school sector where, with the exception of TanenbaumCHAT, there is less need to find ideologically aligned specialists. Notably, Pressman, a Conservative day school with a strong commitment to Hebrew, and the two Modern Orthodox schools—Hillel Torah and the Hebrew Academy—which aspire to find appropriate religious role models who also can teach high levels of Jewish studies and/or Hebrew—are perennially in search of mission-appropriate staff.

In this context, Pressman and Hillel Torah have adopted bold, constructive solutions. First, they have restructured their middle school curriculum to separate Hebrew from Judaic studies, thereby expecting different types of expertise from prospective faculty. Hillel Torah has also invested considerably in the recruitment and training of *shlichim* to prepare them to work with American students. The school has been proactive as well in forming a close relationship with families at the local Yeshiva University Kollel, attracting successful teachers in that way. Pressman has pursued a different approach: it invests a great many resources in professional development, working with a who's who list of outside providers to ensure that those it hires, many of whom are Israeli Americans, are well prepared to work with the school's students. The Hebrew Academy faces a perpetual challenge to make strong hiring decisions in Jewish studies as well as in general studies because it is hard-pressed to offer salary and benefits packages comparable to what teachers can make at local public schools.

Financial and human resource challenges also place still more pressure on tuition costs. As a consequence, in most schools, teachers command salaries of between $40,000 and $60,000 a year; TanenbaumCHAT is again an exception, with senior teachers earning more than $100,000 (Canadian). At most schools, additional benefits are on offer. For example, Darchei Torah has gained a national reputation for taking care of its faculty in this respect. Still, it is telling that take-home pay is not enough for some teachers to pay full tuition for even one of their own children in the schools that employ them. No wonder it is difficult for some schools to recruit teachers. In a great many instances, those who teach in day schools are not the primary breadwinners in their own families, meaning that for schools, like Hillel Day School and Akiva, that lie outside the major Jewish population centers, there is almost no chance of recruiting classroom teachers or support specialists from out of town. Schools hope to get lucky, but invariably they're fishing for talent in very shallow pools.

Though no school in our sample is in danger of going out of business on account of this challenge, all struggle to find the personnel who can deliver the Judaic, social-emotional, and academic outcomes they promise. If they can't do so, their very raison d'être and the extensive financial investment they require is moot. For these reasons, the stakes couldn't be much higher.

Principals and Principles

A final challenge to day schools concerns the hiring of first-class heads of school (or principals, as they are called in some school sectors). Almost all of the nine schools we examined are blessed with stable, high-quality leadership. The stability and quality of the individuals heading up schools are fundamental contributors to the making of good schools.

Two factors ultimately underpin everything else: the quality of the school's most senior personnel and the clarity of the school's educational vision. Ultimately, these merge in the person of the head of school, a highly visible individual who embodies the school's educational vision.

Here are a few examples in the schools we observed. At Brandeis Marin, Peg Sandel models what it means to embrace a Jewish identity, take it seriously, and make it joy filled, while making space for others who see their Jewishness in different terms. This is the Jewish vision she has brought to the school and has encouraged others to embrace. Jonathan Levy at CHAT models what it means to be a Jewishly and civically well-educated Canadian day school alum. A former school guidance counselor, he embodies and advances the fusion of values integral to CHAT's identity as a community academy. Similarly, Menachem Linzer at Hillel Torah brings his persona as a guitar-playing intellectual with a commitment to learner centeredness and a passion for Israel and Jewish learning to his work. Finally, at Akiva, Daniela Pressner demonstrates how seriousness about one's own Jewish choices can be fused with an inclusiveness for all without having to surrender one's own identity, the central Jewish message of the school.

The ease with which it is possible to offer these examples (and would have been to cite others) highlights, first, the extent to which most of these nine schools are animated by distinctive and unambiguous Jewish purposes. We don't need to check their mission statements to know what they stand for. More often than not, their purposes are evident in their policies and practices. Second, these easily chosen examples underscore the central role played by the school's senior educational professional—head of school, Rosh Yeshivah, or principal, whatever his or her official title—both in advancing and embodying those purposes. For parents and students and for community members outside the school, principled principals embody what their schools aim to achieve.

Coda: Day Schools during the COVID-19 Pandemic

As we put the finishing touches on this book, the world was turned upside down by the COVID-19 pandemic. Jewish day schools were widely praised for the speed and effectiveness with which they responded to the turmoil created by the virus. In some cases, they shifted to remote learning in as little as one day and then delivered a rich program of learning and community gathering for the rest of the 2019–20 school year. Surveys of day school students found high levels of appreciation for the efforts made by their schools, especially when they compared their own experiences to those of peers in public schools.[7]

With the start of the following academic year in August 2020, the great majority of day schools made arrangements to reopen their doors while strictly adhering to local health guidelines. Investing heavily in equipment and staff, they prepared themselves for every eventuality: in-person, hybrid, or fully remote learning. Again, the readiness and adaptability of schools were resoundingly applauded.

Against this backdrop, we were curious to see how the nine schools in our study fared. How had they coped in the face of the academic and social-emotional challenges that confronted their students and teachers? Were they among those schools experiencing robust and even growing enrollment going into the new academic year, or were they finding the going harder? In late September 2020, we reached out to the heads at all nine schools, asking them to provide a picture of their school's responses since the onset of the pandemic. We were especially curious to learn whether there was continuity or a complete break from their way of functioning in the pre-COVID times.

Strengthened through Stress

To be sure, the day-to-day experiences of students was radically different from what we had observed when they attended classes with no concern about health precautions, protective masks, and social distancing. How could it be otherwise when schooling either had to be conducted from home or was constrained by various layers of personal protection and social distancing? And yet, the nine schools in our sample were able to continue their work. If they suffered a decline in enrollment, it was only marginal. In some schools, the drop-off occurred mainly in the early childhood centers. A few actually benefited from transfers from public schools or new arrivals as families relocated to escape urban settings in the Northeast. As a result, their enrollments increased. In Nashville, for example, Akiva saw a year-on-year increase of almost 20 percent.

Even more striking, the distinctive culture that we had observed at each school prior to COVID-19 strongly shaped their responses during the health crisis. Ironically, at a historical moment perceived to have been truly exceptional—a proverbial black swan occurrence—the responses of schools and the strengths they displayed were anything but exceptional, by which we mean they were fully consistent with patterns established pre-COVID. Precisely those assets that schools had built up in recent decades, often at great expense and occasionally in the face of some resistance, have been especially valuable under emergency circumstances. For example, the integration of technology into their programs—what we have characterized as "educating for the twenty-first century"—and investing in meeting the social and emotional needs of children—what we called "caring for souls"—have become priceless resources. If parents previously questioned the price tag for some of these features and the staff needed to maintain them, they were now seeing the value in such investments. If COVID-19 constituted a giant stress test, then the assets schools had built up not only helped them get through this moment but flourish too.

For example, in recent years, the Hebrew Academy in Miami Beach had invested in serious professional development opportunities for its teachers, especially in upgrading their proficiency in blended learning. With this foundation, teachers were able to pivot to remote learning within a day. Even more striking, they displayed a great receptivity to new online learning programs. Rabbi Bossewitch, the innovation officer, reported that teachers were now sharing with each other and the administration new approaches they came across on their own. In short, they were primed by earlier training to seek out and adopt new ways of teaching appropriate to the pandemic situation.

Hillel in Detroit had built up an impressive physical plant with many enticing nooks and crannies for students to explore, such as a greenhouse, vast makerspace, and a robotics lab. This attention to the uses of space translated during the pandemic into extensive investments in new spatial configurations when the school reopened for in-person classes. The grounds of the school were enhanced to ensure the health safety of students. Hillel managed to set aside different spaces for what it called "separate communities"—different grades and divisions were isolated in their own pods.

Several schools, including Brandeis Marin and Hillel Day School, used the summer months to work on intensive professional development and instituted a new learning management system to help parents keep track of each child's assignments. "Trust is the most important asset a school has," reported Peg Sandel. Ensuring transparency and working together with parents were priorities in these schools before COVID-19 struck. These priorities pushed the schools to invest in additional means to keep parents in the loop during the health crisis, and parents responded warmly. More broadly, Jewish day schools had developed pre-COVID-19 an active program of regular communication with their students' families. They therefore were well positioned to build on those communications resources during the crisis. Recall, for example, the role of Hillel's school head as "communicator in chief." Other school heads also worked hard to maintain lines of communication with school families. Not surprisingly, parents responded appreciatively.

The investment in staff members to attend to the social and emotional lives of students that have characterized most of our nine schools pre-COVID also provided resources during the health crisis. Schools were acutely aware that the social isolation necessitated by lockdowns or social distancing were crushing to some students. Fortunately, the schools could call on experienced personnel to work with students and their families to ease some of the stresses. The Pressman Academy, with perhaps the largest counseling and social and emotional learning staff of all the schools, adopted trauma-informed practices that they delivered online to students. Most of the schools also organized virtual and distanced community gatherings to mark holidays, festive occasions, and especially graduation. At Brandeis Marin, every graduate was invited to speak at commencement. The staff at Akiva gained affirmation for how well they had supported students when parents told them of their children's distress when the school year ended. School had truly been a source of comfort during a challenging time, and children didn't want it to end.

The situation in the more traditional yeshivot, the Rav Teitz Mesivta and Yeshiva Darchei Torah, was especially challenging. Their communities were hard hit by the pandemic, with staff and students suffering losses in their families. Transferring to remote-learning platforms was also difficult when they had long resisted the invasion of the Internet into their families' lives. Darchei Torah, typically, was one of the more innovative institutions in its sector. The Yeshiva purchased tablets loaded with Zoom for every student, enabling a video connection within a closed network that kept the worst of the Internet at bay. Unfortunately, it does not seem to have been an entirely satisfying experience for either students or educators. At the Rav Teitz Mesivta, the approach was less about technology and more about providing a great deal of one-to-one interaction between *rebbeim* (Judaic studies teachers) and their students and by offering nighttime learning sessions when the boys were looking for company and interaction. At a time when the school was in the midst of a shift to a more student-centered model of education, the pandemic provided an opportunity to actualize such commitments in an especially meaningful fashion.

Priorities that anchored the practices of specific schools in normal times continued to be important in these abnormal times. At TanenbaumCHAT in Toronto, serving a high school population intensely anxious about its college competitiveness, the school invested a special effort in continuing to offer a full course load, first remotely and then, from September 2020, through an ingenious hybrid quad-mester system that minimized students' in-person interaction with their more than thirteen hundred fellow students (a significant increase in number since we had visited). While ensuring that no student's academic program would suffer, the school doubled down on its extracurricular offerings from cooking classes with *shlichim*, Yom Haatzmaut Zoom events for more than seven hundred people, to a grand graduation ceremony on wheels for more than two hundred students dispersed across Toronto, necessitating a proverbial military operation to pull off successfully. In effect, COVID-19 saw the school doubling down on the duel dimensions of its community academy identity

At Hillel Torah in Skokie, the story of how the school evolved its response to the pandemic strongly resembles the ways in which its education was transformed over the previous decade. The response was led from the front by the principal, Menachem Linzer, including enlisting the board's cooperation and prioritizing emotional support for students and teachers, a hallmark of his leadership. The school was typically methodical in how it navigated the transition. It started out with a modest set of remote learning classes, a kind of beta model, and then week by week, with frequent surveys of students, teachers, and parents, Hillel Torah progressively refined its approach to all classes. It reestablished daily Tefila, including on Sunday mornings by student demand. The approach to reopening was similarly calibrated, guided above all by a clear sense of purpose, in this case a kind of Maslow pyramid that prioritized, first, the physical health and safety of students and staff, then their social and emotional well-being, and then the academic integrity of the program. As during more normal times, what happened during the pandemic period at the school can be readily traced to its core principles.

Still Fundamental: Principles and Principals

The specific response of each school to the pandemic embodies, then, the features that make each distinctive—what we previously identified as the principles underpinning its particular direction. Enacting and articulating those principles are the responsibility of school heads, those we previously referred to as the "principals." In the best of times, heads of school shoulder a tremendous weight of responsibility. During the pandemic they were responsible for planning and implementing their school's response. It is astounding how many took it upon themselves to do their own research to determine what would be best for their school. They immersed themselves in the literature, consulted with colleagues, and talked with health experts. Ultimately they set a direction around which, in many cases, they also needed to build support. When we talked with them, they expressed deep pride in what they had accomplished; as one of them said, "It has been the most heart-warming experience of my career to see the kids so comfortable in school when the world outside is so uncomfortable." School heads were committed to opening in-person learning as the fulfillment of their school's educational mission. They did so in the full recognition that grave matters of health were on the line, as were the financial viability and Jewish commitments of their schools. The stakes for day school education were already high; during the health crisis, they were higher still.

Appendix

Day School Sectors by the Numbers

By the 2018–19 school year, there were an estimated 906 Jewish day schools in the United States,[1] and 57 in Canada.[2] These schools may be classified according to ideology.

The largest number of schools and students are found in the so-called Haredi sector (*Haredi* literally refers to "those who tremble before God"). This sector is made up of schools with one or the other of two broad orientations: Hasidic or Yeshivish. Schools under Hasidic auspices enroll the larger contingent in this sector. Inheritors of an eighteenth-century mystical strain of Judaism, Hasidim divide themselves into at least two dozen sects, each with its own leader. Numerically, the second largest group are the historical antagonists of the Hasidim, the spiritual descendants of their Lithuanian opponents. These are the Yeshivish, whose lives are oriented around upper-level academies of Torah study (yeshivas, places where males in their post–high school years study all day). Though often lumped together under the ungainly, and insulting, sobriquet labeling them as "the ultra-Orthodox," the subtle but very real distinctions in customs, garb, allegiances, and ways of living that characterize these different subpopulations loom far larger to insiders than their commonalities.[3] What their schools do have in common is a minimalist approach to general studies; strict gender separation; an ambivalence at best toward Zionism; a discomfort, if not suspicion, of those outside their communities, including Jews who do not share their approach; distinctive dress codes; and a predilection in Hasidic quarters to conduct their religious studies in Yiddish. According to the most recent census of Jewish day schools, two-thirds of Jewish day school students in the United States are enrolled in Haredi schools, whereas in Canada the Haredi sector comprises closer to one-third of all enrollments.

These schools are augmented by a considerably smaller number of students in Modern Orthodox and Centrist Orthodox schools. As the term *Modern Orthodox* suggests, these schools are far more open to the wider world than are Haredi schools and are more likely to offer strong general studies classes. Modern Orthodox schools in fact pride themselves on the successful placement of graduating students in America's elite colleges and universities, as is evident from the advertisements they place every spring in local Jewish newspapers proudly announcing that new graduates have successfully won admission to top Ivy League schools and public universities. Modern Orthodox schools also are likely to have coed classes, certainly for general studies and in some cases also for Judaic studies. They are unabashedly Zionist in their commitment to nurture in their students a strong connection to the state and people of Israel. Haredi schools by contrast do not grant legitimacy to the government of Israel because many of its leaders are not religious, but those schools do connect their students to fellow Haredi Jews in Israel.

Falling somewhere between the Modern Orthodox and Haredi schools are the Centrist Orthodox ones. These eschew coeducation, have strict rules of dress, particularly for girls, and hew a middle course when it comes to college education: they encourage their students to attend a small set of Jewish or local colleges and are wary of their students going on to places without large contingents of Orthodox students.

And finally, one growing sector of Orthodox schools is the network sponsored by the Chabad Hasidic movement. These schools are almost exclusively for students from non-Orthodox homes. They attend Chabad day schools either because those schools are the only Jewish day school in town or because their parents have some connection to Chabad. The Avi Chai census reports also include immigrant/outreach schools and special education ones, both categories almost entirely run under Orthodox auspices. They are quite small and have experienced shrinking enrollment.

Combining these figures with those of the Haredi schools, it is apparent that Jewish day schools are overwhelmingly an Orthodox phenomenon in the United States insofar as such schools enroll roughly 87 percent of Jewish day school students. On the high school level the imbalance is even greater. Only 10 percent of high school students in Jewish day schools attend a school under non-Orthodox auspices in the United States. That is not the case in Canada, where close to 40 percent of students in Jewish day high schools attend institutions not under Orthodox auspices.

Where are the other students to be found? The largest contingent of non-Orthodox day school students is enrolled in so-called community or pluralistic schools. As their name implies, these schools are designed to serve a wide swathe of the Jewish population and thereby strive to teach respect for diversity and pluralism in Jewish life. Students learn about the different strands of North American Judaism and how families in their schools celebrate Jewish holidays, attend different types of synagogues, or may be secular and Zionist. Israel serves as an important glue holding such schools together because it is a common denominator in an otherwise diverse parent body. For this reason, learning about the geography, history, and culture of Israel is an integral aspect of Jewish education in these schools.[4] That said, many community day schools require prayer on a daily basis, but may offer students a choice of the prayer style to be followed or may expose students to prayer as it is done in each of the Jewish religious movements. Community day schools enroll slightly under 7 percent of all Jewish day school students in the United States; in Canada, one-third of students in Jewish day schools are in community schools.

Reform Judaism has merely eleven schools under its auspices in the United States and one in Canada; none is a high school. And the Conservative movement's Schechter network, with thirty-two day schools in the United States and two in Canada, has seen its base shrink as many schools merged with or redefined themselves as community day schools in order to appeal to a broader spectrum of the local Jewish population.

As for ideology and curriculum, Reform and Conservative day schools are committed to high levels of general studies classes, both because their parent bodies insist on it and because most of their students go on to public or private upper schools. On the Jewish side, day schools under Reform auspices stress the ideology of that movement and generally offer only a very limited number of classes per day devoted to Jewish studies; Hebrew-language study is stressed. Schools under Conservative auspices devote between 30 and 40 percent of the school day to Jewish studies, daily prayer, and a strong commitment to Hebraic and Jewish literacy, more so than any other non-Orthodox schools, including the community ones. Both types of schools are entirely coed, have fairly loose dress codes, and tend to teach about religion with a very light touch, acknowledging the diversity of religious practices observed by the families of children enrolled in their schools.

The total enrollment of school-age students in Jewish day schools enumerated by the AVI CHAI Foundation's most recent census (dating to 2018) comes to 273,172 children.[5] Based on the 2013 Pew survey and more recent estimates, there are approximately 1.1 million Jewish children in the United States between the ages of five and eighteen. This means that slightly fewer than 16 percent of Jewish children of school age in the United States were enrolled in a day school in 2018.[6] The proportion of Canadian Jewish children enrolled in Jewish day schools is approximately 27 percent, while in the largest communities of Montreal and Toronto, this figure may reach over 40 percent.[7]

Glossary

Amida
> Literally, the prayer recited while standing; on weekdays, also referred to as the Shmoneh Esrei, Eighteen Benedictions, recited thrice daily.

Ashkenaz/Ashkenazi
> Hebrew name for German-speaking lands. Ashkenazi Jews descend from individuals whose families passed through Germany and then spread throughout Europe.

Ba'al Tefila
> Prayer leader.

Beis medrash
> Yeshiva study hall.

Borchu
> The call to prayer that initiates the most sacred part of the prayer service.

Bracha (pl. brachot)
> A blessing or benediction.

Chesed
> Social action, kindness, or caring for others.

Chinuch
> Education.

Chumash
> The Pentateuch.

Davening (daven)
> Praying (pray).

Derech Eretz
> Respect for others.

Dvar Torah (pl. Divrei Torah)
> A Jewish teaching (lit. a word of Torah).

Eretz Yisrael
> The Land of Israel.

Gemara
> Commentary on the Mishna/part of the Talmud.

Haggadah
  Liturgical work recited during the Passover Seder commemorating the exodus of Israelites from Egypt.
Halacha
  Jewish law.
Hashem
  God.
Hashkafa
  Religious ideology.
Hevruta (pl. Hevrutot)
  Learning partner(s).
Ivrit B'Ivrit
  Teaching Hebrew texts while speaking in Hebrew.
Kabbalat Shabbat
  Welcoming the Sabbath
Kippa/kippot
  Yarmulke; skullcap.
Kiruv
  Literally, drawing closer; religious missionizing.
Klal Yisrael
  The Jewish people.
Kosher/Kashrut
  Traditional Jewish dietary laws and customs.
Limmud Torah
  Torah study.
Limmudei chol (abbr. chol)
  General studies (lit. secular studies).
Limmudei kodesh (abbr. kodesh)
  Jewish studies (lit. holy studies).
Maariv
  Evening prayer service.
Makerspace
  A space in schools designated for students to create artifacts connected to their studies, especially in the areas of science and engineering, but at times also in connection with Jewish studies material.
Masechta (masechet)
  A tractate of Talmud.
Menahel (pl. menahelim)
  Principal(s).
Mesivta (pl. Mesivtos)
  High school(s).

Mincha
  Afternoon prayer service.
Navi
  The Prophets.
Parasha
  Weekly portion of the Pentateuch (Torah).
Project-Based Learning (PBL)
  An approach to learning in which students engage in problem-solving on their
  own or with classmates.
Rebbe (pl. Rebbeim)
  Rabbi-teacher(s).
Seder
  A learning session (seder). In the context of Passover (Seder), a meal in which
  the exodus from Egypt is recounted.
Sefarim
  Jewish religious books.
Sefer Torah
  Torah scroll.
Sephardi
  Jews whose ancestors originated in the Iberian peninsula and then scattered
  throughout the Mediterranean basin after forced expulsions.
Shabbaton (pl. Shabbatonim)
  Shabbat retreat(s).
Shacharit
  Morning prayer service.
Shaliach (pl. shlichim)
  Teacher (lit. emissary) hired from Israel.
Shaliach tzibur
  Prayer leader.
Shiur
  Class on Jewish matters.
Sh'ma
  The prayerful affirmation of God's oneness.
Shomer Shabbat
  Jews who observe the customs and restrictions of the Sabbath day punctiliously.
Siyum
  Celebration to mark the completion of a body of learning.
Social and Emotional Learning (SEL)
  Helping students develop self-awareness, self-control, and interpersonal skills
  that are vital for school, work, and life success.

STEAM
  Science, technology, English language, arts, and math.
TaL AM
  A Hebrew language curriculum for lower-school students.
Talmid (pl. Talmidim)
  Student(s).
Talmud
  The written version of what once was an oral discussion of Jewish law and lore;
  the foundation of traditional Jewish study.
Tanakh
  The Hebrew Bible, consisting of the Pentateuch, Prophets, and Writings.
Tefila
  Prayer.
Tefillin
  Phylacteries.
Torah She B'al Peh
  The oral law.
Tzedaka
  Charity.
Tzitzit
  Ritual garment fringes.
Yeshiva/Yeshovos
  Orthodox Jewish day schools or higher-level academies for post-high school
  males.
Yeshivish
  Aligned with an ultraorthodox house of study.
Yom Ha'atzmaut
  Israel Independence Day.
Yom Hazikaron
  Israel's Memorial Day, commemorated on the day preceding its Independence
  Day.
Yom Yerushalayim
  Commemorates Israel's unification of Jerusalem during the Six-Day War
  of 1967.

Notes

Introduction

1. Quoted in Jenna Weissman Joselit, "A History of Jewish Day Schools," August 29, 2018, https://www.tabletmag.com/jewish-life-and-religion/268651/the-rise-of -jewish-day-schools.

2. Letter to the Editor, *Commentary* (February 1954).

3. Peter Beinart, "The Rise of Jewish Schools," *Atlantic* (October 1999), https://www.theatlantic.com/magazine/archive/1999/10/the-rise-of-jewish -schools/377816./

4. Jethro Berkman, "Day School Education for Student Thriving," *Jewish Philanthropy*, November 14, 2019, https://ejewishphilanthropy.com/day-school -education-for-student-thriving/.

5. United Jewish Communities and JESNA, *Task Force on Jewish Day School Viability and Vitality* (New York: JESNA, 1999), 3.

6. *A Portrait of Jewish Day Schools and Yeshivas: A Benchmark Report* (New York: Prizmah, 2020), 10.

7. Alex Pomson, "Day Schools in the Liberal Sector: Challenges and Opportunities at the Intersection of Two Traditions of Jewish Schooling," in *International Handbook of Jewish Education*, ed. Helena Miller, Lisa Grant, and Alex Pomson (New York: Springer, 2011), 723.

8. Given all the intervening influences of family, environment, life experiences, college and university study, economic necessity and life partners, it is impossible to gauge the long-term impact of day schools other than to generalize from the higher likelihood that products of day school (as compared to other forms of Jewish education) become active participants in Jewish life—a pattern repeatedly found in survey research—and by hearing how individuals describe the role day schools played in their own life course.

9. Data on midcentury numbers are hard to come by. The estimate of day schools as of 1960 is based on a count of Orthodox day schools appearing in Shani Bechhofer, "Day Schools in the Orthodox Sector—a Shifting Landscape," in *International Handbook of Jewish Education*, ed. Helena Miller, Lisa Grant, and Alex

Pomson (New York: Springer, 2011), 731, and approximations of the number of non-Orthodox schools, as well as Canadian ones.

10. Mordechai Besser, *A Census of Jewish Day Schools in the United States, 2018–19* (New York: AVI CHAI Foundation, 2020).

11. No comparable census of Canadian Jewish day schools similar to the census of U.S. schools conducted by the late Marvin Schick and most recently Besser, *A Census of Jewish Day Schools*. A less extensive count of enrollments at Canadian Jewish schools was conducted by Dan Held, who graciously shared his data with us. An earlier national survey of Jews in Canada did find that 43 percent of all Canadian Jews had attended a day school for at least nine years; it's hard to know whether this proportion is currently holding steady. And it is clear that in the two largest Canadian Jewish communities—Toronto and Montreal—rates of attendance are considerably higher than 43 percent. See Robert Brym, Keith Neuman, and Rhonda Lenton, *2018 Survey of Jews in Canada* (2018), https://www.environicsinstitute.org/docs/default-source/project-documents/2018-survey-of-jews-in-canada/2018-survey-of-jews-in-canada--final-report.pdf?sfvrsn=2994ef6_2, 35. The survey also found higher percentages had attended day school with each younger age cohort.

12. Detailed enrollment and school numbers are in the appendix at the end this book.

13. Sarah Lawrence Lightfoot, *The Good High School: Portraits of Character and Culture* (New York: Basic Books, 1983), 11.

1. Progressively Maintaining the Middle:
Hillel Torah Day School, Skokie, Illinois

1. In Orthodox circles, women generally do not attend weekday services.

2. Besser, *A Census of Jewish Day Schools*, 1.

3. Israel's Memorial Day for its fallen soldiers, Independence Day, and the day commemorating the reunification of Jerusalem in 1967.

4. This refers to the teaching of the Pentateuch, books of Prophets, Jewish law, and the major sections of the Talmud.

2. A Forward-Looking Community School:
Hillel Day School, Detroit, Michigan

1. Hillel was among the first schools we observed in spring 2018. Since then, several of the administrators, including the school's head, described in this chapter have left the school. Given high rates of turnover in Jewish day schools, these developments are unsurprising, and to one extent or another, they affect all the schools we observed.

3. The School as a Gateway:
Brandeis Marin, San Rafael, California

1. The temple is located on the same campus as the school.

2. "B'nai Mitzvah—The Milestone Year: FAQ's, Guidelines and Resources," Brandeis Marin, n.d., 1.

3. See "A Portrait of Bay Area Jewish Life and Communities," Jewish Community Federation and Endowment Fund of the Bay Area (2018). The following website is the source of the data reported here. https://jewishfed.org /community-study.

4. The claim was made by someone at the school that among Marin County Jews with children under age five, 98 percent are intermarried. This figure could not be verified.

5. Drew Himmelstein, "Brandeis Schools in S.F., Marin Go Their Separate Ways," *Jewish News of Northern California*, September 18, 2015, https://www.jweekly .com/2015/09/18/brandeis-schools-in-s-f-marin-go-their-separate-ways/

6. For eighth graders, the Israel trip is one additional facet. A good deal of that year is devoted to preparation for the two-week trip in late February. Though some time is devoted to exploring the complexities of the Israeli-Palestinian conflict and Israeli geopolitics, the main focus of the preparation is to attune students to Israeli street art, especially graffiti. Upon their return, they write papers about what they observed.

4. Nurturing Students' Reflectiveness and Wellness:
The Pressman Academy, Los Angeles, California

1. The early history of non-Orthodox day schools in Los Angeles and the factors accounting for the founding of such schools are detailed in Sara Smith, "Shul with a School: A History of the Development of Non-Orthodox Jewish Day Schools in Los Angeles" (PhD diss., New York University, 2017). Chapter 6 is devoted to the early years of Beth Am.

2. See Alex Pomson and Jack Wertheimer, *Hebrew for What? Hebrew at the Heart of Jewish Day Schools* (New York: Avi Chai Foundation, 2017), https://avichai.org /knowledge_base/hebrew-for-what-hebrew-at-the-heart-of-jewish-day-schools/.

3. Camp Ramah is the summer camping movement of the Conservative movement.

5. Doing More with Less: Akiva School, Nashville, Tennessee

1. In these respects, and in many of the specifics described in this section, the educational experiences at Akiva resemble those Deborah Meier touted as

special benefits of small schools in her influential account of the Central Park East Schools: *Power of Their Ideas: Lessons for America from a Small School in Harlem* (1995; reprint ed., Boston: Beacon Press, 2002).

2. Ibid.

6. Recentering the Centrist Orthodox Day School: Rav Teitz Mesivta Academy, Elizabeth, New Jersey

1. Heshy Kleinman, *Praying with Fire* (New York: ArtScroll Mesorah Publications, 2006).

2. During the year following our visits to the school, Rabbi Neuman secured a significant donation to enable the furnishing of a specially designed bes medresh space. Bringing about this change has sent out a strong message about the school's reviving fortunes. It tangibly improves student engagement in daily seder.

3. As noted above, Rabbi Neuman was subsequently able to secure the funds to fulfill this goal. Additionally, about eighteen months after our site visits, thanks to an unprecedented mix of public and private funds, the mesivta opened a new, fully equipped STEAM center. This was another landmark strongly signaling the transformation taking place at the school.

4. From September 2019, eighteen months after we visited, all students are required to deposit their phones in a specially designated locker at the start of the school day. They can take them out only during lunchtime. The phones are then returned to them at the end of the day. This policy change is perhaps the most dramatic indicator of how much progress Rabbi Neuman has made in advancing the cultural change he is leading.

7. It's All in a Name: The Anne & Max Tanenbaum Community Hebrew Academy of Toronto, Toronto, Canada

1. Paul J. Shaviv, *The Jewish High School: A Complete Management Guide* (Principal Press, 2010), 118.

8. How a Day School Transforms Itself: Hebrew Academy (RASG), Miami Beach, Florida

1. The Hebrew Academy was named after its founder and first principal, Rabbi Alexander S. Gross, hence RASG.

2. In contrast to criticism graduates voiced about the academic quality of the school during the latter part of the twentieth century, many alumni continue to appreciate the warm atmosphere created by the school and good friendships they formed while at the Hebrew Academy.

3. Was the school head brought by the board with the understanding he would make these changes, or was he the driving force? The exact dynamics at work some dozen years before this study was conducted go beyond the scope of this chapter.

4. Some Haredi and Chabad families do send their children to the Hebrew Academy because they are disenchanted with the low level of general studies instruction at Haredi yeshivas, especially the lack of college preparation those schools offer.

5. The horrific school shooting in Parkland, Florida, occurred in Broward, the neighboring county.

6. In 2019–20 over twenty-seven hundred Jewish students in Florida benefited from state tax incentives and support for special needs, including some students at the Hebrew Academy. https://teachcoalition.org/fl/20-million-state-scholarships-sends-2700-jewish-children-florida-day-schools-yeshivot/.

9. The Yeshiva as Teiva (Ark): Yeshiva Darchei Torah, Far Rockaway, New York

1. Hebrew transliteration in this chapter mirrors the Ashkenazi pronunciation employed by members of the Darchei Torah community.

2. John Dewey, *Experience and Education* (1938; reprint ed.: New York: Free Press, 1997).

3. Yaakov Bender, *Chinuch with Chessed: A Veteran Mechanech Answers Pressing Questions* (Brooklyn, NY: ArtScroll Mesorah Publications, 2013), 339.

4. Ironically, many of these parents are graduates of Modern Orthodox day schools themselves. Their parents sent them to yeshiva in Israel after high school, and they returned seeking a different, less worldly education for their own children. This has resulted in a situation today where their parents (now grandparents) are uncomfortable with their offspring attending a yeshiva that does not mark Yom Haatzmaut in a special way or does not invest heavily in Hebrew-language education.

5. Bender, *Chinuch with Chessed*, 366.

6. As noted, a sizable minority of those grandparents are religiously more moderate than their own children. They're willing to contribute to their grandchildren's tuition. They are more reluctant to donate to an institution that doesn't fully align with their values, especially in respect to its relationship with the State of Israel.

Conclusion: Vital Jewish Day Schools

1. Sarah Lawrence Lightfoot, *The Good High School: Portraits of Character and Culture* (New York: Basic Books, 1983).

2. A. Pomson and R. Schnoor, *Back to School: Jewish Day Schools in the Lives of Adult Jews* (Detroit, MI: Wayne State University Press, 2008).

3. Jean Twenge, *Generation Me: Why Today's Young Americans Are More Confident, Assertive, Entitled—and More Miserable Than Ever Before* (New York: Simon and Schuster, 2006).

4. Greg Lukianoff and Jonathan Haidt, *The Coddling of the American Mind: How Good Intentions and Bad Ideas Are Setting Up a Generation for Failure* (New York: Penguin Press, 2018).

5. See Jack Wertheimer, ed., *The New Jewish Leaders: Reshaping the American Jewish Landscape* (Waltham, MA: Brandeis University Press, 2011).

6. Dan Perla, "A New Frontier in Alterative Tuition Programs," November 29, 2019, https://prizmah.org/blog/new-frontier-alternative-tuition-programs.

7. Rosov Consulting, "Has Remote Learning Set Back Jewish Day School Students?" (2020), https://prizmah.org/knowledge/resource/has-remote-learning-set-back-jewish-day-school-students.

Appendix: Day School Sectors by the Numbers

1. All data on day school numbers in the United States cited in this appendix are drawn from the most recent day school census sponsored by the Avi Chai Foundation and reported in 2020, Mordechai Besser, *A Census of Jewish Day Schools in the United States 2018–19* (New York: Avi Chai Foundation, 2020). They refer to the 2018–19 school year. The data cited appear in Tables 1 and 2 in Besser's Book.

2. Our thanks to Dan Held of the Koschitzky Centre for Jewish Education at the UJA Federation of Greater Toronto for furnishing data he collected on Canadian Jewish day school enrollments. We are responsible for categorizing his data. Complicating efforts to estimate the size of the Haredi sector in Canada is the significant population of students in Montreal attending Sephardi day schools, which does not map easily onto the Modern Orthodox/Haredi spectrum.

3. For more on these groups, see Jack Wertheimer, "What You Don't Know about the Ultra-Orthodox," *Commentary* (July–August, 2014).

4. The role of Israel as a common denominator in all kinds of Jewish schools that may lack other kinds of commonalities uniting their parent bodies is explored in Alex Pomson, Jack Wertheimer, and Hagit HaCohen-Wolf, *Hearts and Minds: Israel in American Jewish Day Schools* (New York: Avi Chai Foundation, 2013).

5. The census includes four-year-olds enrolled in early childhood program. Because many Jewish day schools do not offer this option, we have excluded the roughly nineteen thousand four year-olds from the total figure.

6. The estimate of Jewish children of school age is based on the Pew study, "Survey of U.S. Jews," conducted in 2013 and subsequent estimates by researchers at the Cohen Center at Brandeis University.

7. The total number of Jewish school-age children is Canada is based on Robert Brym, Keith Neuman, and Rhonda Lenton, *2018 Survey of Jews in Canada* (Toronto: Environics Institute, 2019), 11–12. These are rough approximations based on estimates of Jewish children from birth to age fourteen and for ages fifteen to twenty-four. Among adults surveyed, 34 percent of Canadian Jews claimed they had attended a day school, a figure that reached 54 percent and 43 percent, respectively in Montreal and Toronto. There is no reason to assume that enrollments are the same for the current generation of school-aged children. Note too that the Canadian survey was conducted only in the four largest Jewish communities, with a total estimated population of 84 percent of all Canadian Jews.

Index

Academic Enhancement Program (AEP)
(Hebrew Academy), 221–22
academies, features of, 177.
See also specific schools
achrayut (Rav Teitz Mesivta Academy),
260
ahavat yisrael (Akiva School), 261
Akiva School (Nashville, Tennessee):
ahavat yisrael at, 261; alumni of,
136; background of, 140; challenges
of, 141; community significance of,
139–41, 267–68; community within,
124–25, 133; compromise readiness
within, 133–34; connections and
exceptions of, 142–43; COVID-19
pandemic and, 279; daily assemblies
at, 126; demographics of, 95;
diversity within, 124; enrollment of,
122–23, 257; family attractiveness
of, 265; fundraising of, 139–40;
future of, 141–42; highest common
denominator aim at, 129–31; hiring
challenges at, 275; inclusion at, 125,
132; Jewish Federation and, 123–24,
139–40; Jewish studies at, 129–31;
Kids4Kids at, 127, 137–38; leadership
of, 124, 131–33; origin of, 123;
overview of, 122; parents of, 129–30,
133–34; prayer policy at, 142–43;
resources within, 136; responsibility
within, 135–39; ritual at, 125–29;

siddurim (prayer books) at, 126;
size benefits at, 134–39, 142; social
learning within, 135; sports at, 136;
STEAM classes of, 136; teacher role
within, 138–39, 142; Tefila at, 126–27;
tuition of, 139–40, 273–74; unique-
ness of, 122–23; values of, 127, 131–33;
Yom HaShoah (Holocaust Memorial
Day) ceremony at, 127–28, 255
Alumni of Pressman (Pressman
Academy), 116
American Israel Public Affairs Commit-
tee (AIPAC), 117
Amida (Brandeis Marin), 70
Anne & Max Tanenbaum Community
Hebrew Academy (Toronto,
Canada). *See* TanenbaumCHAT
antisemitic incidents, education
regarding, 85–86
Aramaic language learning, 5
Arie Crown Hebrew Day School, 39

Bender, Yaakov (Darchei Torah), 232–34,
238, 239–40, 243, 245, 249–52, 258
Bes Hamedresh level, 22
Bishvil Ha-ivrit curriculum, 19, 87
blended learning, 206–7, 213, 223, 278
Bnei Akiva Schools (Toronto, Canada),
184
bnot sherut, 28–29, 33–34
Bonayich curriculum, 19–20

Borchu, 70
Bossewitch, Avi (Hebrew Academy),
 212–13, 228, 278
Boycott, Divestment, Sanctions (BDS)
 movement, 72
Brandeis Marin (San Rafael, California):
 academic achievement emphasis
 at, 83; Amida at, 70; Borchu at, 70;
 community of kindness within, 78;
 community within, 270; connections and exceptions at, 94–96;
 COVID-19 pandemic and, 278–79;
 criticism of, 94; culture at, 77;
 curriculum at, 78, 84–85; diversity
 within, 71; educational approach at,
 79, 95; enrollment of, 73, 76–77, 95,
 257; environment location of, 72–73;
 family attractiveness to, 67; festival
 curriculum at, 86–87; general
 studies at, 80–83; growth of, 76–78;
 guidelines at, 75; Hebrew language
 learning at, 77–78, 87–89; Hevruta-
 style learning at, 86; inclusiveness
 of, 94; integration plans at, 77; JCAT
 program at, 86; Jewish Community
 Center and, 74; Jewish studies at,
 74–75, 83–87, 89–91; leadership
 within, 80–81, 276; mission of, 76;
 music at, 69–70; overview of, 69;
 parents of, 74, 75–76, 78–80, 91–94;
 progressive educational approach at,
 82–83; project-based learning at, 78;
 recruitment tactics of, 78–80; siddur
 (prayer book) use at, 86; Standards
 and Benchmarks Program and, 84;
 student project at, 256; teacher role
 within, 77, 93; Tefila at, 69–71, 75,
 86, 93; tension within, 82; Tzedakah
 project of, 69, 71, 79
Brandeis School of San Francisco, 73
Brudny, Rabbi, 250

Bruriah, enrollment at, 149
Bryner, Rebbe, 245
B'yadeinu (In Our Hands) (Pressman
 Academy), 102

Cadena Initiative, 215
Canada, Jewish day school statistics
 within, 6, 284–85
cellular phones, challenges with, 162,
 168, 170–71
Centre for Differentiated Learning
 (CDL) (TanenbaumCHAT), 180
Centrist Orthodox schools, 5, 284
Centrist Orthodox Yeshiva high
 school, 147, 149–50. See also Rav
 Teitz Mesivta Academy (Elizabeth,
 New Jersey)
Chalav U'devash curriculum, 87
chesed (Darchei Torah), 238–40, 260
Chidon class (Hillel Torah North
 Suburban Day School), 30–32
Chumash study (Darchei Torah), 246
Common Core (Hillel Day School), 49
communal life, day school role within,
 3, 267–71
community day schools, 5, 174, 183–85.
 See also specific schools
Community Kollel (Yeshiva University),
 36–37
community of kindness (Brandeis
 Marin), 78
congregational-based model (Pressman
 Academy), 120
Congregation Sherith Israel, 123
Conservative sector, 5, 285.
 See also specific schools
cooperative learning experiences
 (Pressman Academy), 99
Council program (Pressman Academy),
 103
counseling, 102, 180

COVID-19 pandemic, 277–81
cross-curricular studies (Pressman Academy), 113–15
curriculum: Bishvil Ha-ivrit, 19, 87; Bonayich, 19–20; Book of Genesis as, 85, 106; of Brandeis Marin, 78; of Centrist Orthodox Yeshiva high school, 147; Chalav U'devash, 87; Chidon class (Hillel Torah), 30–32; within day schools, 5, 6–7; diversity within, 8–9; of Dvarim (Deuteronomy), 130; Gemara class within, 18, 35; of the Hebrew Bible, 84, 113–14; of Hillel Day School, 49, 51–52, 53; of Hillel Torah, 28–30; of the innovation hub (Hillel Day School), 55–56; of the Kohelet (Ecclesiastes), 114; math (Rav Teitz Mesivta Academy), 168–69; of the midrashim, 84; of the Mishna, 53–54, 113–14, 205–6; of Modern Orthodox schools, 19; of Pressman Academy, 103; progressive educational approach within, 82–83; Rak B'ivrit, 87; Siyyum within, 58; Social, Emotional and Ethical Learning (SEE Learning), 103; TaL AM, 19, 106–7; of the Talmud, 110, 186, 193–94, 216–17, 256; technology and, 108; of textual puzzles, 159–60; of the Torah, 84, 113–14, 261; of Torah She B'el Peh (oral law), 35; of the Tractate Bava Kama, 193–94

daglanut, 34–35
Darchei Torah (Far Rockaway, New York): appeal of, 235–38; atmosphere of, 231–32; background of, 232–35; behavioral demands at, 253; chesed at, 238–40, 260; Chumash study at, 246; community within, 269–70; connections and exceptions at, 252–53; COVID-19 pandemic and, 279; diversity within, 242–44; educational challenges within, 244–48; emotional needs within, 258; enrollment of, 257; expectations at, 235–36; facilities of, 236–37; financial challenges of, 274; funding for, 248–49; Gemara class at, 246; general studies program at, 240–42; Jewish studies at, 252, 256; leadership within, 249–52; Mesivta Beis Medrash at, 230–31; overview of, 230, 252–53; parents of, 267; personal stories within, 244–48; student services at, 236–38, 252–53; student-teacher relationship at, 247; tuition at, 248; Weiss Vocational Center at, 236–37, 259; Yeshiva Gendola at, 234
diversity, 71, 99, 115–17, 124
Dvarim (Deuteronomy) curriculum, 130

early childhood center (ECC) (Hillel Day School), 47–48
Early Childhood Center (ECC) (Pressman Academy), 118
emotional learning, 102–5, 120, 222
enrollment: of Akiva School, 122–23, 257; benefits of, 257; of Brandeis Marin, 73, 76–77, 95, 257; of Bruriah, 149; of Darchei Torah, 257; of Hebrew Academy, 212; of Hillel Day School, 44; of Hillel Torah North Suburban Day School, 20–21, 40–41; limitations to, 7; of Pressman Academy, 97; statistics of, 285; of TanenbaumCHAT, 175, 195, 196–97
Entrepreneurship for Kids (EFK) (Hebrew Academy), 215
ethnic diversity (Pressman Academy), 115–17

Far Rockaway, New York, 231–32, 235, 264. *See also* Darchei Torah (Far Rockaway, New York)

Federation of Jewish philanthropy, 64

festivals, curriculum regarding, 86–87

financial aid, 7

fishbowl (Hillel Day School), 55

flipped learning, 57, 100

focus groups, 161, 190

Freedman, Joan, 53–54

Freedman, Steve, 45–46, 48, 49–52, 65, 66, 67

Friedman, Tamar (Hillel Torah), 23–24, 29, 32, 36

Gemara class, 18, 35, 153–54, 246

gender segregation, 5, 17, 216–17

general studies program: of Brandeis Marin, 80–83; of Darchei Torah, 240–42; of Hebrew Academy (RASG), 213–15; importance of, 43, 60; of Pressman Academy, 110–13; of TanenbaumCHAT, 186–87

Genesis, Book of, curriculum using, 85, 106

"God talk," at Jewish day schools, 115–16

grading system, 62, 178

Guttenberg, Shaye (Hebrew Academy), 227–28

Halacha, 47

halacha philosophy, 38

Haredi sectors, 5, 283. *See also specific schools*

Hasidic sectors, 5, 6, 283. *See also specific schools*

Hebrew Academy (RASG) (Miami Beach, Florida): academic emphasis at, 211–13; Academic Enhancement Program (AEP) at, 221–22; background of, 208–9; blended learning at, 206–7, 213, 223, 278; board role at, 224–25; challenges of, 207–8, 222–24, 272; connections and exceptions at, 228–29; criticism of, 268–69; diversity within, 208–11; emotional needs within, 258; enrollment of, 212; Entrepreneurship for Kids (EFK) at, 215; gender segregation within, 216–17; general studies program at, 213–15; Hebrew language learning at, 217–18; hiring challenges at, 275; Israel commitment at, 219–20; Jewish studies at, 216–19, 226, 256; leadership at, 224–25, 271; learning specialists within, 259; mini-mester at, 214; Mishna study at, 205–6; Mishnayot Behirot (Mishna Study Made Clear) at, 206–7; overview of, 205, 228–29; parents of, 223; personalized learning at, 213; religious observance at, 210; school-family care within, 212; security at, 223–24; shilichim at, 218; social and emotional learning at, 222; Socratic method use at, 216–17; STEM activities of, 212; student need meeting at, 220–22; student perspective within, 225–27, 256–57; Talmud curriculum at, 216–17; teacher role within, 206, 218–19, 222–23, 227; technology use at, 205–6, 214–15, 226; Tefila at, 218–19; tuition of, 274

Hebrew Bible, curriculum regarding, 84, 113–14

Hebrew language learning: of Brandeis Marin, 77–78, 87–89; of Hebrew Academy, 217–18; of Hillel Day School, 53, 57; of Hillel Torah, 28–30, 33–35, 121; of Pressman Academy, 105–9, 120–21; proficiency approach to, 107; of TanenbaumCHAT, 180; teaching of, 9; of Yeshiva schools, 5

Hevruta-style learning, 86, 110

high-level learning, 108–9

Hillel Day School (Detroit, Michigan): affiliation of, 46–47; alumni of, 65–66, 258; benefits of, 65–66; community within, 61–65, 270; conflict within, 46–47; continuing professional education at, 67–68; COVID-19 pandemic and, 278–79; curriculum of, 51–52, 53; dress code of, 45; early childhood center (ECC) at, 47–48; educational approaches at, 44, 49–50; educational vision of, 49–52; enrollment of, 44; family attractiveness to, 65–67, 264–65; features of, 43; Federation of Jewish philanthropy and, 64; financial status of, 64–65, 273; fishbowl within, 55; flipped learning at, 57; funding of, 64, 67; grading system at, 62; Hebrew language learning at, 53, 57; hiring challenges at, 275; innovation hub at, 55–57, 62–63; Jewish studies at, 57–61; leadership within, 45–48, 52–54, 67, 263, 271; makerspace at, 55–57, 256; Melisa Michaelson at, 54; Mercaz at, 55, 58–59; parents of, 45–46, 50, 61–63, 65; physical spaces at, 54–57; priorities of, 60; problem-based learning at, 60; project-based learning at, 58; reward system at, 60–61; Siyyum at, 58; staff of, 46; strengths of, 62; student services at, 259; teacher role within, 51–52, 60; Tefila at, 58–59

Hillel Torah North Suburban Day School (Skokie, Illinois): alumni of, 258; bnot sherut at, 28–29, 33–34; Chidon class at, 30–32; connections within, 41–42; COVID-19 pandemic and, 280; daglanut at, 34–35; daily curriculum at, 18; educational blending at, 22; educational level at, 41–42; educational microclimate of, 20–21; educational philosophy at, 23; enrollment of, 20–21, 40–41; features of, 17, 21; flywheel effect at, 24; Gemara class at, 35; Hebrew language learning at, 28–30, 33–35, 121; Israeli significance at, 33–34; Jewish studies within, 30–32, 37–38; leadership at, 23–24, 42, 67, 271; limmudei kodesh experience at, 36; mission of, 25, 39–41; parental advocacy at, 27, 267; popularity of, 19; reputation of, 28; restorative circles at, 258–59; senior team of, 24; shaliach couples at, 26–27; shilichim at, 28–30; STEM activities at, 25; teacher role within, 275; teacher salary at, 27; tekkes at, 34–35; Torah She B'aal Peh (oral law) teaching at, 35; volunteer leadership of, 26–28; Yom Haatzmaut at, 32–33, 34–35, 255

imagination (Hillel Day School), 49–50

immersion, 1, 105–9

innovation hub (Hillel Day School), 55–57, 62–63

Internet, influence of, 170

Israel, 33–34, 219–20, 284–85

Israelis, education viewpoint of, 7

Jewish Community Center (Brandeis Marin), 74

Jewish day schools: affordability of, 272–74; challenges within, 272–76; claustrophobic atmosphere of, 257; community building within, 256–58, 264–65, 267–72;

competition within, 184; criticism of, 1, 2; cultural virtuoso nurturing within, 255–56; emotional and academic needs at, 258–59; financial challenges at, 7, 272–74; future of education at, 262–63; "God talk" at, 115–16; hiring challenges at, 274–75; historical overview of, 4–7; Jewish value modeling within, 259–61; mission of, 7; parental benefits at, 263–67; priorities within, 7–9; social networks within, 256–58; statistics of, 6, 283–85; success within, 1–2

Jewish Educational Center (JEC) (Elizabeth, New Jersey), 148, 149

Jewish Federation, 123–24, 139–40

Jewish studies: of Akiva School, 129–31; of Brandeis Marin, 74–75, 83–87; challenges within, 9; of Darchei Torah, 252, 256; of Hebrew Academy (RASG), 216–19, 226, 256; of Hillel Day School, 57–61; of Hillel Torah, 30–32, 37–38; pluralism within, 59–60; of Pressman Academy, 109–10; of Rav Teitz Mesivta Academy, 256; student assessment within, 89–91; of TanenbaumCHAT, 180, 183, 186–87, 190–91, 193–94, 256, 261

Kabbalat Shabbat (Pressman Academy), 116

Kids4Kids (Akiva School), 127, 137–38

kikkar, 55

Kohelet (Ecclesiastes), curriculum regarding, 114

Kolbe, Maximillian, 128

learning styles, education regarding, 83

Legacy Heritage Foundation, 84

Levy, Jonathan (TanenbaumCHAT), 181, 197–99, 276

Lichtenstein, Aharon, 21

Lightfoot, Sarah Lawrence, 11, 254

limmudei kodesh, 20, 36

Linzer, Menachem, 21–23, 27, 36, 37–38, 40, 276

The Lord of the Flies (Golding), 85

Lowinger, Chaim Shlomo, 234

makerspace (Akiva School), 136

makerspace (Hillel Day School), 55–57, 256

Marin County, California, 72–73

menschlichkeit (Pressman Academy), 261

Mercaz (Hillel Day School), 55, 58–59

Mesivta Beis Medrash (Darchei Torah), 230–31

Mesivta Chaim Shlomo, 234

Michaelson, Melisa (Hillel Day School), 54

midrashim, curriculum regarding, 84

Midrash Rabbah, 79–80

mincha (service) (Hillel Torah), 17

mini-mester (Hebrew Academy), 214

minyan (prayer service) (Hillel Torah), 17–18

Mishna, curriculum regarding, 53–54, 113–14, 205–6

Mishnayot Behirot (Mishna Study Made Clear), 206–7

Modern Orthodox Jews, 6, 39–40

Modern Orthodox schools, 5, 19, 20, 209, 283–84. See also specific schools

Moot Beit Din (Pressman Academy), 110

music, 69–70, 106

Nachshon, 70

Nashville, Tennessee, 125, 133, 140, 143.

See also Akiva School (Nashville, Tennessee)

Neuman, Ami (Rav Teitz Mesivta Academy), 152, 154–55, 157–58, 162, 163–65, 167, 170, 171

New York Jewish Federation, 233

non-Orthodox day schools, 5

Palestinians, Jewish viewpoints regarding, 72

Parenting Institute (Pressman Academy), 266–67

personalized learning (Hebrew Academy), 213

philanthropy (Hillel Day School), 64, 67

pluralism, within Jewish studies, 59–60

policies, challenges within, 8

The Power of Their Ideas (Meier), 142

Pressman Academy (West Los Angeles, California): AIPAC and, 117; Alumni of Pressman, 116; assistance program at, 118; auxiliary staff at, 104; community within, 118–19; congregational-based model of, 120; connections and exceptions at, 120–21; cooperative learning experiences at, 99; Council program at, 103; counseling services at, 102; COVID-19 pandemic and, 279; criticism of, 268; cross-curricular studies at, 113–15; cultural identity within, 99; director of wellness at, 102; diversity within, 99, 115–17; ECC at, 118; emotional learning at, 102–5, 120; enrollment of, 97; ethnic diversity within, 115–17; facilities of, 119; family groups at, 103; flipped learning model at, 100; general studies program at, 110–13; Hebrew immersion at, 105–9, 120–21; Hevruta-style learning at, 110;

high-level learning at, 108–9; Jewish studies at, 109–10; Kabbalat Shabbat at, 116; leadership of, 99–102; menschlichkeit at, 261; Moot Beit Din at, 110; as neighborhood school, 98; overview of, 97; Parenting Institute, 266–67; parents of, 102, 104, 118–19; pillars of education at, 105–15; prayer focus at, 115; priorities of, 98; project-based learning at, 111; rabbi role within, 98; religious diversity at, 115–17; social learning at, 102–5, 120; sports at, 97; STEAM classes at, 100, 112–13; student data measurement at, 100; student voices at, 258; TaL AM curriculum (Pressman Academy), 106–7; Talmud curriculum at, 110; teacher learning at, 67–68; teacher role within, 100, 111–12, 116, 275; technology use at, 101; Tefila at, 115, 116, 255–56; Temple Beth Am and, 98; tuition of, 98–99, 104, 117–18. SEE Learning at, 103

Pressner, Daniella (Akiva School), 129, 130–31, 132–33, 137, 276

problem-based learning (Hillel Day School), 60

professional education, 67–68, 81

proficiency approach, to Hebrew language learning, 107

progressive educational approach (Brandeis Marin), 82–83

project-based learning, 58, 78, 111, 213

rabbis, 98, 115–16, 125

Rak B'ivrit curriculum, 87

Ramaz Upper School, 22

Ravsak (Hillel Day School), 46

Rav Teitz Mesivta Academy (Elizabeth, New Jersey): achrayut at, 260; bes medresh (yeshiva study hall) of seder at, 155; cellular phone challenges at, 162, 168, 170–71; challenges of, 150, 152–54; connections and exceptions at, 172–73; COVID-19 pandemic and, 279–80; educational changes at, 169–70; financial challenges of, 166–68, 173; focus groups of, 161; Gemara class at, 153–54; homosexuality viewpoint at, 158–59; Jewish studies at, 256; leadership at, 67, 168; math instruction at, 168–69; overview of, 147, 148–51; parents of, 170, 173; physical facilities of, 167; prayer at, 151; schedule of, 150–51; Seder at, 156–57; sports at, 150–51; STEM activities of, 155, 173; student focus at, 154–57, 158, 159–60, 163–65, 258; student-teacher conferences at, 161–62; student voice at, 160–62; teacher role within, 153–54, 157–60, 169; textual puzzle approach at, 159–60; uniforms of, 151; video games and, 162; vision of, 154–55; Yom Haatzmaut and, 158

reform auspices, 5

Reform Judaism schools, 285

Reform sectors, 5

religious diversity (Pressman Academy), 115–17

responsive classroom approach, 24–25

restorative circles, 25

ritual, 125–29

Rothblum, Erica (Pressman Academy), 100–102, 104–5, 119

Rube, Saul (Hillel Day School), 54

Salanter Akiva Riverdale (SAR) Middle School, 22

Sandel, Peg (Brandeis Marin), 73–76, 78–81, 84, 85, 95, 266, 276, 279

Sauber, Noach (Rav Teitz Mesivta Academy), 152, 157

Schechter Conservative day school system, 46

scholarships, 7

school-family care (Hebrew Academy), 212

sectors, 4–7

Seder, 37–38, 83–84, 156–57

Shabbat, 8

Shabbatonim (TanenbaumCHAT), 189, 190

shacharit (service) (Hillel Torah), 17

shaliach couples (Hillel Torah), 26–27

Shapiro, Pinchas (Rav Teitz Mesivta Academy), 152

Shaviv, Paul, 191

shilichim, 28–30, 218

siddur (prayer book), 86

siddurim (prayer books), 126

Siyyum (Hillel Day School), 58

Social, Emotional and Ethical Learning (SEE Learning) curriculum (Pressman Academy), 103

social learning, 102–5, 120, 135, 222

Socratic method, 216–17

Solomon Schechter day schools, 5

Spanish language learning (Brandeis Marin), 87–88

sports, 97, 136, 150–51

Standards and Benchmarks Program (Brandeis Marin), 84

standing on guard, 32–33

STEAM classes, 8, 100, 112–13, 136

Steinberger, Merav (Brandeis Marin), 84, 86, 88

STEM activities, 25, 155, 212

student-teacher conferences (Rav Teitz Mesivta Academy), 161–62

TaL AM curriculum, 19, 87, 106–7

Talmud, curriculum regarding, 110, 186, 193–94, 216–17, 256

TanenbaumCHAT: academic intensity at, 178–81; admissions policy of, 179; as an academy, 176–78; background of, 174–75; Centre for Differentiated Learning (CDL) at, 180; challenges at, 272; classroom example at, 191–92; community care within, 183–85, 257–58; connections and exceptions at, 200–201; counseling program at, 180; COVID-19 pandemic and, 280; criticism of, 184–85; discipline at, 177–78; diversity within, 190; enrollment of, 175, 195, 196–97; extracurricular participation within, 181–83; facilities of, 176–77; features of, 175–76; flash points of, 185–90; funding for, 175; general studies program at, 186–87; grading scale at, 178; Hebrew language learning at, 180; Jewish practice at, 187–90, 269; Jewish studies at, 180, 183, 186–87, 190–91, 193–94, 256, 261; leadership within, 188, 197–99, 271; overview of, 200–201; prayer at, 126; retention rate at, 179–80; Shabbatonim at, 189, 190; student experiences at, 199–200; student services at, 259; success concept at, 181–83; support system at, 180; teacher role within, 177–78, 188, 191–95; teacher salary at, 275; Torah study at, 261; tuition of, 195–97, 273; vision of, 67

teachers: as Hebrew language speakers, 28–29, 32; protesting by, 46; responsive classroom approach of, 24–25; as sage on the stage, 9;

training for, 67–68; uncertainty of, 60; unconventional methods of, 56

teaching methods, 9

technology: challenges within, 263; curriculum regarding, 108; of Hebrew Academy, 205–6, 214–15, 226; integration of, 278; Pressman Academy's viewpoint of, 101; through COVID-19 pandemic, 279–80

Tefila: of Akiva School, 126–27; of Brandeis Marin, 69–71, 75, 86, 93; of Hebrew Academy, 218–19; of Hillel Day School, 58–59; of Pressman Academy, 115, 116, 255–56

Teitz, Rabbi, 148–49

tekkes, 34–35

Temple Beth Am, 98, 117

Torah, curriculum regarding, 84, 113–14, 261

Torah Im Derech Eretz (Torah U'Mada), 19

Torah She B'el Peh (oral law) (Hillel Torah), 35

Torah U'mesorah, 4

tuition: of Akiva School, 139–40, 273–74; of Darchei Torah, 248; effects of, 20; of Hebrew Academy, 274; of Jewish day schools, 184; of Pressman Academy, 98–99, 104, 117–18; statistics of, 2; of Tanen-baumCHAT, 195–97, 273

Tzedakah project (Brandeis Marin), 69, 71, 79

UJA Federation of Toronto, 175, 195–96

United States, Jewish day school statistics within, 6, 283–85

University School of Nashville (USN), 141

Weiss Vocational Center (Darchei
    Torah), 236–37, 259
Winton, Nicholas, 128

Yeshiva Gendola (Darchei Torah), 234
Yeshiva schools, 5

yeshiva sectors, 6
Yeshiva University, 36–37
Yiddish, 5
Yom Haatzmaut, 32–33, 34–35, 158, 255
Yom HaShoah (Holocaust Memorial
    Day) ceremony, 127–28, 255